VICTORIAN NOVELISTS AND
THEIR ILLUSTRATORS

VICTORIAN NOVELISTS AND THEIR ILLUSTRATORS

J. R. HARVEY

NEW YORK UNIVERSITY PRESS

NEW YORK 1971

First published in Great Britain by
Sidgwick and Jackson Limited

Copyright © J. R. Harvey

Library of Congress Catalogue Card Number: 73–136209

SBN 8147 3358 1

Made and printed in Great Britain by
William Clowes and Sons, Limited
London and Beccles

For Leta

Contents

Illustrations

Introduction

This exhibition had poems as other exhibitions have paintings or statues – yellow poems about the sun and blue ones about the sea, poems in three dimensions, poems that flashed and moved and sang. The poets also were on show, being wild and untrammelled and very affable; and the crowd, anxious not to miss anything, hovered at a safe distance. We knew only one man there, and we worked our way round to where he sat, behind a trestle table, with his poem in front of him. It was in a little wooden box like a television, with a wide, low screen. On the right of the screen were the letters 'oom' and on the left other letters would roll up, each making a word ending in 'oom'. We waited and saw OOM – BLOOM – GLOOM – MUSHROOM – DOOM. Our friend explained that he was combining literature and visuals. Combination was the theme of the exhibition: the arts must collaborate to be truly alive and truly 20th-century.

The various arts do seem now to make just one vast reservoir of undirected life, constantly throwing up new creatures. Yet the very versatility of our artists is ambiguous. Perhaps many men want to be universal men; but if a man has a hard-won spontaneity and mastery in a given art, he would surely feel his richer possibility lay within the art, not outside it? So it may be, rather, that artists are nomadic because they are desperate – in which case the question of collaboration touches deeply their actual vocation.

In the past, hybrid forms like opera have quickly found their own new centre and integrity; but the integrity came when the art-form knew what it was there for. An artist might have new things to do, and might need to change the forms he worked in, but he could not do significant work without a large faith that his art-form was made for such work, with or without him. In the combination of literature and 'visuals' such a faith can be seen, for instance, in the illustrated novel of the 19th century – the monthly-part novel of Dickens, Thackeray, and their rivals, illustrated by Cruikshank and 'Phiz'.

The successful collaboration here suggests that for two arts to work as one, it is not necessary for them to merge as completely as they did in our friend's poem, but that, on the contrary, if they run parallel but distinct they can do more, they have more variety of attack. They should keep their own integrity within the large integrity. It is true that illustrations to fiction are often accessories after the fact, and that though they may be good pictures, they do not belong to the novel in the sense that without them the novel would not be complete. But it is precisely in this respect that the serial novels are so unusual: they do show text and picture making a single art.

It is, however, only in special circumstances that such oneness can be achieved, and the theme of the present book could be conveyed in the question: what circumstances are needed, to make true co-operation possible? The serial novelists profited from one great precondition: they and their artists had a common background in a mode of visual art that was chiefly concerned to make fighting points about human character, motive, and action. From the Middle Ages to the 19th century such an art was practised continuously in the popular satiric print, and was practised with genius (though with very different kinds of genius) by Bruegel, Hogarth, Gillray, and Cruikshank. The father of this art in England was Hogarth, whose profound resemblance to Dickens was solemnly intimated by Forster. But Dickens was not alone in his awe of Hogarth; his competitors wrote fictional versions of the Progresses and found prose equivalents for Hogarth's visual techniques. Chief among them was Thackeray, who also admired the caricatures of Gillray and was trained as an etcher by Cruikshank. Dickens himself has been called a caricaturist, and certainly there is reason to think that the brightly coloured caricatures that filled many shop-windows in London, when he roved the streets as a child, affected the way he saw life and the way his imagination worked. The caricatures did more than encourage him to exaggerate, however; they fostered also his 'animism', his way of giving life to the inanimate things around him. The whole imaginative synthesis of the 'Dickens vision' coincides surprisingly with that of the caricatures. And at the same time his responsive imagination went further back, beyond Hogarth, to absorb and recreate what he found in Bruegel and Holbein.

On the one hand, the serial novelists were conversant with a vigorous and elaborate form of pictorial narrative; on the other, the illustrators with whom they worked derived from Hogarth through late 18th-century caricature. Their immediate master was James Gillray, and though Gillray *was* primarily a caricaturist, and limited the generality and depth of Hogarth's art, he added a new economy and vitality in technique, and he turned the cumbersome allegorical habit of Hogarth's imagination into lively visual metaphor. He was more than a caricaturist in many ways, and he passed on to the illustrators strengths and finenesses that are not normally allowed him. At the same time the illustrators could easily return to the qualities of Hogarth that had been dissipated in political satire, and

[2]

though Cruikshank began life finishing etchings left by Gillray before his madness, he emulated Hogarth all through his subsequent career. The imaginations of author and artist naturally had recourse to the same pictorial idiom, which was devoted not merely to showing appearances, but also to making lively points about behaviour and character. Moreover, author and artist worked for a public which did not easily imagine what it read, and so found illustrations a valuable aid, and which was accustomed to 'read' its pictures – to pore over the prints of Hogarth and the caricaturists gradually working out a wealth of non-visual significances.

The common inheritance meant that the imaginations of author and artist could almost fuse in moments of inspiration. The work of Phiz, for instance, shows many changes of style, almost as though different artists were succeeding each other in him, but each of these changes peculiarly suits the novel in which it first appears, and corresponds to something that was new in Dickens's writing at that stage. Phiz's successive metamorphoses show how much and how intimately he submitted his imagination to Dickens's control, and how much interest and energy Dickens invested in the illustrations. Between them, they developed a visual art of great communicative power, a live part of the novel with important functions entrusted to it by the novelist.

The actual working conditions of author and artist involved constant contact, the artist drawing while the author was still writing. The artist might even prepare his illustration first, and the author simply write up his text from it, transposing into the novel a whole scene that the artist had imagined on his own initiative. One well-known novelist of the time often worked in this way, though his 'illustrator' has never had recognition for the help he gave.

The book is not chiefly about the personal contacts of author and artist, however, but about the contact of their arts. Previous approaches to the subject have been heavily biographical, giving useful but piecemeal accounts of the personal relationships of writers and artists, and little has been said about the illustrator's *art* and the way it works in the novel. This is a pity, for it is here, rather than in the personal interest, that the distinction of the illustrated serials lies. They vindicate the view that text and picture *can* truly work together. That view needs defending at the present time because when one thinks of what illustration can do, one inevitably thinks chiefly in terms of modern illustrations, and modern illustrations are not equipped to be integral parts of the novel: there is so little common ground between the things that matter most for the visual artist and those that matter most for the writer. The illustrations in the monthly parts had faults of melodrama and cramped technique from which we are emancipated, but they embody an economy of standards different from that which prevails now, and one that is worth preserving because it shows how illustrations, while retaining their integrity as visual art, can extend the preoccupations of a novelist. The illustrations of Cruikshank and Phiz were not confined to the vivid suggestion of character and mood; they could develop a novel's themes subtly, delicately, and powerfully, and in essentially visual terms. Their mannerisms are of the past, and the specific historical conditions that encouraged them are not likely to recur, but their inheritance and activity defines certain general conditions which must hold for any true collaboration of distinct arts, and a sense of their priorities should be sustained for the light it sheds, should there be in the future a question of novel and picture working as one.

In preparing this book, I have been dependent on, and have received very gratefully, the help of experts in a variety of fields, and of the owners or keepers of much unpublished material. My study of material in America — and a great deal of the relevant material is now in America — has had to be done at a distance, and I should particularly like to thank the keepers of the following collections for their great help in supplementing the available catalogues with detailed descriptions of their holdings: the Arents Collection, New York Public Library; the Baker Memorial Library, Dartmouth College; Boston Public Library; Cornel University Library; Haverford College Library; the Houghton Library, Harvard; the Henry E. Huntington Library and Art Gallery; Indiana University Libraries; University of Iowa Libraries; University of North Carolina Library; the Free Library of Philadelphia; the Pierpont Morgan Library, New York; Stanford University Library; the Miriam Lutcher Stark Library, University of Texas; University of Virginia Library; the Widener Collection, Harvard; Yale University Library.

I should also like to thank Mrs Alan Stern for letting me go through the Dexter Collection, which is in her possession; Mr Eric Hawksley for showing me the Samuel Williams drawing of Little Nell; Professor Etlinger, Mr Anthony Gross, Mr Philip James, Mr Graham Robertson at the Victoria and Albert Museum, and Mr Trapp at the Warburg Institute for advice on technical points; David Barker for his instruction of my own attempts to learn how an etching should be etched; Mr Arthur Sale for reading and commenting on the manuscript; the Editors of the Pilgrim Edition of *The Letters of Charles Dickens* for giving me access to the complete files of Dickens's correspondence, and especially Graham Storey for his patient reading and generous criticism of early drafts; and my wife, for reading the manuscript many times over, and for many reasons besides.

Since this book is not so much about Dickens himself, as about the general use of illustration in fiction from the 1830s to the 1850s, attention is largely confined, so far as Dickens is concerned, to the long, principal partnership in which almost all the significant uses of illustration occur — the partnership with Hablôt Browne. There are special complications with the covers of the monthly parts, which were engraved before the novel began, and the frontispieces, which were etched only as it ended, and these topics are reserved for a more specialist study;

the same is true of the use of illustrations in the Christmas books, and the diplomatic complexities of the relationship with, for instance, Robert Seymour. A good deal of information on these subjects is, in any case, already in print. There is of course much else that remains, and needs, to be said. The field of 19th-century illustration is rich, and teems with heterogeneous incidents. A single book could not give a comprehensive report of them all; but it may try to define the central line of growth, and to locate the large single pattern in which the diverse episodes fall into place.

I

Barbaric Origins:
Illustration and the Form of Publication

'I think a better and more striking subject would be the headless body of Catherine Howard lying in an open coffin, within the chapel of the Tower . . . and two persons present, Henry VIII and the executioner. This, if well done, would be grand and ghastly – affording deep shadows and strong effects.'[1]

The historical novelist, William Harrison Ainsworth, is giving instructions to his illustrator. His enthusiasm could well surprise a modern reader, for nowadays one does not imagine a novelist taking any interest in the illustration of his work, if it has any illustrations. But the situation was very different for the 19th-century authors whose novels came out, once a month, in serial parts. Dickens strikes the common note when he writes to Phiz, his regular illustrator, 'the first subject which I am now going to give is very important to the book'.[2] The subject in question is that of the plate 'Major Bagstock is delighted to have that opportunity' (1). Describing the future Mrs Dombey, Dickens says exactly what character he requires, inside and out:

'. . . the Major introduces Mr. Dombey to a certain lady, whom, as I wish to foreshadow dimly, said Dombey may come to marry in due season. She is about thirty – not a day more – handsome, though haughty-looking – good figure. Well dressed – showy – and desirable. Quite a lady in appearance, with something of a proud indifference about her, suggestive of a spark of the Devil within. . . . Wants a husband. Flies at none but high game. . . .'

Although in this prescription Dickens leaves some discretion to his illustrator, it is clear that he has a very definite impression in his own mind of the picture he wants to see. He says of the lady's mother:

'Mother usually shoved about in a Bath chair by a Page who has rather outgrown and outshoved his strength, and who butts at it behind, like a ram, while his mistress steers herself languidly by a handle in front.'

From these instructions Phiz (H. K. Browne) drew a careful sketch, which he sent to Dickens. Dickens criticized it, suggested alterations, and sent it back; Browne then prepared the etching. The whole exchange shows a degree of enthusiastic collaboration that would have been most irregular in any other form of novel, though it was common practice in the monthly parts. The present chapter asks, therefore, the large first question the monthly parts provoke: how was it the illustrations came to be there at all?

1. H. K. Browne, 'Major Bagstock is delighted to have that opportunity'.

The question is challenging because at the time that Dickens began his career, the traditional novel had little place for pictures. In the 1830s the novel proper would normally come out in three or four small volumes. Occasionally there might be an elegant frontispiece, but usually there were no illustrations at all. And for two decades more the three-volume novel continued to resist illustration.[3] Even the serial writers themselves, if they issued a work in three volumes, renounced illustration. Thackeray, who illustrated his serial novels himself, had no pictures in *Esmond*.

Sir Walter Scott may represent the attitude of the earlier three-volume novelist to illustration. None of his Waverley novels had any pictures when they first came out, though various collected editions had vignettes and frontispieces. As Scott had wanted to be a painter in his youth, and was a friend of Wilkie, Allan, and Haydon, one might have expected him to be interested in illustration for its own sake. But he was interested only if the pictures helped make the money he needed so badly. Late in life, the success of other illustrated works, such as Rogers's poems, put him on the alert;[4] but his attitude was simply that he 'must try to make the new edition superior by illustrations and embellishments as a faded beauty dresses'.[5] He pressed strongly for illustrations when he found the faded beauty's dress had realized £13,000.[6]

It made little difference to the first edition of a three-volume novel whether there were illustrations or not. But with the monthly-part novel the illustrations were not merely desired, they were needed. When the publisher, Richard Bentley, commissioned one monthly-part novel, his only stipulation about the actual text was that it 'contain at least two striking scenes adapted for graphic illustration'[7]. And when Charles Lever's 'Harry Lorrequer' papers were to be brought out in parts, the author himself maintained that 'much if not all the success to be hoped for depends on these [illustrations]'.[8] Similarly, the experienced novelist, William Harrison Ainsworth, told R. S. Surtees that he had 'no doubt whatever of the success of [*Mr Sponge's Sporting Tour*] when brought out with illustrations'.[9]

The illustrations mattered so much partly because they were a good advertisement. The pictures were displayed in the shop-windows as each new episode appeared, and they could catch a reader or put him off. But this factor alone does not explain why illustrations kept their importance when a novel, or an author, was so well established that advertisements could not radically affect the sale.

Another factor, however, was the essentially visual character of much of the comedy. Although some reviewers did not care for the plates, others made such claims as that 'it is the pencil, not the pen, which completes the vivid conception we undoubtedly possess of [Pickwick's] personal appearance'.[10] The pencil made the comic fancy a reality one could laugh at:

'The success of many . . . passages is due in a great measure to the skill of [Browne] in embodying them . . . how tame, without that, would be such situations as those in which he is detected holding Mrs Bardell in his arms, or represented peeping through the bed-curtains at the unknown lady at the inn!'[11]

Character and situation had to be seen to be funny, and it is evident that for some readers they had to be drawn to be seen.

It is, however, only certain sorts of comedy that must be seen to be funny. The standard resource of the *Pickwick* plates is the violation of dignity: we see the showy sportsman, Winkle, trying to placate a fractious horse, Tupman and the Spinster Aunt discovered in their *tête-à-tête* by the Fat Boy, 'Mr Winkle's Situation when the Door Blew To'. Mr Pickwick is especially vunerable and is seen, for instance, 'in Chase of his Hat' and 'in the Pound'. He repeatedly gets on the wrong footing with respectable ladies: he is squeezed like a lemon behind the door at 'The unexpected breaking up of the Seminary for young ladies'; Mrs Bardell flops into his arms in the middle of a decorous conversation (43); and, finding himself in the bed of an unknown lady – the days of Fielding being past – he peeps through the bed-curtains in comic dismay.

These plates show that whatever Chesterton or Stephen Marcus may say of the heroic saintliness of Pickwick,[12] to a large extent he is the hero of the book because it is supposed to be especially funny to see a plump, prosperous, elderly man in *contretemps* where all his dignity is lost. In the text he does acquire a more heroic aura in his encounter with the law, and this is reflected in several plates which are quite without slapstick suggestions, and which simply show poor Pickwick, in the indignation of innocence, amid the cynical lawyers ('Mr Pickwick and Sam in the Attorney's Office', 'The First Interview with Mr Serjeant Snubbin', 'The Trial' [46]). But two late illustrations – 'The Warden's Room', in which Pickwick, in bed, suffers from the racket his fellow-prisoners are making; and 'The Rival Editors', in which, as the text describes, Pickwick is battered by both combatants – show that right up to the book's end Dickens himself made the most of Mr Pickwick as a butt.

In comedy of this kind the illustration might actually take over from the text at the crucial point. In a number of short stories in M. H. Barker's *The Old Sailor's Jolly Boat*, the writer carefully prepares the ground for a ludicrous climax, and then simply hands the reader over to the artist:

'It was fully evident, by the contortions of his face and body, that he was suffering great agony from the burning, and which our friend Robert Cruikshank has so well depictured'.[13]

Robert Cruikshank had been in just this position when he worked with Pierce Egan. Egan will describe not so much the humorous situation in his story, as the plate which depicts it, and he invites the reader to laugh simply by telling him how much the onlookers shown in the plate are laughing: thus he says that

[9]

one plate shows 'the Fat Knight enjoying the scene, and laughing like fun at LOGIC's disaster'.[14] So the crowd of laughing onlookers in a number of the *Pickwick* plates had work to do; for a corresponding effect in the prose there is the long, laughing paragraph in Chapter VI, 'Meanwhile the round game proceeded. . . .'

A reliance on actual drawings is reflected also in the 'extra illustrations' which various artists prepared for *Pickwick* as it came out. They were based on the assumption that many episodes in the text cried out for pictures, [15] and they were offered as a comic entertainment in their own right. They were directed partly to 'the thousands who read, but did not purchase the work'[16] and would do, for many readers, in lieu of the text.

In the 1830s the print-shop was still a going concern, and the 'extra illustrations' were comic prints similar in subject and style to those of Rowlandson and Gillray. *Pickwick* had never, in any case, been far removed from this rough tradition of visual humour. Dickens said 'I put in Mr Winkle expressly for the use of Mr Seymour',[17] and Winkle remained Seymour's inept Cockney Sportsman well after Seymour's death. A reader seeing Pickwick chasing his hat might recall Gillray's 'Windy Weather' and similar prints. Noticing Pickwick on the ice and Winkle fallen down, he might turn up – in the huge portfolios that were still common[18] – Gillray's series of skating misfortunes. When Pickwick is carried in a wheelbarrow, the reader might recall a plate like Rowlandson's 'Dr Drainbarrel conveyed home in a wheelbarrow': the resemblance is strengthened when the plump Pickwick gets drunk and is carried away unconscious.[19]

Dickens shared and wrote for a rough popular taste that was formed and strong. When it first came out, *Pickwick* fell at once into the familiar context of London's street entertainments. Henry Vizetelly was not recording a new scene when he described the city's response to *Pickwick*:

'"Pickwick" was then appearing in its green monthly numbers, and no sooner was a new number published than needy admirers flattened their noses against the bookseller's windows, eager to secure a good look at the etchings, and peruse every line of the letterpress that might be exposed to view, frequently reading it aloud to applauding bystanders.'[20]

Thackeray had described the print-shops thus:

'. . . to ponder for an hour before that delightful window in Sweeting's Alley! in walks through Fleet Street, to vanish abruptly down Fairburn's passage, and there make one at his "charming gratis" exhibition. There used to be a crowd round the window in those days, of grinning, good-natured mechanics, who spelt the songs, and spoke them out for the benefit of the company, and who received the points of humour with a general sympathising roar.'[21]

Dickens's original commission for *Pickwick* had been simply to provide the letterpress for a series of comic prints by the caricaturist, Robert Seymour.[22] This practice was not uncommon: William Combe had produced the Dr Syntax cycles in this way. Rowlandson would send him a comic design each month, and he wrote the verses to explain it without even knowing what the next month's subject would be. Even in the 1830s, wood-engraved copies of Rowlandson's prints were still being issued, with new texts got up for the occasion. In the preface to one such work, W. H. Harrison's *Humourist* (1831), the author speaks of 'the Embellishments, to which, after the manner of Annuals in general the matter has been adapted'. Orthodox professionals took such commissions as a matter of course. When Lady Blessington asked Harrison Ainsworth to 'illustrate' an engraving for her *Book of Beauty*, Ainsworth replied, in a deferential flutter: 'Rest assured that my best efforts shall be used to make my illustration of the engraving you have been good enough to send me worthy of the pages of *The Book of Beauty*.'[23] It suited Ainsworth's comfortable sense of his talent and versatility to work in this way. Even when planning his own serial venture, 'The Lions of London', he treated his writing self in a cavalier style:

'Let [Leech's] design be either architectural . . . or let him take an historical bit, the execution of Catherine Howard or a scene of a dungeon or gloomy room in the Tower . . . Any scene of this sort, to which I can write a ballad or story relating to the Tower in Henry 8th's reign for No. 1.'[24]

Dickens, however, had no intention of writing up anyone else's pictures. When the Seymour plan was put to him, he insisted that he should write his own story and Seymour should illustrate *that*. To Seymour himself he was alternately peremptory and patronizing, and he had no qualms about telling him to redraw a design. 'The furniture of the room you have depicted, *admirably*,'[25] he said of one illustration, being generous rather than ironic. When Seymour died (with the second issue) the amount of text was doubled, from sixteen pages to thirty-two, and the number of etchings halved, from four to two. Dickens did not, however, try to reduce the number of illustrations below two, and there is no evidence that he wanted to. It was a question not of dismissing the artist, but of wresting control from him and putting him in his place. Seymour's successor, H. K. Browne, was younger than Dickens, little-known, and pliable; and the collaboration was harmonious and happy. Now Dickens's authority was secure, he unbent, and would forget his own text in his eagerness to make the illustrations as comical as possible. Discussing the sketch for 'Mr Winkle's Situation when the Door Blew To' he wrote: 'Winkle should be holding the Candlestick above his head I think. It looks more comical, the light having gone out.'[26] As Kitton points out, Winkle had put the candle down by this stage.[27] If Dickens had resented the illustrator's presence, we would have expected him to confine the artist to subsidiary subjects and to keep the high points of comedy for himself; and in any case we might expect an author to keep a comic dénoument in reserve, rather than let an illustration give it away. But as Browne often had the comic climax of a number – the point where one paused, and just gave oneself up to laughter – it appears that Dickens accepted readily the need for visual aids.

We may now see how it was that illustration came to figure so largely in fiction, when the formal novel in three volumes was so little interested in pictures. Illustration was introduced by *Pickwick*, and no resistance was offered because *Pickwick* was not regarded as a novel. Dickens himself, while writing it, referred to his next work, intended for three volumes, as his 'first Novel',[28] while reviewers of *Pickwick* did not know what to call the new genre.[29] But the success of *Pickwick*, far beyond the author's and publisher's expectations, caused a radical change in the publishing of fiction in England. Among the major repercussions was Dickens's own decision to stay in monthly (or weekly) parts, so that the career in three volumes that he had planned was in fact pursued only by David Copperfield. Another consequence was that the young Thackeray, who had some training and experience as an artist, found ready to hand a medium in which illustration and text worked closely together. Other novelists were also drawn into illustrated monthly parts, so that it presently became an inescapable fact that monthly parts were a form of the novel, and that illustrations were a part of it.

It should be said that in the general diversion of talent into monthly parts, the initiative came more from the publishers than from the authors themselves. In Dickens's case, the publishers were especially quick off the mark. Chapman and Hall commissioned a sequel within the first eight months of *Pickwick*, so that Richard Bentley, who shrewdly tried to buy up Dickens's periodical writing within this time, had to make an exception of the future *Nicholas Nickleby*.[30] When Bentley lost Dickens he quickly commissioned an imitation of *Nickleby*; a resemblance to 'the work recently published under the title of Nicholas Nickleby' being stipulated in the contract.[31] As it happened, the author in question, Henry Cockton, was already engaged on yet another imitation of Dickens, so that Bentley, who was always trying to monopolize the talents he employed, had again to make an exception.[32]

As Kathleen Tillotson observes, the new form had distinct advantages for the publishers: 'high circulation, spreading and elasticity of costs, payments from advertisers . . . independence of lending libraries'.[33] The risk involved in publishing a new novel was much reduced. The number of copies printed could be varied from month to month as the novel's popularity fluctuated, and if it did not succeed it could be brought to a convenient close. The agreement with Cockton mentioned earlier allowed Bentley to require 'the said work to be completed in eight instead of thirteen numbers'. By Bentley's later standards this arrangement was rigid. In the agreement with the Rev. W. H. Maxwell for the novel that later became *Hector O'Halloran*, Bentley stipulated that he should 'be at liberty to require the said Revd W. H. Maxwell to produce any further number of monthly parts beyond ten but not exceeding eight more as he may judge necessary'.[34]

The Irish publisher, M'Glashan, saw what might be done with the comic articles about 'Harry Lorrequer' that had been appearing intermittently in the *Dublin University Magazine*. The author, a young doctor called Charles Lever, wrote to a friend: 'M'Glashan proposes . . . to publish H. L. in monthly numbers with illustrations like the "Pickwick", in preference to a 2-vol. form; in which I thoroughly coincide.'[35] Published in imitation of *Pickwick*, with illustrations by Browne, the new serial was so successful that the tireless Bentley was soon commissioning a work each monthly part of which was to be 'of the same size and page and type as a work called Harry Lorrequer'.[36] There were imitations of imitations, evidently.

The preamble to Lever's *Arthur O'Leary* shows the pressure Lever felt to follow in Dickens's steps, and the exasperation this pressure could cause. O'Leary himself protests vigorously: 'Was I to exhibit in ludicrous situations and extravagant incidents, with "illustrations by Phiz", because I happened to be fat, and fond of rambling?' Yet he does exhibit in such situations, though the illustrations are by Cruikshank, not Phiz. Phiz, however, became Lever's regular illustrator in the following novels. They came out in monthly numbers, each with two etchings. If it had not been for *Pickwick*, Lever would not have written fiction of this kind, or made a large use of illustration. As it is, Browne illustrated more of Lever's novels than of Dickens's, and this partnership makes a useful parallel to the better-known one in that it enables one to assess just what effect a particular author had on the illustrator's style and method.

The foxhunting novelist, Robert Smith Surtees, was similarly changed by *Pickwick*'s success from a periodical journalist into a monthly-part novelist. Again it was the publisher's idea. George Tattersall wrote to Surtees in 1843: 'Ackermann thinks that a sporting work in monthly numbers on the lines of the *Pickwick Club*, &c., would answer.'[37] But with the misfortunes and delays that dogged Surtees all through his career, he did not break into illustrated monthly parts until *Mr Sponge's Sporting Tour* (1852–3). More serials followed, however, and his partnership with John Leech makes a further parallel to that of Dickens and Browne. Leech's illustrations were pleasantly unusual in that they were coloured. Ackermann had at his command the vast hand-colouring industry that had decorated Rowlandson's prints. The printed etching would be passed down a line of women, one touching in a red jacket, the next a yellow waistcoat, the next the blue sky. Author and artist took advantage of the opportunities offered by Surtees's subject, and brought in the 'scarlet' whenever they could.

It was ironic that Surtees should follow in Dickens's tracks, for the original Jorrocks series in the *New Sporting Magazine* had provided Dickens with a number of ideas for *Pickwick*, particularly in the court scene.[38] Similarly, though Dickens was supposed to have been indebted to Pierce Egan's *Tom and Jerry*, Egan himself imitated *Pickwick* in *The Pilgrims of the Thames*. His hero, Peter Makemoney, is, like Pickwick, a retired businessman, prosperous, rotund, benevolent, and – unusually for an Egan hero – innocent. He and his companions embark on an educational ramble through the countryside, interrupted by tales of a tragic and dramatic cast.

Actually, the influence on *Pickwick* of *Tom and Jerry* is far from apparent. The original scheme with Seymour involved no special debt to that work. The Cockney Sportsman was a well-established figure of popular humour, and though Egan was a sporting character, neither Tom, Jerry, nor Bob Logic could be called Cockney Sportsmen. It is hard to imagine what evidence could be adduced to show the fifteen-year-old work influencing the transition from the Seymour scheme to the final *Pickwick Papers*. Hood had feared the book 'was only a new strain of Tom-and-Jerryism' because he had heard 'that one of the Prominences was a stage coachman & the other a Boots', but when he read the book he found this impression to be false (and in any case neither a stage coachman nor a boots were prominences of *Tom and Jerry*).[39] Dickens himself was nettled rather than embarrassed by the comparison, and there is no evidence to suggest that without Egan's work we should not have had Dickens's. If Dickens is indebted to any work by Egan, it is rather to the sequel, *The Finish to Tom and Jerry*, which Egan produced ten years later: a number of the episodes are similar, and the 'Fat Knight' who travels the country with three fast young men seeking adventure is first encountered at a place called Pickwick.[40]

But the debt to Egan was small at best, and one might, at this point, venture to contradict the customary account of the evolution of the monthly-part novel, with its large continuity running back to Egan and its insistence on commercial success. For to have such an effect on the form of English fiction as Dickens had, more was needed than the commercial success *Pickwick* enjoyed. *Tom and Jerry* had that, but *Tom and Jerry* was not imitated by novelists, whereas *Pickwick* combined commercial success with a qualified literary success, and many novelists followed suit. Egan was not treated as a *writer*; but Dickens, though not quite a 'novelist', was acclaimed as 'a new and decidedly original genius',[41] and wrote so well that he became almost at once a classic of our comic prose. He challenged comparison with Fielding and Smollett in a way that Egan did not: 'The renown of Fielding and of Smollett is that to which [Dickens] should aspire.'[42] He quickly won a reputation as a power for good that could never have pertained to Egan: 'beneath all the slang, we see in Dickens' dialogues, a substratum of moral principle'.[43] Thus he soon won recognition for the monthly part as a plausible unit of fiction in a way that Egan could never have done.

There was, however, a danger for the monthly part in the very success of

Pickwick in establishing the form. The publishers of several magazines quickly responded by running illustrated serial novels in their papers, and the monthly part, as a form separate from the magazine, ran the risk of being made redundant as soon as its feasibility was proved. The assault from the magazines came at an early stage. In November 1836, when *Pickwick* had been running for only eight months, Dickens was engaged to edit *Bentley's Miscellany* and bound to write for no 'other periodical publication whatever', except for *Pickwick* and its commissioned sequel. In *Bentley's Miscellany* appeared *Oliver Twist*, with illustrations by George Cruikshank. Such illustrations were new in the magazines, and make clear the affinity with monthly parts. Similarly, when the *Monthly Magazine* began a continuation of *Pickwick*, G. W. M. Reynolds's *Pickwick Abroad*, the style of the illustrations was close to that of the *Pickwick* plates. These were the first illustrations the magazine had, apart from the occasional engraving for a factual article, and a brief run of steel-engraved portraits in 1837. *Pickwick Abroad* was also the first serial in the magazine to run to such length, or to take such a prominent place; fiction had played a minor part before, and had mostly taken the form of occasional tales.

In a sense, this sequel brought the monthly parts of *Pickwick* within the framework of a monthly magazine. There was a fitness in this, for it was in the *Monthly Magazine*, in December 1833, that the first sketch by 'Boz' had appeared. But if the *Pickwick* parts had thus come into the magazines, they did not stay there, for in February 1838 *Pickwick Abroad* began publication in monthly parts. The two versions ran side by side for five months, and then, with the June issue, *Pickwick Abroad* left the magazines. The July issue made no mention of the disappearance, but in the later months of the year the magazine carried enthusiastic notices of the part-issue *Pickwick Abroad*.

To judge from the original preface to the serial, Reynolds's first intention had been to conduct his story through 'twenty numbers of the Monthly Magazine'. The discontinuance of the story suggests that at this date monthly parts had little to fear from competition with the magazines. But we should not conclude that serialization in the magazine was a failure; it seems, rather, that Reynolds wished to exploit such success as it enjoyed in a way that brought him a better sort of credit. In the July issue there began *Alfred de Rosann; or, the Adventures of a French Gentleman by G. W. M. Reynolds, Author of 'Pickwick Abroad' &c*. There was continuity in the French interest, and the new serial was presented in the same way that *Pickwick Abroad* had been. We may infer that illustrations had proved a good investment, for the first instalment contained – in the same style as the *Pickwick* plates – not two, but five etchings. Evidently Reynolds was prodigal of his resources here, for the number of plates diminished sharply as the story proceeded. Nevertheless, an intimate relation between text and plate developed, and a striking integration of the two arts comes at the end of the second instalment: the last page of type and the final etching face each other, and the last words of the text make it clear that the illustration itself is the real last paragraph of the chapter (2).

However, *Alfred de Rosann* ended after six months, and with it ended Reynolds's editorship of the *Monthly Magazine*. His successor, John A. Heraud, had little interest in fiction, and under his aegis there were few stories and no plates. But whatever this change signified for Reynolds in particular, it was not generally taken to show that his experiment had failed. For at the same time that Heraud took over the *Monthly Magazine*, the *New Monthly Magazine* – a quite separate paper – began to present fiction in the way Reynolds had done. Mrs Trollope's *The Widow Married* began in 1839, soon to be joined and succeeded

cern by their countenances, that there was not a warrior amongst the martial throng, whose heart was not softened at the melancholy tragedy about to be enacted. Heroes that have bled at Wagram, Austerlitz, Jena, and Arcole, and that have trampled upon conquered thousands beneath the banners of Napoleon, can still drop a tear at the sight of a fellow-creature's sufferings!·

No sooner had the soldiers taken up their station as described, than the convicts were chained in couples as a precautionary measure against the inclination to create a tumult, which invariably possesses a lawless multitude on such occasions, and were then conducted to the large square to be spectators of François' execution; while Edouard, whose excuses could not totally overcome the sagacity of the prison-doctor, was himself doomed to witness a sight of which he was the cause. As he had just left the hospital he was not shackled; and, as if his evil genius were determined to torment him, or rather to place temptation to fresh crimes in his way, as will appear by the result, he found himself in the front rank nearest the guillotine. When he was perceived by his immediate neighbours, a repetition of the previous day's reproaches and gibes commenced; but an order from one of the inspectors soon enforced a strict silence.

All was now prepared; the presence of the victim was alone required to complete the sad ceremony. At length he came, supported by two priests, and listening to their holy consolations with the utmost attention. His face was death-like pale—his limbs trembling—his glances bent downwards. The conduct of Edouard had put the seal upon his former misery; his heart was broken—his energies were gone—hope was blasted within him. His head was bare—it had not been necessary to cut the thin white locks that still hung down his neck; for they were few, and could offer no impediment to the force of the deadly weapon soon to sever them. He looked not to the right, nor to the left—and all present guessed wherefore he chose to cast his eyes upon the ground. But Edouard stared at him with undisguised brutality, as he passed; and the care-worn appearance of the old man failed to produce any effect upon the ruthless boy.

We love not frequent digressions from the thread of our narrative— we are not one of those authors who are fearful of giving the public too much for their money, or who are unable, from lack of imaginative powers, to keep up an unbroken chain of interesting anecdote, and are consequently obliged to supply many pages of rhodomontade and useless pathos—or else we should take advantage of this opportunity for giving our reader a fine lecture on ingratitude. But we will allow the crisis to work its own effect, free from laboured comments on our part, and unencumbered with the introductory solemnity of many touching words. In order that the merits of the artist may be better understood, the force and meaning of his picture should strike at once, and occupy the mind ere the slightest syllable of explanation be uttered. ·

(*To be continued in our next.*)

[16]

by further serial novels; and while there had been almost no illustrations in the magazine before, *The Widow Married* was illustrated in the style of the *Pickwick* plates by the rejected *Pickwick* illustrator, R. W. Buss; who was joined, in the following year, by Browne himself. Similarly, *Ainsworth's Magazine* asserted its relation to the monthly-part novel by giving fiction a prominent place, and including two etchings in each number.

Without the inspiring example of *Pickwick*'s success, the *Monthly Magazine*, *New Monthly*, *Bentley's Miscellany*, and *Ainsworth's Magazine* would not have featured illustrated serials prominently, and the latter two might not have existed. The example of *Ainsworth's Magazine* may prompt the thought that for a novelist to run his own magazine, and serialize his own works in it, was a natural development of the monthly-part novel. Yet this was not what the public wanted most,

2. 'Alfred Crowquill' (A. H. Forrester), 'The Execution of the Parricide', with accompanying text (*The Monthly Magazine*, August 1838).

[17]

as Dickens realized when he launched his weekly, *Master Humphrey's Clock*. When it was discovered that the new paper was just a collection of short stories and short serials, the circulation dwindled, and was restored only when Dickens converted the magazine into the serialization of, first, *The Old Curiosity Shop*, and then *Barnaby Rudge*. After the opening issues almost every number consisted solely of the latest instalment of novel.

A monthly-part novel was not just a magazine-serial without the magazine. Yet it has often been assumed that the monthly-part novel was simply this, and that this was why it died. The magazines are supposed to have chased the monthly parts from the field, as soon as editors and public realized that magazines could offer all the monthly parts did, and more.[44] And it is true that in the 1860s the shilling magazines prospered while the monthly parts declined. But the magazines did not wait till the sixties to attempt their take-over. They began at the start, in the late thirties, and the monthly parts held their own.[45]

The self-sufficiency of the monthly parts suggests that the chief motive of a reading public is not simply to get two things for the price of one. Above all the reader wants a single powerful story that takes his imagination and fills it with living people and issues, so that he follows the evolving fate of the characters, as he follows a drama in his own life. Though bulky, loose, and spreading, the major monthly-part novels were coherent enough to take this hold; and with such a story the magazines could not compete, whether they offered many lesser serials, or many various items by a major novelist. Recalling modern sagas on the media, we may reflect that this answering to the general need does not in itself tell us very much about quality. But it does show the firm base on which a monthly-part novelist could enjoy an encouraging sense of autonomy and purpose. Illustrations were an integral part of the form, and could share this confidence. The beginnings of this collaborative art were primitive, but they were in some ways propitious, for text and picture could not have combined in a closer and more lively way than they did in realizing, jointly, a climax of far-fetched comedy. The connection with the satiric print made this possible; but here it must be said that things of far greater value than slapstick came down to the monthly-part novel from the satiric print. They do not show at the start: Dickens and Browne only gradually realized their inheritance. But that inheritance was rich and strong, and it is time to say what it was.

2

Gillray to Cruikshank:
Graphic Satire and Illustration

The years round 1800 saw an explosion of new life and colour in English book-illustration. After decades of copper-engraving, a host of new techniques were available. Lithography, mezzotint, and aquatint were developed; wood-engraving was reborn and practised by Bewick and his pupils with a brilliance that soon made it the chief medium of illustration in England and on the Continent. Innumerable etchings of picturesque ruins, the Lake District, and Cambridge Colleges, beautifully toned in aquatint and coloured by hand, were issued from Ackermann's Repository. Cotman used etching alone for the large drawings of his 'Architectural Antiquities' and Blake used relief-etching, glowingly coloured by hand, for his Prophetic Books. The failure of Cotman and Blake to find a market reminds one that the explosion was often not a commercial one. Fuseli's Milton Gallery had failed; Alderman Boydell's Shakespeare Gallery, which offered a specially commissioned masterpiece for every great scene, failed with the Napoleonic Wars, as it depended on export, and had to make up its losses with a lottery. Even Thornton's *Temple of Flora* lost money, and lost more on the subsequent lottery. Turner and Constable on the other hand enjoyed great success when their paintings and water-colour sketches were reproduced by the new medium of steel-engraving. Turner trained a whole school to close-etch and engrave his designs, and each year produced one of his Annual Tours; he was exceptionally fortunate in that he could incidentally satisfy the popular taste for the grand and the picturesque, while using the same prints to realize the oneness he was coming to feel between his human nature and the non-human energies in nature and the cosmos.

From all this productive ferment, the novel held aloof. Such illustrations as were to be found in fiction continued the gentle art of the 18th-century copper engraving, and perpetuated the style of the prolific Thomas Stothard. As a rule illustrations in Stothard's manner are exquisitely worked, though they scarcely allow room for sharp observation. The full-length figures often occupy less than half the height of the plate, the remaining area being filled in with uniform ruled lines or the clustered curlicues standing for soil and foliage. Faces are standardized and Grecian, and the body is liable to imitate the best statues. Grace and delicacy are bought at some cost; William Blake thought privately of Stothard that 'He has obeyed the Golden Rule, Till he's become the Golden Fool'.

In 1823 it was discovered that steel plates could, with quite as much profit, print illustrations as well as bank-notes. The chief effect of this development, for the illustration of fiction, was to make the traditional notations finer still: stipple became like a fine dust, and the small curved lines for clothes, flesh, sky, and wall were reduced to a microscopic scale. As a result some of the illustrations have a dense velvety pile one wants to stroke, but the style of drawing remained squarely in the copperplate tradition.

One might well ask how, from such a start, there developed the kind of illustration seen in the monthly-part novels, with its character, humour, and lively observation. The clue of course is that the serial illustrators came into the

3. James Gillray, 'Wife and no Wife'.

art from outside, from one of the most distinct and colourful forms of print flourishing at the turn of the century. Cruikshank and Seymour were not trained book-illustrators, but caricaturists turned illustrator, and the father of their art was not Stothard but Gillray. A background in political satire may not sound the most fertile or encouraging soil for illustration to grow in; but in Gillray's hands caricature involved far more than derisive distortion, and finer powers than the simple, abundant vigour that has been emphasized in the recent revivals of his work. An admirer may tell you that his grossness is vindicated by his energy, when the point is rather that in his best work he is not gross. In a number of prints one can point to the delicate fineness of the hands, the elegant sway in the slim figures and the spring in their feet.

To see what *could* be done in this savage genre, and done easily and naturally, one has only to look at the hands and faces in 'Wife and no Wife' (3) and 'The Morning after Marriage' (4). The delicacy of the drawing suits the quietness of the total effect, and it is a talent for something more than satirical sarcasm that hangs those pictures on the walls, and places a draped and almost concealed Christ immediately behind the officiating priest so that his shadow falls on the nailed feet, and, in the second plate, contrasts the lacklustre lovers, in their

4. James Gillray, 'The Morning after Marriage'.

disarray of clothes and furniture, with the orderly and wholesome domestic framed in the pool of light outside the dingy room.

Gillray's ease in quiet irony is not the only way in which he transcends caricature; he shows also an energy and largeness of imagination that makes his low art of party politics capable of grandeur. His command of the Sublime shows not so much in plates like 'Light expelling Darkness' (5), which merely arranges the usual sublime furniture of chariots and hovering allegories, but rather in such a piece of original creation as 'Disciples catching the Mantle' (6). That print covers a great distance, and every figure is rendered in clear, immediate detail, yet the impression given is not at all confused or cramped. Foreground and middle-ground are packed, and Pitt's chariot fills the sky, yet the design seems majestically spacious. The chariot itself combines in a miracle of quick, delicate etching the suggestions of fire, whirlwind, billowing cumulus cloud, and a huge wave sweeping upwards. It seems really to *be* a chariot of the elements, and makes its effect without any ponderous emphasis of Romantic storm-cloud or gratuitous dazzle of cosmic radiance: just one clear beam makes straight for Pitt, and diffuses a softer light across the sky.

The sublimity achieved is, of course, a sublimity of the comic spirit: Gillray's humour is pervasive and includes the charioteer. But though there is a good deal of sceptical and boisterous amusement at the rhetoric, vanity, and squalor of politicians, the total effect of the satire is neither simple nor negative. Gillray had lampooned Pitt in the past – his face was a gift – yet it is clear that in executing this obituary satire he was moved by a sense that the great minister's life, now completed, was a genuinely dignified and impressive achievement. The face is still a caricature, and not a flattering one, but just for this reason it is more convincing than in 'Light expelling Darkness', where Pitt is made handsome and classical. Though the plate takes sides, the pervasive, genial irony forestalls any impression of partisan narrowness; it suggests a breadth and emancipation of spirit.

The prevailing comic mood does not, however, prevent the grandeur from being powerfully conveyed. Gillray lived through what was later called the Romantic Movement, and the chariot of the elements, the surging horses, and the whole mobile composition recall the visionary art of Blake and Fuseli. Gillray contemplates the vision in a spirit different from theirs, but his attitude is not mocking. 'Disciples catching the Mantle' shows how he could accommodate a Romantic sublimity, wonderfully realized, to his own broad, ironic, and more-than-Romantic outlook. That outlook was, none the less, that of an 18th-century satirist with tough, stringent, Juvenalian sensibility. And what distinguishes Gillray among artists of his time is that the part of him that belonged to the 18th century was not at odds with the part of him that responded to the Romantic Imagination: the unusual synthesis he achieved can perhaps best be described by saying that it is where he seems most Romantic that he most resembles the poet Pope. When

5. James Gillray, 'Light expelling Darkness'.

DISCIPLES *catching the* MANTLE ; — *the Spirit of Darkness overshadowing the People of* P...

6. James Gillray, 'Disciples catching the Mantle'.

he invokes the Sublime, he turns the imagination of a Fuseli to his own ends, and the resulting combination of irony and magnificence recalls the *Dunciad*. The wild and fantastic play of his imagination shows a fertility in startling juxtapositions that answers to the charged incongruities and antitheses of Pope's wit. The lines:

> 'Before her, *Fancy*'s gilded clouds decay,
> And all its varying Rain-bows die away.
> *Wit* shoots in vain its momentary fires,
> The meteor drops, and in a flash expires.
> As one by one, at dread Medea's strain,
> The sick'ning stars fade off th'ethereal plain . . .'[1]

have surely entered into the inspiration of 'Titianus Redivivus' (7). The composition includes irradiated clouds in great profusion, a rainbow, and, to the right, a number of meteors that are, very clearly, the stars falling down. The same plate calls to mind the lines:

> 'And now had Fame's posterior Trumpet blown,
> And all the Nations summon'd to the Throne.
> The young, the old, who feels her inward sway,
> One instinct seizes, and transports away. . . .
>
> The gath'ring number, as it moves along,
> Involves a vast involuntary throng,
> Who gently drawn, and struggling less and less,
> Roll in her Vortex, and her pow'r confess.'[2]

There are three posterior trumpets just beneath the rainbow, and behind the principal painters a huge crowd can be seen, clamouring round the base of the rainbow, and sweeping, in one rushing movement, up the rainbow and under the skirts of the girl painter. In Gillray's estimation the seated painters are the Dunces of the art-world, and the painter on the right goes so far as to call himself a Dunce. The plate as a whole is an appropriate pictorial equivalent of the poem.[3]

Gillray's literary interests informed his art. If novel-illustration presently brought his school closer to literature, it had never been very far removed in any case. A lively dramatic quality was encouraged by Hogarth himself: 'I have endeavoured to treat my subjects as a dramatic writer: my picture is my stage, and men and women my players.'[4] Gillray commands a rich comic rhetoric of posture – his figures are constantly striking attitudes – and a facility in racy dialogue. His politicians are living dramatic creations in their own right. Fox is a positive joy to him, and becomes a rich, Quilp-like figure of lusty, irrepressible, and endlessly inventive villainy. The way in which Gillray subtly varies the expression of the

[25]

7. James Gillray, 'Titianus Redivivus'.

thick mouth, the huge stubbly jowls, the great nose, the mobile brows, and the bleary but humorous eyes gives us, in the full series of prints, a caricature-Fox who is still human and real, however distant the actual Fox may now be.

Not only does Gillray show a writer's feeling for active character, he was also, for a visual artist, unusually well-read.[5] One cannot help noticing how full his pictures are of dialogue, quotations, and innumerable allusions to Shakespeare and Milton. In 1806 he was praised for 'his large knowledge about every subject in literature'[6] and it was characteristic of him to take up arms, on Shakespeare's behalf, against the vulgarization of Boydell's Shakespeare Gallery.[7] He had the right to do so, for his own inventiveness in metaphor shows the fertility and power of a great poet.

It is worth stressing here that Gillray's metaphors do not belong simply to the effervescence of comic imagery that a political situation suggested to him. On the contrary, they play their strongest part where the caricaturing is poignantly simple and grave. In 'John Bull and his Dog Faithful' (8) the Faithful Pitt, party-political *raison d'être* of the plate, does not loom very large. Attention and compassion are concentrated on John Bull, the representative Englishman, and the depth of Gillray's identification with his countrymen is given in the fact that John Bull's face is Gillray's own. This John Bull contrasts shockingly with the sturdy, corpulent John Bull that Gillray and others normally drew. He is wasted,

8. James Gillray, 'John Bull and his Dog Faithful'.

ragged, blind, and short of a hand and leg. As he tries to stumble forward, he is hampered by a dog (with Sheridan's head) who has sunk his teeth into the wooden leg; another dog is tugging at his coat. The wooden leg looks very like a bone, making, in the sombre humour of the plate, a special attraction for the dog. John Bull's reduction to a walking skeleton is thus brought home with the harshest metaphor, for the dog Sheridan is biting not so much a wooden leg, as the bared bone of John Bull. Allegory, emblem, and symbol had been used elaborately by Hogarth and his Continental predecessors, since the main purpose of their art was to speak to their public; and in Gillray's hands these conventions turn to poetic metaphor as his art comes fully alive. In this respect he is a more remarkable artist than Hogarth, for the lucid naturalism of Hogarth's manner frustrates metaphor. If Hogarth paints a wooden leg it must look exactly and only like a firm piece of timber.

The contrast between the artists in ease in metaphor corresponds to the technical difference in their styles. The lively brevity of Gillray's notation makes metaphorical transformations easy. Hogarth's own more respectable style can seem staid and overworked by comparison; certainly the effect is to emphasize the solidity and single fixed identity of what he draws.

This contrast must not, of course, stand for the complete comparison of Hogarth and Gillray. One can speak seriously of Gillray and Rowlandson practising 'the art of Hogarth', for Hogarth effectively founded English graphic satire, and Gillray, Rowlandson, and Cruikshank took innumerable themes, motifs, and technical practices from him.[8] But it is clear that in the hands of Gillray and Rowlandson the art of Hogarth has gravely diminished in scope. This shrinkage is too well-known to need emphasis, and there has seemed more point, for the present, in suggesting that this change was not merely diminution, that there is growth also, and that in Gillray we see something of the visionary and poetic intensity of the earlier satires – especially those of Bruegel – on which Hogarth drew.

This description still leaves out of account, however, the central inheritance that did come from Hogarth. Hogarth had established for the English artist the possibility of being not only a popular entertainer and an observer and celebrator of the life of the times, but of being a satirist in the Roman tradition: an autonomous and authoritative critic whose word must be heeded. The visual satirist could take himself seriously as an artist.

Without such a faith in his art, it is unlikely that Gillray would have developed his imaginative and poetic strengths – what point would they have had? The value of a sense of vocation shows if we put Gillray's work beside that of Rowlandson. Rowlandson has made his reputation by being, in his satiric drawings, quite a different kind of artist: a delicate penman and water-colourist, with a sensitive feeling for landscape. The most appallingly obese toper may always be praised for the flowing beauty of his outline. Easy-going and adrift, Rowlandson put all his devotion as an artist into the liveliness, sparkle, and delicacy of his water-colours; and in his drawings we can see what a marvellous draughtsman he was, for a few relaxed, mobile lines faultlessly realize the solid body and distributed weight of his subjects, and all their vital motion. Yet with the etching needle he can be more slovenly than one would have believed. His outline can wander without decision or flow, and may be swamped by a mass of shading, flattening the figures, and failing to suggest a plausible light-source. His usual style of shading consists of wavy lines alternated with dotted lines, an easy-going version of the formal dot-and-lozenge manner of the copper-engraver, and it seems always to have contented Rowlandson; at any rate, he was never tempted to develop a subtler range of effects.

Looking through the *Microcosm of London* and the *Dr Syntax* series, even an enthusiast must be troubled by the artist's habitual refusal to take pains. It may be that etching was uncongenial. One needs only a little experience to appreciate how the needle may have hampered even a great artist, when his gifts were such as Rowlandson's. The needle was always to be moved firmly, against a slight resistance from the ground, and it must be hard to achieve that extreme lightness and quickness of touch, which has so much to do with Rowlandson's felicity as a draughtsman. Also, the needle responds very little to changes of pressure that can make a pen line taut and muscular at one point, and as fine as a hair the next: each line is uniformly thick or thin, depending on the time in the acid. Yet there are etchings where Rowlandson clearly has used the needle in a masterly way, and where the hardness of the etched line simply gives a crispness to the graceful drawing; examples are chiefly to be found in *The English Dance of Death*, a series which, to judge from Combe's preface, Rowlandson took to heart far more than his usual commissions. The finer plates here show that it was not from incapacity that Rowlandson was normally so perfunctory.

So one talks of the hackwork Rowlandson had to do – why should he bother? Yet Gillray always bothered, even though many of his political commissions would have been mere drudgery, had he not transformed them. His mature style is sufficiently free and relaxed, but scarcely ever untidy. He developed a wonderful variety of notations in response to the particular feel and character of whatever object he was drawing. The quality of the local technique reflects the general confidence of purpose in the artist, his instinctive belief, or disbelief, that his work matters. Rowlandson's loose and jovial linework shows that he enjoyed doing his comic prints, but he seems to have enjoyed them as a kind of artistic slumming. Gillray reminds us that one did not have to take this attitude. The satiric draughtsman could have a different sense of himself as an artist.

Though both artists were admired, the difference between them was clearly felt by their contemporaries and successors, and shows in the immense influence Gillray had. Rowlandson, by contrast, made almost no mark. Going through the works of the forgotten figures of that time – H. and W. Heath, C. J. Grant,

Robert Cruikshank, and others – one continually finds instances of Gillray's customary notation: in posture and expression, bagged knees and trouser-seats, folds of feminine muslin, even the little lines flecking the wall.[9] Other styles can be found, such as that of the sporting artist, Alken, but deviations from Gillray's manner are individual, and there was no alternative shared style of distinctive character.

For the world of lusty comic entertainment, primarily visual, amid which the young Dickens grew up, Gillray was *the* formative genius. Although disreputable by Victorian standards, he remained a live popular classic well into the Victorian period. In 1818, John Miller and W. Blackwood issued for the popular market, in serial parts, copies of Gillray's engravings. In its rough way, the facetious commentary they provide is aware of Gillray's more serious affinities, for it remarks of 'The Fashionable Mama': 'Rather Hogarthian this, for under the mask of ridicule the satirist points a moral.' Thomas McClean brought out a two-volume edition, from the original copper plates, in 1830. And in 1851, H. G. Bohn, adding to McClean's set of original plates, brought out a mammoth edition which was evidently a feasible publishing venture, although colossal, unwieldy, and priced at £10. (Bohn's edition is perhaps the best place to study Gillray's drawing, since the plates are carefully printed, and uncoloured; it should perhaps be added that nowadays individual plates from Bohn, recoloured, are sometimes to be found masquerading as originals, and seem expected to do well out of it.)

Gillray shaped the style of the popular comic artist, Robert Seymour, the first illustrator of *Pickwick*. Seymour executed some political satires but his special province was the misadventures of Cockney Sportsmen, and Gillray had preceded him with his four consecutive prints of Cockney Sportsmen 'marking Game', 'Shooting Flying', 'Re-charging', and 'finding a Hare'.

More important, there is the direct continuity between Gillray and the artist who dominated book-illustration in Dickens's time, George Cruikshank. Cruikshank began as a political caricaturist, working for Gillray's publisher, Mrs Humphrey. He had actually to complete some of the etchings that Gillray had started before his final breakdown.[10] He also re-engraved a number of Gillray's prints for Hone. In the details of the drawing, in the whirling compositions, and in the remarkable elasticity of people's bodies – as in the violent sense of fun, decidedly pre-Victorian – some of Cruikshank's early works might almost be by Gillray. He absorbed Gillray's characteristic humour, even his delighted ingenuity in satirizing sartorial 'Monstrosities' (a term they both use).

Above all, Gillray taught him how to learn from Hogarth, and from his two predecessors Cruikshank gained his notion of the essential autonomy and self-sufficiency, as popular entertainer and moralist, of the visual artist. The Hogarthian vocation betrays itself in the recurrent use of the form established by Hogarth, and used on several occasions by Gillray,[11] the Progress.[12] For Cruikshank, when

[30]

he was determined to show how much more than a book-illustrator an artist could be, it was the form he had to use.[13] From the beginning of his career, Cruikshank was encouraged in the belief that he could be another Hogarth. Professor Wilson wrote in 1823:

'Here lies genius; but let him do himself justice – let him persevere and *rise* in his own path ... Let him, in one word, proceed – and, as he proceeds, let him think of HOGARTH.'[14]

In his maturity he was widely acclaimed as 'the modern Hogarth'.[15] He was praised for 'that story-teller's power which was so much Hogarth's and his own'.[16] One reviewer of *Oliver Twist* judged that 'Sikes attempting to destroy his dog' and 'Fagin in the condemned Cell' 'proved a range of power perhaps unrivalled since Hogarth'.[17] Surrounded by such praises, Cruikshank might naturally have seen himself in this light. His ambition was not to illustrate beautifully the works of a congenial author, but to exert the influence of an authoritative moralist on the mass of unregenerate mankind. The fineness of the artist was readily sacrificed to the crusader's needs: *The Bottle* was 'executed in a very coarse style – in order that it might be printed at the steam press – so that an edition might be sold cheap, to the Million'.[18]   Hogarth had similarly said of his *Four Stages of Cruelty*: 'The leading points in these as well as in [*Beer Street* and *Gin Lane*], were made as obvious as possible, in the hope that their tendency might be seen by men of the lowest rank. . . .'[19] Having completed *The Bottle*, in which in six frames an insidious sip of wine at Christmas leads to decay, murder, and madness, Cruikshank was attracted by J. M. Scollier's suggestion that he produce a sequel 'illustrating the upward tendency of the Pledge – by beginning *No.* 1 with a house divested of furniture and all in confusion – and onward to pledge signing to the comforts of domestic life'.[20] Cruikshank was less optimistic, and in the actual sequel, *The Drunkard's Children*, the protagonists follow their father to disgrace and death.

Cruikshank claimed the same independence and authority when he illustrated books, and so long as his authors conceded the pride of place to him there was no difficulty. Authors, for their part, were very ready to concede. They wrote deferential prefaces in which they apologized for writing at all, and pleaded Cruikshank's illustrations as the best excuse. The most remarkable tribute comes in the Mayhew Brothers' novel *The Greatest Plague of Life* (1847). The 'authoress', a young married woman, describes her visit to her publisher, who gives her 'a letter to that highly-talented artist, Mr George Cruikshank,' and tells her

'that Mr Cruikshank was a man of such versatile genius, that he was sure that the drawings from his intellectual pencil would be quite in keeping with the book. . . .'[21]

The entire third chapter of her book is devoted to her visit to Cruikshank, who is good-looking ('a fine picture set in a muscular frame'), 'exceedingly kind' to his lady visitor ('for he appears to have a great partiality for animals of all kinds'), and moral (in his first remark, he said 'that he needn't ask if my interesting little work was to be "moral"').[22] Cruikshank's services were a great asset to a new publication, and his sense of his own value would have been further strengthened by such letters as that in which J. L. Gardner beseeched him to provide 'the very great addition and improvement' of his illustrations before any steps were taken to have the work in question published.[23]

If an author should be less amenable, there was some danger of friction. In the preface to his first book, *Sketches by Boz*, Dickens had followed common practice in paying tribute to Cruikshank:

'Entertaining no inconsiderable feeling of trepidation, at the idea of making so perilous a voyage in so frail a machine, alone and unaccompanied, the author was naturally desirous to secure the assistance and companionship of some well-known individual, who had frequently contributed to the success, though his well-earned reputation rendered it impossible for him ever to have shared the hazard, of similar undertakings. To whom, as possessing this requisite in an eminent degree, could he apply but to GEORGE CRUIKSHANK?'

After his success with the first series, however, Dickens resented the idea that he needed any assistance, and Cruikshank was hurt by this new independence. When the second series of *Sketches* was due, he wrote to the publisher, Macrone:

'I did expect to see that Ms. from time to time in order that I might have the privilege of suggesting any little alterations to suit the Pencil but if you are printing the book all that sort of thing is out of the question. Only this much I must say that unless I can get good subjects to work upon, I will not work at all.'[24]

Dickens wrote in anger to Macrone, who presumably had sent him Cruikshank's letter: 'I have long believed Cruikshank to be mad; and his letter therefore, surprises me, not a jot. . . .'[25] The anger, on both sides, was short-lived; and with *Oliver Twist* it is noticeable that Dickens seriously applies himself to giving Cruikshank the 'good subjects to work upon' that he asked for:

'Moreover, I think I have hit on a capital notion for myself, and one which will bring Cruikshank out.'[26] (To Cruikshank) 'I think you will find a very good subject at page 10, which we will call "Oliver's reception by Fagin and the boys".'[27]

He tries to see the subjects from an artist's point of view, and to assess their feasibility as illustrations:

'I find on writing it, that the scene of Sikes's escape will not do for illustration. It is so very complicated, with such a multitude of figures, such violent action, and torch-light to boot, that a small plate could not take in the slightest idea of it.'[28]

Cruikshank responded by making a strong illustration out of this subject in spite of Dickens's misgivings. But with the last illustration in the novel, Dickens did what he had never done before: he rejected it completely, and ordered Cruikshank to do another.[29]

The difficulties were not lasting, but, equally, they were more than mere passing explosions of artistic temperament: they reflect a sustained fight for control. There was a real risk, for Dickens, of being overshadowed. Reviewers were anxious to make such a claim for Cruikshank as: 'Surely we might claim a sort of authorship for Cruikshank too, for what to us would have been *Peter Schlemihl* without his illustrations?'[30] And although Dickens made a name for himself in his first book, *Sketches by Boz*, in a number of the reviews that acclaimed the new talent, there is a tendency for the high tributes to slide in Cruikshank's direction rather than Dickens's:

'The majority of these very pleasant sketches have already appeared in the columns of the *Evening Chronicle*, and the interest which they excited has, it seems, induced the author to publish them in their present form, with appropriate graphic illustrations by George Cruikshank, whose genius, like the purse of Fortunatus, is inexhaustible.'[31]

Some felt that the highest praise they could bestow on Dickens was to say that he was as good as his illustrator:

'[the *Sketches*] are replete with talent: and when we say that we are left in doubt whether we most admire the racy humour and irresistible wit of the "sketches", or of the "illustrations" in George Cruikshank's very best style, our readers will agree that we could not well give higher commendation.'[32]

The *Spectator* review announced that 'BOZ is the CRUIKSHANK of writers'.[33]

Dickens had to make it clear to the world, and to Cruikshank, that he was the author and Cruikshank the illustrator. But in this assertion a great deal was involved, for the illustrator had a privileged position with a public that was not adept at visualizing what it read; moreover, the illustrator was accustomed, in prints and comic serials, to originate character, to arrange plot, to provide dialogue, and to inform with moral significance. The artist's realm of creation had a large dramatic side which overlapped with that of the novelist, and in this overlapping area Dickens had to rule alone if his genius were properly to fulfil itself in the kind of publication he had chosen. He had not only to reverse the roles of author and artist; he had, while retaining the illustrations on which his public to some extent depended, to take over a large part of the artist's creative function. For there is a further stage that has not so far been mentioned: Dickens could not abandon illustration; he had rather to become the illustrator in all but execution, and this is what he does. The great advantage of H. K. Browne was that with his youth, inexperience, and receptive and malleable character he was ideal for Dickens's purpose: he was still unformed.

But Cruikshank *was* formed, and one may surely understand how natural it was for an artist with Cruikshank's background to resent bitterly the second place he had to take. A Hogarthian wholeness of achievement had been impossible for Gillray, but in his intense, creative, and highly individual satire, he could at least maintain a self-sufficiency of some moral substance. Cruikshank could not do even this. The independent satiric print was dying, and he refused to work for *Punch*. Book-illustration was the only outlet for his talents, but in book-illustration he must sacrifice what mattered most in his vocation, his creative and moralizing independence. He did not give in, but fought all his life a fight which he must have known to be hopeless. We see the fighting in the various abortive magazines he launched: each one failed.[34] We see the fighting too in the insistent desire to play the leading role in the serial novels he illustrated: he claimed in later years that he had originated *Oliver Twist* and many novels by Ainsworth. Cruikshank's desire to usurp his novelists is well-known as an aberrant nuisance, and I have wanted to show that, far from being simply a function of his conceit and eccentricity, this desire is understandable and deserving of sympathy. Everyone said he was the new Hogarth, and he must surely have felt he had the right to be not less than an equal in any collaboration.

The position of illustrator must place stresses on an artist of any school, but for Cruikshank the strain was exceptionally severe. If the result had been the delusion, sustained by a desperate will, that he had originated the novels he illustrated, we might understand how the intolerable pressure on his genius, applied with steadily increasing force over a number of years, contributed to his decay. Certainly there is delusion in his claims; there is no evidence that he did originate *Oliver Twist* or make a large contribution to the text (though the specific claims he made were more qualified and less deluded than they have been taken to be; the intricacies involved are discussed in Appendix II). But just for this reason it needs to be said that with certain other novels he contributed far more to the text than the original idea. In respect of Ainsworth's novels he has never had justice. Not only did he furnish Ainsworth with many incidental touches, but he suggested climatic scenes, realized them in detail, and sent his novelist elaborate instructions for the writing up of whole episodes. Ainsworth frequently followed these suggestions with minimal changes, though he never gave proper acknowledgement for the help he received (he could scarcely afford to). Far from bearing out the idea that Cruikshank was mad, the partnership with Ainsworth shows how very much an artist of Cruikshank's school could contribute to a novel, given the chance.

Cruikshank was first provoked to public assertion in April 1872, when a dramatization of Ainsworth's *The Miser's Daughter* opened at the Adelphi. Cruikshank wrote to *The Times* expressing his surprise that his name had not been mentioned in connection with the production, and explaining that 'this tale of the *Miser's Daughter* originated from me, and not from Mr Ainsworth'. Ainsworth replied: 'I content myself with giving the statement a positive contradiction.'[35] Cruikshank was not abashed; he repeated the claim for *The Miser's Daughter*, and went on to announce:

'I am also the sole originator of what is called *Ainsworth's Tower of London*, as well as another work bearing his name. . . .'[36]

Again Ainsworth responded with a brief denial:

'I disdain to reply to Mr Cruikshank's preposterous assertions, except to give them, as before, a flat contradiction.'[37]

At this point the correspondence was closed by the Editor, but Cruikshank had said, in his second letter, that he was preparing for the press 'a full, true, and particular account of all the professional transactions between Mr Ainsworth and myself', and this presently appeared. In *The Artist and the Author* Cruikshank went through Ainsworth's novels one by one, stating just how much he felt he had contributed to each; and the point at issue may best be raised by taking first a novel where Cruikshank's claim is moderate:

'No. 2. "Jack Sheppard", illustrated by me, and published in monthly parts in "Bentley's Miscellany". This story *originated from Mr Ainsworth*, and, when preparing it for publication, he showed me about two or three pages of manuscript on "post paper", and *I beg that it may be observed that this was the only bit of manuscript written by this author that I ever saw in the whole course of my life*.'

Letters from both Ainsworth and Cruikshank, in the Widener Collection at Harvard, show the kind of collaboration Cruikshank offered. With the tracing for 'Audacity of Jack Sheppard' (9), Cruikshank sent the following note:

'I enclose the tracing of the second subject – I suppose Wood to be transfixed with astonishment – he is lifting up his spectacles. I thought it would be a point for you to describe him as reading the Bible aloud* – as Jack enters. – Winnifred in tears and if you do not approve of this, old Wood must read it to himself. The flowers on the Mantleshelf are *drooping*: (i.e.) not fresh gathered. a handkerchief is thrown over the birdcage – Mrs. Wood's portrait has been removed...

[35]

9. George Cruikshank, 'Audacity of Jack Sheppard'.

*Our excellent and Re.ᵈ friend the Prebend would no doubt pick you out a good passage.'

Each of Cruikshank's details 'tells a story' in the way he had learned from Hogarth. Clearly Hogarth's manner lent itself not only to the illustration of fiction, but to the writing also, for the details go straight into the text with an appropriate commentary that is scarcely distinguishable from the kind of popular elucidation that Hogarth's own paintings received at this time:

'[Wood] had much ado to maintain his self-command. His wife's portrait had been removed from the walls, and the place it had occupied was only to be known by the cord by which it had been suspended. The very blank, however, affected

[36]

him more deeply than if it had been left. Then, a handkerchief was thrown over the cage, to prevent the bird from singing; it was *her* favourite canary. The flowers upon the mantel-shelf were withered and drooping – *she* had gathered them. All these circumstances – slight in themselves, but powerful in their effect, – touched the heart of the widowed carpenter, and added to his depression.

Supper was over. It had been discussed in silence. The cloth was removed, and Wood, drawing the table as near the window as possible – for it was getting dusk – put on his spectacles, and opened that sacred volume from which the best consolation in affliction is derived, and left the lovers – for such they may now be fairly termed – to their own conversation.'[38]

The conversation of the lovers is punctuated by appropriate texts, read out loud by Wood, and perhaps chosen by the excellent and Reverend friend:

"'*No doubt*,'" said Wood, who had again turned over the leaves of the sacred volume, – "'*no doubt this man is a murderer, whom, though he escaped the seas, yet vengeance suffereth not to live.*'"

"No feelings of consanguity shall stay my vengeance," said Thames, sternly. "I will have no satisfaction but his life."

"'*Thou shalt take no satisfaction for the life of a murderer which is guilty of death, but he shall surely be put to death,*'" said Wood, referring to another text.'

The other illustration for this number was 'Jack Sheppard visits his Mother in Bedlam' and Cruikshank evidently decided the mad woman's dress, for, continuing the same letter, he wrote:

'For fear you might not recollect the attire of Jack's Mother I will just state that her head which is *shaved* is bound round with a *rag* in which some straws are stuck for ornament. a piece of old blanket is tied over her shoulders and the remainder of her dress is a petticoat.'

And the text reads:

'A piece of old blanket was fastened across her shoulders, and she had no other clothing except a petticoat. Her arms and feet were uncovered, and of almost skeleton thinness. Her features were meagre, and ghastly white, and had the fixed and horrible stamp of insanity. Her head had been shaved, and around it was swathed a piece of rag, in which a few straws were stuck.'[39]

Evidently the illustrations were produced at a stage when Ainsworth had worked out only the most basic development of the plot. Cruikshank then realized the scene in detail by himself; and Ainsworth described the scene with the picture before him, and incorporated the details in it as they arose. This account fits the one given by Ainsworth himself:

'In no instance did he even see a proof. The subjects were arranged with him early in the month, and about the fifteenth he used to send me tracings of the plates. That was all. . . .'[40]

In explanation of this arrangement, it should be pointed out that the time it took to etch a plate (the etching ground had to dry, and the acid to bite the plate slowly) and to print it (the plate had to be re-inked and wiped by hand before every impression) meant that the illustration needed to be drawn well before the printer needed the actual text. And there is no evidence that Ainsworth had the kind of conscience, as an artist, that would have made him resent the way in which Cruikshank made his task easier. When he had to defend himself from Cruikshank's charges of indebtedness, Ainsworth complained that Cruikshank 'was excessively troublesome and obtrusive in his suggestions'.[41] But this was said some years later, and in special circumstances; in the letters written while the novels were coming out, there is not the slightest sign of any resentment in Ainsworth.

In the case of *Jack Sheppard* the partnership began on the friendliest footing, with a genial 'Christening dinner' for 'little Jack Sheppard'.[42] Ainsworth admired without reservation the first illustrations.[43] There is no need here to claim that Cruikshank 'originated' the novel, because he himself did not claim that; but then, Cruikshank claimed no share in *Jack Sheppard* at all, while it is clear that he contributed far more to that novel than Ainsworth's 'flat contradiction' implied.

With the following novel, *Guy Fawkes*, the position was similar;[44] it was with *The Tower of London* that Cruikshank made his most ambitious claim:

'No. 4. "The Tower of London", the ORIGINAL IDEA of which was SUGGESTED by me to Mr. Ainsworth, and also *illustrated* by me, and published in monthly numbers. In this work Mr. Ainsworth and I were *partners*, holding equal shares.'

There is no clear evidence as to who had the original idea, though it is true that in Bentley's agreement for the work Ainsworth and Cruikshank were '*partners*, holding equal shares' – a conspicuously unusual arrangement in the Bentley Papers.[45]

Cruikshank then goes on to make claims so radical that they would, if true, grievously compromise Ainsworth as an author:

'I have now most distinctly to state that Mr. Ainsworth *wrote up to most of my suggestions and designs*, although some of the subjects we jointly arranged, to introduce into the work; and I used every month to send him the *tracings* or *out-*

lines of the *sketches or drawings* from which I was making the etchings to illustrate the work, *in order that he might write up to them*, and that they should be *accurately described*. And I beg the reader to understand that all these *etchings or plates were printed and ready for publication before the letterpress was printed*, and sometimes even before the Author *had written his manuscript....'*

The claim sounds outrageous;[46] and yet it seems no more than the simple record of the truth when it is considered in the light of two remarkable letters in Cruikshank's hand. The relevant illustration is 'Sir Thomas Wyat attacking the By Ward Tower' (10).

10. George Cruikshank, 'Sir Thomas Wyat attacking the By Ward Tower'.

'London Sept. 16th. 1840.

My Dear Ainsworth,

 The Party under the command of Sir Thos. Wyat were divided into *two divisions* – one of which proceeded along "Thames St." – the other by "Tower

[39]

St." – the "Bulwark Gate." was soon carried & the *wooden* houses adjoining in flames – "*in no time.*" a terrible struggle takes place at the "Lions Gate" Sir Thomas succeeds in forcing this gate also – and drives all before him – and before the Portcullis of the "Middle Tower" can be lowered it is *propped* up by a piece of timber, Wyat dashes across the Bridge amongst the vanquished who are flying to the "Bye Ward Tower." from which issue the three Giants – in Helmets – & Curass Og, & Magog (armed with *Maces* – Gog has a Partizan – Og knocks about in fine style & bundles a lot of fellows over the wall Magog (who has a shield) has enough to do to keep back, Wyat. who tries to gallop over him, one well aimed & desperate blow from Sir Thomas – would have brought down the Giant had he not caught it on his shield – at the same instant an awful crack from Magogs Mace splits the scull of the Noble Animal upon which Sir Thomas was mounted – the fall of their leader, daunted the attacking party – the moments delay gave the treating party time pass into the gate way of the Byward & Lower the Portcullis – during this affair Xit had mounted on the wall – in a most noble manner – & whilst flourishing his sword and daring them to come on. he perceives some one who had been thrown into the Ditch endeavouring to climb the wall – he calls out to him to surrender – which he does This may be a person of consequence . . .
NB there are two more Horsemen besides Sir Thos. upon the Bridge – (in armour of course).
PS. Sir Thos.'s party had taken possession of the Middle Tower – from which they fired upon those who were firing from the Byward so now I leave you in the "*thick* of it" – the post of honour! so fire away! my boy – fight on! and success attend you.'⁴⁷

'Sunday Evg.

My Dear Ainsworth. –

I enclose the tracing for the "Gog" – which has cost me some trouble, as I made two drawings and was much puzzled which to choose – however this one *must* do –
as it is highly improbable that little "Xit" would be in armour I send you a sketch of the manner in which I have dressed him up. His helmet being *much* too large for him and surmounted with a *very fine* plume of feathers – [there are two sketches of Xit, one of them in the same pose as in the plate.]
I am in a dreadful state of anxiety about my plates. there is such a *frightful* quantity of work in them – Hoping you are getting on well – and that you are all well

I remain

Yours truly

Geo. Cruikshank.'⁴⁸

In the corresponding passage in the novel, Ainsworth did little more than paraphrase Cruikshank's letter. The most striking feature of Ainsworth's version is that he added so little. To show this, however, quotation *in extenso* would be necessary, and, as the passage in question is a long one, it is given in an appendix (Appendix III).

The By Ward Tower episode was not an incidental one: it belongs to the climax of the novel. And to that climax Cruikshank made two further contributions. Referring to the illustration which *was* finally called 'The Death Warrant' he wrote:

'Had we not better change the title to "*The Death Warrant*"? mind there is *no dagger* Simon grasps his sword with his *left* hand. The *Right* arm is merely extended *& the hand clenched* — '[49]

and Ainsworth wrote accordingly:

'Repressing a cry of alarm, she called Renard's attention to the object, when she was equally startled by his appearance. He seemed transfixed with horror, with his right hand extended towards the mysterious object, and clenched, while the left grasped his sword.'[50]

Cruikshank also rearranged the final scene of Jane's execution. In a letter to Ainsworth, he discusses a revision of the sketch for the illustration 'Jane meeting the body of her husband on her way to the Scaffold' and it is clear that this involved changes in the text itself, as to the way in which Jane came upon her husband's body:

'These few lines in case I should not see you — the first sketch of Jane meeting the body of her husband is thus. . . . Now as the bearers would certainly not (nor could they) carry the body up the *stairs* — they must of course take it up *the road* — and as they would do this *without being seen until they came up close to the scaffold* the other appears more *natural* — and will group better thus. . . .'[51]

Cruikshank's instructions about Mauger — 'Mauger (who must come *limping* back with indecent haste). he is going up the steps, & looking at his victim' — are also carried into the text:

'While this took place, Mauger, who had limped back as fast as he could after his bloody work on Tower Hill, — only tarrying a moment to exchange his axe, — ascended the steps of the scaffold, and ordered Wolfytt to get down.'[52]

In the short notes, as in the long letters cited earlier, what is most striking is the easy authority of Cruikshank's tone; the text shows that his authority was respected.

With others of Ainsworth's novels the position is at best conjectural;[53] but it is no conjecture to say that in the episode of Wyat's attack on the Tower, the creative effort of imagination was all Cruikshank's; and it was not an isolated case. If Ainsworth habitually relied on Cruikshank in this way, then his indebtedness here is, in any case, much more important than it would be if he had simply taken his first ideas from Cruikshank. Ainsworth himself evidently felt he had been less than fair to him, for after complaining that the artist 'was excessively troublesome and obtrusive in his suggestions'[54] and noting that Dickens was similarly troubled, he immediately added:

'It would be unjust, however, to deny that there was wonderful cleverness and quickness about Cruikshank, and I am indebted to him for many valuable hints and suggestions.'[55]

But 'hints and suggestions' is hardly a fair summary of the way in which Cruikshank took imaginative possession of the story, and realized the climax.

The fact that, in other respects, Cruikshank was worse than eccentric in his late years, only makes it more necessary not to consign to lunacy a challenging claim like that for *The Tower of London* without close inspection. A reappraisal of his relationship with Ainsworth may suggest also that the claims for *Oliver Twist* be reviewed with more sympathy and care than they have received up to now.[56] As to why Cruikshank so repeatedly pushed himself to the fore, and so anxiously insisted on his rights, it is hoped that the preceding account showed that this is not surprising in an artist with his training.

His immediate master was Gillray, and his ancestor – the artist he must emulate above all – Hogarth. The careers of these two artists defined the kind of genius that Cruikshank discovered in himself, and the independence he assumed with authors would not have seemed ridiculous if he had remained a print-artist; the self-sufficiency as popular entertainer-cum-moralist enjoyed by the print-artist had been encouraged by an enthusiastic public. But when these qualities were transferred to book-illustration they became unreasonable: the change from being a print-artist to being a book-illustrator – even the best book-illustrator – put Cruikshank's genius into a Procrustean bed. And though Cruikshank felt the limitations and fought against them, the change was irreversible.

Yet this switch, which was Cruikshank's personal tragedy, was extremely propitious for a novel with serious pretentions (such as Ainsworth's never had). The value of a figure like Gillray in the background of the serial illustrators should now be clear. His relaxed, quick, and lively style of etching was ideally suited to the demands of serial illustration, far more so than the minutely worked and painstakingly solid manner of Hogarth himself. Gillray's art could be rebarbative, but it engaged a fertile comic invention, based in a thorough familiarity with the heterogeneous details of everyday life. It was an art that specialized in the economic and emphatic presentation of individuals (not only, or primarily, ugly ones), of 'character'. 'Character' lives in this mode with a largeness of expression and gesture that tends to the theatrical; and with its profuse allusion to literature, its ancient vocabulary of symbol and emblem, and its poetic strength of metaphor, it is clearly, as art, very literary. But the ease, spontaneity, and adequacy with which these characteristics express themselves in etching shows that the literary bent did not entail any deadness in the visual art. Properly to describe this art, we need an equivalent term, in art-criticism, to 'wit' – one that combines the modern, 18th-century and also 17th-century senses of the word. Gillray's descendants were wonderfully equipped to illustrate the novels of Dickens and Thackeray.

And although Cruikshank's career was a continuous defeat, a particularly poignant irony emerges when it is seen that he had common ground with the novelists in a way that he seems never to have realized. For the monthly-part novelists were not at odds with the Hogarthian tradition of graphic satire: on the contrary, they were, in a sense, in it.

3
Bruegel to Dickens:
Graphic Satire and the Novel

From Hogarth's day to Cruikshank's, graphic satire had been one of the most vital of the English arts, but when Cruikshank left the print-shops for book-illustration, the art lost its autonomy. It would not be true to say that it died at this time, but it survived only with greatly diminished scope and vitality. Yet in another field this declining art sprang up unexpectedly, and thrived. The affinities between the monthly-part novel and graphic satire were many, varied, and deep; and it was in the novel, rather than in actual pictures, that this long-established mode of visual imagining came to lead its most robust life.

Dickens himself knew so well the work of the caricaturists and of their founding father, Hogarth, that certain idiosyncrasies of the Dickensian 'vision' were simply the natural result of his immersion in graphic satire. He was deeply impressed by Hogarth's strong sense of the artist's duty to the world, and he imagined many of his more powerful scenes as Hogarth might have painted them.[1] And Dickens was far from being the only novelist of that time who drew frequently on the 18th-century artist.

In his own day, Hogarth's art had immediate repercussions on literature.[2] Plays and novels were made from his series as they came out, and both Smollett and Fielding would refer their readers to paintings by Hogarth to see what some of their own characters looked like. In *Tom Jones*, Fielding, who was a friend of Hogarth, excuses himself from a full description of Mrs Allworthy with the remark that she has already been drawn 'by a more able Master, Mr *Hogarth* himself . . . in his Print of a Winter's Morning'.[3] Hogarth was still used as a short cut in the 19th century, especially if the scene to be described was chaotic. Mrs Trollope speaks for many when she evokes the mess in one of the character's rooms by remarking that 'had Hogarth himself desired to produce a type of disorder, his imagination could hardly have suggested any object or any disarrangement which might not there have found a model'.[4]

Use of Hogarth was not always so perfunctory. In 1837, Ainsworth planned 'to write a sort of Hogarthian novel – describing London, etc., at the beginning of the Eighteenth Century'.[5] This became *Jack Sheppard*, a novel that has been called 'simply a prose version' of Hogarth's moral series *Industry and Idleness*.[6] Ainsworth himself went so far as to suggest the relationship was the other way round. Late in the novel, Hogarth comes to make a sketch of Sheppard in prison – the scene is shown in Cruikshank's plate 'The Portrait' – and on leaving, an idea occurs to him 'grounded in some measure upon Sheppard's story. I'll take two apprentices, and depict their career. One, by perseverance and industry shall obtain fortune, credit, and the highest honours; while the other by an opposite course, and dissolute habits, shall eventually arrive at Tyburn.'[7]

The novel runs parallel to *Industry and Idleness*. In the chapter headed 'The Idle Apprentice' the moral of Hogarth's series is insisted on several times, in the terms that Hogarth had used. Jack's master upbraids him: 'You want one quality, without which all others are valueless. You want industry. . . . Idleness is the

11. William Hogarth, 'The Fellow 'Prentices at their Looms'.

[45]

key of beggary, Jack!'[8] Ainsworth takes pains to impress on the reader, at the very beginning of his story, that the Idle Apprentice's end awaits Jack Sheppard. Carving his name on one of the beams in the workshop, Jack hopes he will not chance 'to swing on the Tyburn tree for [his] pains'. Even Ainsworth's literary technique, at this point, comes from Hogarth, with pieces of writing taking a prominent place in the picture, and details of inescapable moral point:

'On the bench was set a quartern measure of gin, a crust of bread, and a slice of cheese. Attracted by the odour of the latter dainty, a hungry cat had contrived to scratch open the paper in which it was wrapped, displaying the following words in large characters:— "THE HISTORY OF THE FOUR KINGS, OR CHILD'S BEST GUIDE TO THE GALLOWS." And, as if to make the moral more obvious, a dirty pack of cards was scattered, underneath, upon the sawdust.'

Gaming was an early stage in Thomas Idle's ruin.

12. George Cruikshank, 'The name on the beam'.

The 'hungry cat' comes in by association from the plate Ainsworth clearly has in mind (11), where the Idle Apprentice has a cat at his feet: the cat has the same significance – neglect – in both pictures. In his illustration of the scene (12) Cruikshank follows Hogarth not only in depicting the moment of the master's return, but also in giving great care to the drawing of each tool of the apprentice's trade, and in arranging the written documents so that the spectator cannot help reading them.

The final picture of Jack's death (13) gives further proof that Cruikshank

Jack Sheppard's Farewell to Mr Wood.

Blueskin cutting down Jack Sheppard.

The body of Jack Sheppard carried off by the Mob.

13. George Cruikshank, 'The Last Scene'.

14. William Hogarth, 'The Idle 'Prentice Executed at Tyburn'.

[48]

was working with Hogarth's series in mind. Cruikshank has shifted from his usual frame to a low, wide one which allows him to give a panoramic view similar to that in Hogarth's execution-plate (14); and in the three final frames he surveys the scene from the same vantage-point that Hogarth chose. Both author and artist worked from Hogarth's plates, and each knew the other was doing this: Ainsworth said of Cruikshank's illustrations for this novel: 'From their Hogarthian character, and careful attention to detail, I consider these by far the best of Cruikshank's designs.'[9]

Ainsworth was not alone in making such elaborate reference to Hogarth. The Progress form was in general use among novelists,[10] and the connection with Hogarth was advertised rather than concealed. The most remarkable prose imitation is G. W. M. Reynolds' *The Days of Hogarth*. The novel is illustrated with thirty-six large wood-engravings, all close copies of Hogarth's engravings, and the narrative is so contrived that these seem merely the illustrations to Reynolds' prose. The book has its use, for it shows how closely a spectator of the time was accustomed to 'read' Hogarth's pictures. The first scene of *Industry and Idleness* becomes part of the novel thus:

'It was verging towards noon . . . when Mr. West appeared at the door of the workshop. His countenance beamed with benevolence and satisfaction as the busy noise met his ears: but a cloud suddenly overspread his features, as his eyes rested on the place occupied by Henry Hemmings. For the idle apprentice was leaning back in a sound sleep, his head supported by one of the uprights of the loom; and the cat was playing with his shuttle. A pewter quart-pot close by indicated the nature of the liquor which had overpowered him, and the drowsy influence of which had completely unfitted him for work. Everything about him denoted idleness, improvidence, and depravity. The licentious ballad of "Moll Flanders" was pinned to the frame-work of his loom; in another place a blackened tobacco-pipe proclaimed him to be an inveterate smoker; and on the floor lay the "Apprentice's Guide," a manual of good advice introduced by Mr. West into the factory — soiled, dog's eared, and torn. His hair was matted and uncombed; his clothes were stained with liquor, and rent in several places; — and his entire appearance was that of the dissipated, indolent sloven.

From this lamentable picture the eyes of Mr. West were turned, as if to seek a relief where he knew such a contrast would be afforded, towards the loom occupied by the industrious apprentice.'

The industrious apprentice is described with similar fidelity to the print. Reynolds works through the four Progresses simultaneously: the first four illustrations show the first scenes of, respectively, *The Rake's Progress*, *The Harlot's Progress*, *Industry and Idleness*, and *Marriage à-la-Mode*. The titles of the progresses are incorporated as chapter-headings, and their protagonists are tied together by

[49]

blood and intrigue: the Harlot, for instance, is revealed as the Idle Apprentice's sister. Some characters are renamed, while others keep the names Hogarth gave them, and in general Reynolds adheres to Hogarth's narratives or departs from them without any consistent principle. It is clear, however, that he knew his material well, for he identifies such historical characters as Colonel Charteris, whom Hogarth includes in the first plate of *The Harlot's Progress*.[11]

A venture like *The Days of Hogarth* presupposes a general familiarity with Hogarth's works. Among the populace, Hogarth's lessons were taken seriously and taken to heart. The hero of another novel of the time is at a low point in his fortunes when:

'I entered the inn-parlour, and there, for the first time, saw the prints of Hogarth's apprentices, suspended round the walls. I was minutely examining that which represents, with so much simplicity, chasteness, and force of character, a rich merchant leaning upon the shoulder of the youth, who, by industry and good conduct, has obtained his confidence.'[12]

He is approached by a voluble gentleman, who commends him for studying Hogarth, and presently says:

'"Nothing like beginning early, – commenced myself at fourteen, as warehouse-boy to a Turkey merchant ... what spare time I had was passed in reading, what little money I earned, was spent in books and paper, – bought a set of Hogarth's prints at an old stall, took them for my beacon, as the poet says, and was repaid for it, – was made book-keeper, traveller, and confidential clerk, ..."'

The speaker has practised what Hogarth preached, and his industrious apprenticeship has been rewarded with success. He is well grounded in Hogarth criticism, and quotes Walpole who 'calls Hogarth "a writer of comedy with a pencil, and not a painter"'. Such tributes as this encouraged writers to imitate the artist; and in general, in the great revival of interest in Hogarth at the beginning of the 19th century, it was customary to praise his work in literary terms. In his historic essay in Leigh Hunt's *Reflector*, Lamb repeated Walpole's point with greater weight: '[Hogarth's] graphic representations are indeed books: they have the teeming, fruitful, suggestive meaning of *words*. Other pictures we look at, – his prints we read.'[13] He proceeded to give the literary analogy a depth and dignity it had not enjoyed before. With the humour, he found nobility, tragedy, and grandeur in Hogarth's picture of humanity, and at the same time he called attention to the 'quantity of thought which Hogarth crowds into every picture', and showed how in each scene a powerful meaning is borne out poetically in every detail. Hazlitt made similar claims in his critique of *Marriage à-la-Mode*,[14] and concluded his second paper with a tribute to Lamb that showed he fully endorsed what Lamb had said.[15]

Lamb's essay effectively established Hogarth as a figure of almost unique greatness. At the beginning he related how he 'was pleased with the reply of a gentleman, who being asked which book he esteemed most in his library, answered, – "Shakespeare:" being asked which he esteemed next best, replied – "Hogarth."' Lamb was much impressed by 'that universality of subject, which has stamped [Hogarth] perhaps, next to Shakespeare, the most inventive genius this island has produced'. He found the final scene of *The Rake's Progress* superior to the conclusion of *Timon of Athens*, and comparable to the early scenes of Lear's madness. His strong association of poet and artist provided one of the vital preconditions of Hogarth's effect on the novel: for the young man who, in the 1830s, might aspire to be a dramatic-poetic genius handling the whole of human life there were two towering examples of achievement: Shakespeare, and after him, Hogarth.[16]

How deeply Dickens had absorbed this estimate of Hogarth, and the idiom that expressed it, shows in his Preface to *Oliver Twist*. His sentiments are not original, but the accent is personal and the feeling strong. He lists his great predecessors in the honest treatment of low life and pays stronger tribute to Hogarth than to any novelist, Fielding included:

'On the other hand, if I look for examples and for precedents, I find them in the noblest range of English literature. Fielding, De Foe, Goldsmith, Smollett, Richardson, Mackenzie – all these for wise purposes, and especially the two first, brought upon the scene the very scum and refuse of the land. Hogarth, the moralist, and censor of his age – in whose great works the times in which he lived, and the characters of every time, will never cease to be reflected – did the like, without the compromise of a hair's breadth; with a power and depth of thought which belonged to few men before him, and will probably appertain to fewer still in time to come. Where does this giant stand now in the estimation of his countrymen?'

In associating himself so clearly with the great 'precedent' of Hogarth, Dickens is perhaps responding with an open avowal to the many readers who had, from his first appearance, acclaimed him as a new Hogarth. The *Edinburgh Review* had observed that 'What Hogarth was in painting, such very nearly is Mr Dickens in prose fiction', while the *Examiner* insisted on the likeness in review after review.[17]

Dickens had every reason and encouragement to link his name with that of Hogarth. Though the Preface was contributed to the third edition of *Oliver Twist*, it was not merely a *post hoc* reflection. The original subtitle had been *The Parish-Boy's Progress*, and Dickens had shown his knowledge of Hogarth in the treatment of the thieves.[18] In Dickens's fiction at large Hogarth's influence may be seen in the use of the Progress, in the use of visual accessories to bear out the character and point of a given scene, and in the special concentration on the physical idiosyncrasies of people.

The value of the Progress for a writer with Dickens's temptations and needs is readily understood. At the start of his career he had a dangerous facility in composing episodes and plot as he went, and *Pickwick* and *Nickleby* came to an end because twenty numbers were filled rather than because some profound human process had reached its natural end; the plot provided a specious finality. An attempt was made to unify *Chuzzlewit* with a single meaning, 'the design being to show, more or less by every person introduced, the number and variety of humours and vices that have their root in selfishness',[19] and in the period when *Dombey* was being written, Dickens's anxiety to achieve a clear emancipation from his earlier ramblings and proliferations shows clearly when he tells Forster 'I have avoided unnecessary dialogue so far, to avoid overwriting; and all I *have* written is point.'[20] For a man anxious to tighten the rein on a genius for improvisation, the Progress offered the clarity of outline and the large, simple structure of a story in which a protagonist with one moral characteristic moves steadily in one direction to his consummation in either worldly success or ignominious death. The unified plot devised by Dickens for *Dombey* lacks this grand simplicity, but it may be noted that the career originally intended for Walter Gay was exactly that of the Idle Apprentice. Dickens had planned 'to show him gradually and naturally trailing away, from that love of adventure and boyish light-heartedness, into negligence, idleness, dissipation, dishonesty, and ruin'.[21] Gay's history was to be a moral tale, and the moral was to be that of Hogarth's series, which depended, for its significance, on the fact that Thomas Idle was not vicious initially, but merely easy-going, deteriorating 'by degrees' (and Walter, like Thomas, has a significant surname). The passage just quoted continues:

'To show, in short, that common, everyday, miserable declension of which we know so much in our ordinary life, to exhibit something of the philosophy of it, in great temptations and an easy nature; and to show how the good turns into bad, by degrees.'

Although the material may have been provided by ordinary life, the 'philosophy' is Hogarth's; and although Walter Gay plays a small part in the final novel, Dickens felt, at this stage, that 'this question of the boy is very important'. The idea was not completely abandoned, for, as Forster notes, it 'took modified shape, amid circumstances better suited to its excellent capabilities, in the striking character of Richard Carstone in the tale of *Bleak House*'.

The *Apprentices* series had particular appeal for Dickens, and although he might playfully collaborate with Wilkie Collins in 'The Lazy Tour of Two Idle Apprentices', his own basic outlook is often, in its more serious expression, indistinguishable from Hogarth's. The moral of that series is one of the morals of

David Copperfield: the novel is organized round the contrasted careers of two young men from childhood to, on the one hand, prosperity and fame, and, on the other, failure and death. The local adventures and surprises do not deflect either character from his appointed moral path, and it is noteworthy that when David mentions his evolution as a writer he does not speak of the fire of genius; he merely remarks with quiet self-approval that he has been the industrious apprentice: 'my success had steadily increased with my steady application', 'I worked early and late, patiently and hard'.[22] In his letters of advice to the would-be author, R. S. Horrell, Dickens prescribed care, thoroughness, and hard work, and insisted that 'whatever Genius does, it does well'.[23] David Copperfield, moreover, wins not once but twice the industrious apprentice's traditional reward, his master's daughter's hand. The glamorous Steerforth, on the other hand, attributes his bad habit of life to the want of 'a steadfast and judicious father' and to his resulting inability to settle down to a respectable profession.

'As to fitfulness, I have never learnt the art of binding myself to any of the wheels on which the Ixions of those days are turning round and round. I missed it somehow in a bad apprenticeship, and now don't care about it.' (Chapter XXII)

Richard Carstone is a clearer case, more severely judged, of the Idle Apprentice: the man who cannot settle down to a respectable profession and master it with steady application. The need for industry in the period of training is stressed by Mr Jarndyce at an early stage – '"The course of study and preparation requires to be diligently pursued"' (Chapter XIII) – and emphasized again by Mrs Badger and her husband, when they suggest that Richard abandon medicine (Chapter XVII). And as with Thomas Idle, the incapacity for application goes with the 'careless spirit of a gamester' (Chapter XVII). This condition of mind exposes Richard to a vice which, gaining a small hold at first, grows by easy gradations into an inescapable addiction that kills him. Dickens's art here resembles Hogarth's in the simplicity and relentlessness of that steady progress to a miserable end; and, as in a Progress, Richard's career is presented not in continuous description, but in a succession of scenes each of which depicts him at the next stage down.

The contrast of Industry and Idleness is repeated in *A Tale of Two Cities*, where Darnay very explicitly identifies himself with industry. He tells his uncle, 'I must do, to live, what others of my countrymen, even with nobility at their backs, may have to do some day – work' (ii, Chapter IX), and through steady application he rises in his adopted profession; Carton, on the other hand, is the 'idlest and most unpromising of men', and is upbraided by Stryver for his idleness (ii, Chapter V). The contrast between the two men is pointed by their close likeness in face. Carton, however, pursues a very different career from Thomas Idle, and Dickens's growing dissatisfaction with the simple Industry-Idleness opposition shows in the more interesting contrast the novel contains, that between Carton and Stryver. The two are yoked together in professional inter-dependence, and while Stryver reminds Carton that he is idle, Stryver himself is Industry personified, 'bursting out of the bed of wigs, like a great sunflower pushing its way at the sun from among a rank garden-full of flaring companions' (ii, Chapter V). The contrast here anticipates that in *Our Mutual Friend* where the industrious Apprentice, bent on rising in the world, is shown to apply himself with a bad kind of industry, while the idle Wrayburn becomes the focus of a man's difficult struggle to right the faults in his character that idleness has fostered. By this stage, the simple form of a Progress could not deal justly with the complexities the theme has incurred, and a close correspondence is not to be looked for; yet the way in which Dickens continually returned to the industry-idleness opposition, and only gradually developed a truly individual treatment of it, testifies to the impact Hogarth's series made on his imagination and ethical outlook.

Presumably, however, Forster had more than formal and ethical resemblances in mind when he said that Dickens and Hogarth were similar in genius 'as another generation will be probably more apt than our own to discover'.[24] When Dickens's contemporaries went into detail, they spoke of Hogarthian 'touches', and the temporary illustrator of *Pickwick*, R. W. Buss, found 'a great similarity' between Hogarth and Dickens not only in 'thought and power of description', but also in style;[25] the local techniques of the two artists should therefore be reviewed, in case there should be a general correspondence between them that would explain Forster's cryptic and portentous claim. A convenient working definition of Dickens's procedure is to be found in Taylor Stoehr's *Dickens: The Dreamer's Stance*. He notes that Dickens's descriptions of action are, in a peculiar way, static. While the prose seems to sweep forward with great momentum, Dickens does not actually follow through any central development *in* the action: rather, he curiously seems to 'freeze' the scene, while his mind plays over it, picking out the details at random. They could come in any order, and the unity of effect is imposed by the repetitions of Dickens's prose, which insist that each detail makes the same central point. Mr Stoehr describes these characteristics in an analysis of the Wine-Shop chapter in *A Tale of Two Cities*, which he takes to be representative of much of Dickens's writing, and he observes that 'the method involves a halting of time, a freezing of the scene to allow "photographic accuracy" in the representation of life-going-on'.[26] Thus, to find an adequate way of describing this habit, Mr Stoehr resorts to the cinematic comparison: each detail is an 'ocular fixation', a 'close-up', and the whole procedure resembles that of a director who will break up a scene of action into a succession of close-ups which could come in any order: 'To borrow another cinematic concept, the effect is like that of a montage-cluster, a series of detail shots juxtaposed in time, . . .'[27]

For the anachronistic analogy of the cinema, however, one could substitute the less bizarre comparison of Hogarth's paintings. A man studying a painting by Hogarth sees a host of distinct details, each of which has an almost allegorical burden and requires such close scrutiny that it might well be called an 'ocular fixation'. And the spectator's eye may rove as it pleases, so that the details may be 'read' in any order. Often each small area repeats the one central point, as the omnipresent coronet reduplicates the pride of the Earl through the first plate of *Marriage à-la-Mode* (70), or as the idleness of the Idle Apprentice is manifest in all the articles about him (as G. W. M. Reynolds described).[28] The method of such pictures is strikingly similar to that in the Wineshop passage:

'Hunger was pushed out of the tall houses, in the wretched clothing that hung upon poles and lines; Hunger was patched into them with straw and rag, and wood and paper; Hunger was repeated in every fragment of the small modicum of firewood that the man sawed off; Hunger stared down from the smokeless chimneys, and started up from the filthy street that had no offal, among its refuse, of anything to eat. Hunger was the inscription on the baker's shelves, written in every small loaf of his scanty stock of bad bread; at the sausage-shop, in every dead-dog preparation that was offered for sale. Hunger rattled its dry bones among the roasting chestnuts in the turned cylinder; Hunger was shred into atomies in every farthing porringer of husky chips of potato, fried with some reluctant drops of oil.'

The style is Dickensian, yet the technique is that of Hogarth. In 'Gin Lane' (15), for instance, the hunger, misery, and poverty resulting from drink are borne out in innumerable images. A man crouches down and gnaws a bare bone while a dog gnaws the other end. A tradesman is pawning his tools, a housewife her cooking pots. A corpse is picked off the street and put straight into a coffin. A mother absently lets her child fall over a banister. The houses are tottering, and through the ruined wall of one can be seen a man who has hanged himself.

There is, of course, a difference between Hogarth's print and the passage by Dickens, in that Dickens simply describes people miserable with hunger and repression, while Hogarth depicts a streetful of people crazy for drink. But the chapter from which the passage comes had begun:

'A large cask of wine had been dropped and broken, in the street. . . . All the people within reach had suspended their business, or their idleness, to run to the spot and drink the wine. The rough, irregular stones of the street, pointing every way, and designed, one might have thought, expressly to lame all living creatures that approached them, had dammed it into little pools; these were surrounded, each by its own jostling group or crowd, according to its size. Some men kneeled down, made scoops of their two hands joined, and sipped, or tried to help women, who bent over their shoulders, to sip, before the wine had all run out between their fingers. Others, men and women, dipped in the puddles with little mugs of

15. William Hogarth, 'Gin Lane'.

mutilated earthenware, or even with handkerchiefs from women's heads, which were squeezed dry into infants' mouths; others made small mud-embankments, to stem the wine as it ran; others, directed by lookers-on up at high windows, darted here and there, to cut off little streams of wine that started away in new directions; others devoted themselves to the sodden and lee-dyed pieces of the cask, licking, and even champing the moister wine-rotted fragments with eager relish.'

The situation here is the reverse of that in 'Gin Lane', for here it is misery and poverty that have driven people to drink, while in Hogarth's picture it is the gin that has brought people to misery and poverty. This difference would not have existed for Dickens, however, since in his reading of 'Gin Lane' the drunkenness was merely the result of destitution. He disagreed with Charles Lamb on this point, and said, in an article attacking teetotalism:

'It is remarkable of that picture ["Gin Lane"], that while it exhibits drunkenness in its most appalling forms, it forces on the attention of the spectator a most neglected, wretched neighbourhood. . . . We have always been inclined to think the purpose of this piece was not adequately stated, even by Charles Lamb. "The very houses seem absolutely reeling," it is true; but they quite as powerfully indicate some of the more prominent causes of intoxication among the neglected orders of society, as any of its effects.'[29]

Dickens argued that it was no use telling people not to drink when the appalling conditions in which they lived offered no other consolation. It is hard to think that this is truly the lesson of Hogarth's print. In 'Beer Street', the companion-piece to 'Gin Lane', the same class of people – the small tradesmen – are shown to be happy, prosperous, and fat because they drink beer rather than gin. Their houses are in good repair, and the contrast between the plates suggests that the decay of the houses in 'Gin Lane' is intended more as a result of drink than a cause.

It remains true, however, that the Wineshop chapter in *Two Cities* gives us Dickens's 'Gin Lane', even if it does not give us 'Gin Lane' as Hogarth had originally intended it. And in the full description there is passage on passage that is at the same time pure Dickens and pure Hogarth:

'The trade signs (and they were almost as many as the shops) were, all, grim illustrations of Want. The butcher and the porkman painted up, only the leanest scrags of meat; the baker, the coarsest of meagre loaves. The people rudely pictured as drinking in the wine-shops, croaked over their scanty measures of thin wine and beer, and were gloweringly confidential together. Nothing was represented in a flourishing condition, save tools and weapons; but, the cutler's knives and axes were sharp and bright, the smith's hammers were heavy, and the gunmaker's stock was murderous.'

There are no pictorial trade-signs in 'Gin Lane', although the emblematic signs of pawnbroker, coffin-maker, and spirit-seller assert themselves strongly in the composition; but in other pictures Hogarth made an extensive and elaborate use of trade-signs, particularly in the series *The Times*.

Passages in other novels suggest that 'Gin Lane', one of Hogarth's most horrific pictures, haunted Dickens throughout his writing life. There is the wretched neighbourhood through which Oliver Twist goes to the pauper funeral, or the glimpse of the slums from the train-window in *Dombey and Son*:

'There are jagged walls and falling houses close at hand, and through the battered roofs and broken windows, wretched rooms are seen, where want and fever hide themselves in many wretched shapes, while smoke, and crowded gables, and distorted chimneys, and deformity of brick and mortar penning up deformity of mind and body, choke the murky distance.'[30]

We cannot doubt that Dickens is here describing realities that were often to be seen in his England; but his energy in carrying the one point through many details, his automatic recourse to allegory, his animation of the decayed houses, and his equation of their decay with human decay, suggest that he saw these realities as a constant repetition of 'Gin Lane' in the real world.

Hogarth's practice of intensifying a single meaning by repeating it through a hundred multifarious details was recognized and respected in Dickens's day. The commentaries available to Dickens, such as those of Trusler and Ireland, were chiefly concerned to elucidate such meanings point by point. Yet when this artistic procedure is used by Dickens himself it provokes a different kind of commentary. Mr Stoehr quotes Taine: 'The imagination of Dickens is like that of monomaniacs. To plunge oneself into an idea, to be absorbed by it, to see nothing else, to repeat it under a hundred forms. . . .'[31] A quotation from Lamb's essay on Hogarth will show that monomania is not the only possible explanation for the repetition of an idea under a hundred forms:

'There is more of imagination in [Hogarth's work – Lamb is comparing him to Poussin] – that power which draws all things to one, – which makes things animate and inanimate, beings with their attributes, subjects and their accessories, take one colour, and serve to one effect. Every thing in the print, to use a vulgar expression, *tells*.'

Later, he speaks of 'the dumb rhetoric of the scenery – for tables, and chairs, and joint-stools in Hogarth, are living and significant things,' and one of Dickens's most marked features is, in the phrase of another critic, 'the pervasive animistic magic . . . by which he endows inanimate objects with life'.[32]

Dickens himself supplied an apt formula for his use of multiplied detail in the following passage from *Dombey*:

'He glanced round the room; saw how the splendid means of personal adorn-
ment, and the luxuries of dress, were scattered here and there, and disregarded;
not in mere caprice and carelessness (or so he thought), but in a steadfast, haughty
disregard of costly things: and felt it more and more. Chaplets of flowers, plumes
of feathers, jewels, laces, silks and satins; look where he would, he saw riches,
despised, poured out, and made of no account. The very diamonds – a marriage
gift – that rose and fell impatiently upon her bosom, seemed to pant to break the
chain that clasped them round her neck, and roll down on the floor where she
might tread upon them.

He felt his disadvantage, and he showed it. Solemn and strange among
this wealth of colour and voluptuous glitter, strange and constrained towards its
haughty mistress, whose repellent beauty it repeated, and presented all around
him, as in so many fragments of a mirror. . . .' (Chapter XL)

Dickens, like Hogarth, uses his material details as 'so many fragments of a mirror'; as to the actual use of disorder here, there is a comparable use of riches
strewn about a room, also in a context of mis-mating, in the second plate of *Marriage à-la-Mode*.

Mr Stoehr describes very well Dickens's ability 'to command effects which
are out of the question for most writers, at once realistic in kind and in quantity
of detail, and almost allegorical in the schematization and intensity of rendering'.
But he goes on: 'The blend is dream-like, hallucinatory, super-real' and this is
surely an unnecessary extension? The effects he describes need not seem hallucinatory, but merely traditional, particularly if one considers the way in which
Dickens's prose developed. For in his early writing, the habit of filling in a picture
with significant details is demonstrably related to traditional allegorical habit:

'There was a lean and haggard woman, too – a prisoner's wife – who was water-
ing, with great solicitude, the wretched stump of a dried-up, withered plant,
which, it was plain to see, could never send forth a green leaf again; – too true an
emblem, perhaps, of the office she had come there to discharge.'

In *Pickwick* (Chapter XLI), Dickens can be as explicit as that; in his later writing his use of emblematic detail becomes at the same time more personal and
alive, and more closely woven into his prose. One might expect that in a later
work, an effect comparable with that of *Pickwick* would be achieved by an insistent description of a great many things withering in a general blight, without
any open mention of emblems. And this is how Miss Wade's house is described
in *Little Dorrit*:

'A dead sort of house, with a dead wall over the way and a dead gateway at
the side, where a pendant bell-handle produced two dead tinkles, . . . However,

the door jarred open on a dead sort of spring; and he closed it behind him as he entered a dull yard, soon brought to a close at the back by another dead wall, where an attempt had been made to train some creeping shrubs, which were dead; and to make a little fountain in a grotto, which was dry; and to decorate that with a little statue, which was gone.' (ii, Chapter XX)

But again this passage, though mature and decidedly 'Dickensian', uses a technique similar to that of Hogarth in 'Gin Lane' where the debility of the people is repeated in the disintegration of the houses and the general desolation. We may note that the particular emblem of the withered plant may well have come from Hogarth, who used it in his Tailpiece for the Catalogue of the Exhibition of the Society of Artists at Spring Gardens (16). And among the 18th-century artists who might be counted Dickens's predecessors, this almost allegorical use of visual detail is conspicuous in Hogarth, but hardly noticeable in any novelist.

16. William Hogarth, Tailpiece to the Catalogue of the Exhibition of the Society of Artists at Spring Gardens.

Finally, it may be suggested that Hogarth gave Dickens his visual bearings in looking at the human body, and in particular at the human face. For Dickens is so sharply conscious of the physical peculiarities of his characters that each feature might well be called the subject of an 'ocular fixation'. The features are identified with the personality, and are regularly recalled when the character reappears. Thus, in *Our Mutual Friend*, Podsnap is first described as 'prosperously feeding, two little light-coloured wiry wings, one on either side of his else bald head, looking as like his hair-brushes as his hair' (i, Chapter II). The reader is not permitted to forget these tufts; at the wedding, for instance, Podsnap appears 'with his hair-brushes made the most of' (i, Chapter X). For a novelist, Dickens has a remarkable intentness of eye, and he sees almost every character he creates with the same sharp perception of the physical details that isolate the individual. But it might be said that in this respect, he is simply seeing with Hogarth's eye – with the eye that marked Hogarth himself off from other artists. For it was Hogarth's practice to fill his pictures with crowds, and yet to make each figure distinct from the others and unique in every detail. In so far as Dickens had precedents in literature, they are to be found in such passages as Fielding's description of Mrs Tow-Wouse:

'Her Person was short, thin, and crooked. Her Forehead projected in the middle, and thence descended in a Declivity to the Top of her Nose, which was sharp and red, and would have hung over her Lips, had not nature turned up the end of it. Her Lips were two Bits of Skin, which, whenever she spoke, she drew together in a Purse. Her Chin was pecked, and at the upper end of that Skin which composed her Cheeks, stood two Bones, that almost hid a Pair of small red Eyes.'[33]

But such sharp realization is uncommon in Fielding's work (nor does he recur to the physical details on each successive reappearance of the character, as Dickens does), and in any case Fielding is deeply influenced by Hogarth in his handling of the physical aspects of characterization;[34] the Tow-Wouse passage is introduced with a remark that says, in effect, that Fielding is attempting in prose what Hogarth does in painting: 'Nature had taken such Pains in her Countenance, that *Hogarth* himself never gave more Expression to a Picture.' Admiring Fielding as he did, Dickens was presumably familiar with the tribute to Hogarth in the Preface to *Joseph Andrews*, in which Fielding identifies Hogarth's visual mode with his own literary one and argues that 'the Comic Writer and Painter correlate to each other'. Moreover, his attention would have been directed to Hogarth's treatment of the human face, if any direction were needed, by Lamb's repeated praises: 'there is one part of the figure in which Hogarth is allowed to have excelled . . . I mean the human face'. Again, he speaks of 'all these faces so strongly charactered, yet finished with the accuracy of the finest miniature'. Hazlitt, too, had pointed out the excellence of Hogarth's heads, which 'have all the reality and correctness of portraits', and in which 'he gives the extremes of character and expression', although 'he gives them with perfect truth and accuracy'. It may, therefore, seem reasonable to suggest that the intense scrutiny of Hogarth's work played a large part in alerting Dickens's observation to the physical characteristics of human beings; the narrative use of these characteristics was already to be found in Hogarth's Progresses, where the principal characters are recognized, on each successive appearance, by their physical peculiarities.

Hazlitt, in particular, finds in Hogarth a balance of nature with accentuation, and of truth with the unusual, that corresponds to the balance intended in Dickens's own characterization. Hazlitt observes that Hogarth's faces 'go to the very verge of caricature, and yet never (we believe in any single instance) go beyond it: they take the very widest latitude, and yet we always see the links which bind them to nature'. He says also that 'they exhibit the most uncommon features with the most uncommon expressions, but which are yet as familiar and intelligible as possible, because with all the force they have all the truth of Nature'. Hazlitt's dictum may be compared with Santayana's: 'When people say that Dickens exaggerates, it seems to me that they can have no eyes and no ears.'[35] The position is, however, more complicated than Santayana allows, for whether or not Dickens's creations may be called caricatures, Dickens uses various kinds of exaggeration habitually; and the question of Hogarth's influence is complicated because Hogarth was the declared enemy of any degree of exaggeration, and attacked the methods of caricature in such prints as 'Characters and Caricaturas'. In 'The Bench' (17) he satirized the exaggeration of physical feature (in the studies at the top) and recommended his own exact delineation, in which character was sufficiently expressed. Fielding endorsed Hogarth's distinction in the Preface to *Joseph Andrews*, arguing that 'it is much easier, much less the Subject of Admiration, to paint a Man with a Nose, or any other Feature of a preposterous Size, or to expose him in some absurd or monstrous Attitude, than to express the Affections of Men on Canvas'. But their rigid distinction between 'character' and 'caricature' ignores the ways in which caricature can express character. Caricature need not distort only the physical shape of the head, it can also accentuate expression, and a well-caught expression, although exaggerated, tells the spectator more about the inner man than the outer; moreover, some of the lines that may be used to convey expression do not copy actual puckerings of the skin, so much as record its movements: lines of sneering or frowning may convey, in their quick sweep, the sudden motion of the muscle, rather than the pattern of lines that result from it. In 'The Bench' there is little reason to prefer either version, since the expression is equally well-caught in each; and in the finer works of Gillray and Rowlandson, caricature *is* character. Exaggeration expresses the artist's legitimate delight in noticing and isolating the distinctive feature, while his prey is the whole man and not merely the physique. The exaggerations of

Gillray and Rowlandson do not mislead the spectator about human anatomy, and the faces they draw do not necessarily convey less of the inner life than those of Hogarth. For their part, they clearly did not feel themselves to be at odds with Hogarth, and they were much influenced by him.

Dickens's habitual mode of characterization has the complexity we should expect to result from long immersion both in Hogarth's works and in the caricatures also. Although he brings a uniquely concentrated vision to bear on the physical details of his people, he does not submit these details to physical distortion; yet the reality is presented, none the less, through an elaborate play of

17. William Hogarth, 'The Bench' (Fourth State).

far-fetched comparisons. In a fine caricature, the exaggeration still creates in the mind a real human face, and not an impossible mask; it is a question of emphatic economy rather than distortion, and we instinctively qualify the witty magnifications, while taking the caricaturist's point; and Dickens's conceits work in a comparable way when he describes Mr Bounderby in *Hard Times*:

'A man made out of a coarse material, which seemed to have been stretched to make so much of him. A man with a great puffed head and forehead, swelled veins in his temples, and such a strained skin to his face that it seemed to hold his eyes open, and lift his eyebrows up. A man with a pervading appearance on him of being inflated like a balloon, and ready to start.' (Chapter IV)

Although a real face is fearfully caught here, such a portrayal fits naturally in the context of the many figures of vastly exaggerated bloatedness in the caricatures, Cruikshank's caricature of the sailor whose pigtail was tied so tight that he could not shut his eyes, and Gillray's balloon-man in his print 'Tentanda via est. . .'.

The complexity, however, belongs to Dickens's later years; in his early work, the relationship to caricature is simpler and clearer. The exaggeration is not confined to the conceits of the description, but seriously affects the imagined physique of the person described. Dickens says of the elder Mr Weller's face:

'its bold fleshy curves had so far extended beyond the limits originally assigned them, that unless you took a full view of his countenance in front, it was difficult to distinguish more than the extreme tip of a very rubicund nose.' (Chapter XXIII)

Mr Weller's cheeks could not really be so swollen without some more serious disorder than normal fatness. Such a figure calls Rowlandson to mind, and Dickens's familiarity with 'the works of Rowlandson or Gillray' is evident in his review of Leech's *Rising Generation*.[36] He praises their 'great humour' but then goes on to condemn the 'vast amount of personal ugliness'. Yet although Dickens is a representative Victorian here, conscious of belonging to a more refined and proper age, he may not have disapproved so strongly in his more boisterous days, and before the example of Leech provoked comparisons.[37] For it could hardly be said that in his *Pickwick* phase Dickens confined himself to physical beauty, in the way that Leech is praised for doing. Then, Dickens was amused by obesity, and positively liked fat men: Mr Justice Stareleigh, like many other characters, seems to have stepped straight out of Rowlandson's work:

'Mr Justice Stareleigh . . . was a most particularly short man, and so fat, that he seemed all face and waistcoat. He rolled in, upon two little turned legs, and having bobbed gravely to the bar, who bobbed gravely to him, put his little legs underneath the table, and his little three-cornered hat upon it; and when Mr Justice Stareleigh had done this, all you could see of him was two queer little eyes, one broad pink face, and somewhere about half of a big and very comical-looking wig.' (Chapter XXXIII)

It is not just that Rowlandson peopled his world with preternaturally fat men, while Dickens has his Pickwick, Tupman, Wardle, Fat Boy, Old Weller, and a large subsidiary cast of fat men, such as the three fat men at Dingley Dell; but that when Dickens introduces a new pair of minor characters, he has a habit of making one of them very fat and one of them very thin. It is part of his idiom:

'Just as the clock struck three, there were blown into the Crescent a sedan-chair with Mrs Dowler inside, borne by one short fat chairman, and one long thin one, who had much ado all the way to keep their bodies perpendicular, to say nothing of the chair.' (Chapter XXXV)

'The stout turnkey having been relieved from the lock, sat down, and looked at him carelessly from time to time, while a long thin man who had relieved him, . . .' (Chapter XXXIX)

The contrast is a visual one, and although one could find literary precedents for it – in *Don Quixote*, for instance, which was certainly known to Dickens – it is common only in the fanciful world of caricature. There, it represents an almost mechanical habit in the creation of comic characters, and that is what it is for Dickens. More generally, Dickens resembles Rowlandson in his delight in giving a high-spirited, panoramic portrayal of the varied traditional enjoyments of life. In scope and spirit his art is quite different from the fast slumming of *Tom and Jerry*, and would be characterized more truly by the name of Rowlandson than by that of Pierce Egan.

Dickens was indebted to Rowlandson, for the comic cycles of Dr Syntax were among the precursors of *Pickwick*: the basic notion of a comic antiquarian writing up his tours served for both artist and novelist. Syntax's concern with the picturesque recalls another common characteristic. For it is not the most obvious or natural artistic practice to combine characters consistently imagined in a style of broad comedy and caricature with a landscape-background offered for the simple but intense appreciation of its beauty. Yet Rowlandson often does this, and it may be that he showed Dickens how feasible such a combination could be. Dickens certainly achieves it with remarkable ease, fullness, and beauty in the passage describing Pickwick on Rochester bridge. For all its freshness and sparkle – Dickens is clearly recalling a real scene – the picture painted is a traditional example of the picturesque:

'. . . the green ivy clung mournfully round the dark, and ruined battlements. Behind [the wall] rose the ancient castle, . . . telling as proudly of its own might and strength, as when, seven hundred years ago, it rang with the clash of arms, . . .' (Chapter V)

The term 'picturesque' is used in the final sentence ('heavy but picturesque boats glided slowly down the stream'). Against this lovely background the rotund Pickwick is presently joined by the emaciated and ragged 'dismal man' of the previous chapter, making a composition highly reminiscent of Rowlandson.

Dickens's affinity with the satiric print goes far beyond composition, moreover. It extends to the fantastic realm, in constant ferment, that hovers behind and shows through Dickens's London. His imaginative world is capable of sudden incandescent transformations, and every person, animal, and thing can abruptly take new life. These transformations came easily to Dickens, and they are sometimes more a habit than a vision; yet so often in reading him one is arrested by the thought: through what strange eyes this man saw life, that he could know that blackened, debased, and deprived London so much at first hand, and yet see it so filled with mystery and real magic? If the vision is not his genius, it is inextricably involved with his genius; but a vision of life is an evanescent and fugitive quantity, difficult to come to terms with. It does not invite analysis, and an attempt to resolve it into separate components may take away the life of the vision without giving insight into it. In Dickens's writing, however, distinct features do recur, and a list of them can provide a useful start. The most complete list is perhaps that compiled by J. C. Reid in his lecture-series *The Hidden World of Charles Dickens*. He includes in it dream and nightmare, allegory, parable, fairy-tale figures, men seen as animals, the Devil, Hell, and 'the pervasive animistic magic' that turns things into people and people into things. Reid argues that each of these is an 'archetype' and that Dickens's gifts were of the archetypal kind: he easily saw through the immediate and local to the permanent, primary elements of human experience. Certainly in his writing Dickens had ready access to stratas of experience that few writers have drawn on with such variety and power; and a genius for getting inside the immediate ordinary event and intensifying and deepening it so as to open large perspectives beyond it. But it does, at least, complicate the archetypal case to say that all the items so far mentioned are part of the regular imaginative synthesis of the caricatures and older graphic satire.

To an extent it is the compresence of all the archetypes together that is significant, rather than the coincidence of single items. For one cannot assume an influence simply because fable and parable, personification and allegory were the standard resources of political caricature; or because the incongruous juxtapositions were often realized with a wild inventiveness that made the caricatures seem dreamlike or even nightmarish. But it is remarkable that some of the most compelling features of the Dickensian vision are also among the most forceful presences in the fantasy worlds of Gillray and Cruikshank.

Dickens has, for instance, a habit of charging chairs, sundials, trees, and machines with the vitality and character of human beings. There is a constant dialogue in his novels between object and person, and the inanimate things of the world actively coax, bully, cheer, and frighten his characters. In *Great Expectations* Pip ventures out onto the marshes with the pork-pie he has stolen for the convict:

'The mist was heavier yet when I got out upon the marshes, so that instead of my running at everything, everything seemed to run at me. This was very disagreeable to a guilty mind. The gates and dykes and banks came bursting at me through the mist, as if they cried as plainly as could be, "A boy with Somebody-else's pork pie! Stop him!"' (Chapter III)

And in *Bleak House* the fears and confusions in Esther Summerson's mind make her think that 'the stained house fronts put on human shapes and looked at me' (Chapter LIX).

Dickens's habit of vitalizing what he describes is well-known as a trait that marks him off from other writers. Patricia Gibson describes his sense of 'the inanimate world as animated, self-directing, and even endowed with human feelings and responses' as a 'unique vision'.[38] But the vision was not unique. George Cruikshank had, in his caricatures, frequently identified the human and the inanimate, and 'London going out of Town' (18) shows at once with what vigour and

18. George Cruikshank, 'London going out of Town'.

variety inanimate things came to life in his work. Although there is some engaging humour in the plate – the workmen digging the pit have beermugs for heads – there is too much menace in the advancing hordes to let us suppose the city is animated purely out of whimsical fancy. The plate has with its humour an intensity that suggests the artist had truly felt the expanding city as a dangerous growing creature, or plague of creatures. This weird strength of visionary wit could remind us of many plates by Gillray; viewing such a work as 'London going out of Town' in a longer perspective, however, we might say rather that on this side of his genius Cruikshank belongs with Bruegel.

Cruikshank's animated creations are often frightening, and resemble the composite monsters of a nightmare. In 'Fashionable Movements' some panic-stricken geese run into the sea from three awesome ogres, one of whom is an animated guillotine, while another has a portcullis for a body and shackles for arms and legs. Yet again, although the plate is frightening, it is a caricature, and the monsters are humorously conceived.[39] And the animism of Dickens himself shows just this combination of energetic imaginative vision with a curious play of humour. In *A Tale of Two Cities*, Young Jerry

'had a strong idea that the coffin he had seen was running after him; and, pictured as hopping on behind him, bolt upright upon its narrow end, always on the point of overtaking him and hopping on at his side – perhaps taking his arm – it was a pursuer to shun.' (ii, Chapter XIV)

The 'pictured' coffin is eminently Cruikshankian in its combination of sprightly activity ('hopping') with horror.

Dickens's use of animism can of course seem such an intimate and personal characteristic that one hesitates to ascribe it to any external influence. But the idiosyncrasy of his mature imagination was perhaps only the final rising to the surface, sea-changed and self-renewing, of innumerable impressions that were thrust into his exposed consciousness when a child at large in the London streets. For the print-shops, their windows crowded with brightly coloured caricatures, survived as a popular street-entertainment well into the youth of the Dickens–Thackeray generation. They were one of the vivid events of Thackeray's childhood: he recalled

'Knight's in Sweeting's Alley; Fairburn's, in a court off Ludgate Hill; Hone's, in Fleet Street – bright, enchanted palaces, which George Cruikshank used to people with grinning, fantastical imps, ... where are they? ... How we used ... to stray miles out of the way on holidays, in order to ponder for an hour before that delightful window in Sweeting's Alley!'[40]

There were many such shops, and the crowd at the window seems to have been a permanent feature. There are prints by both Gillray and Cruikshank showing these crowds standing at the shop-windows and gazing with admiration at caricatures by Gillray and Cruikshank respectively. Tom Pinch's dissipation in Salisbury, in *Martin Chuzzlewit*, suggests that Dickens had been accustomed to an even more intense absorption in the pictures in shop-windows; it suggests also

[68]

that his habit of fusing fairy-tale and reality was partly encouraged by the book-illustrations on show there. Some books Dickens could read at home, in isolation from the actual world, but many more were available as enchanted pictures in a busy thoroughfare; he could wander round the real streets with the imaginary scenes vividly superimposed on the vivid London scene, and marrying with it:

'There was another . . . trying shop; where children's books were sold . . . and there too was Abudah, the merchant, with the terrible little old woman hobbling out of the box in his bedroom: and there the mighty talisman—the rare Arabian Nights—with Cassim Baba, divided by four, like the ghost of a dreadful sum, hanging up, all gory, in the robbers' cave. Which matchless wonders, coming fast on Mr. Pinch's mind, did so rub up and chafe that wonderful lamp within him, that when he turned his face towards the busy street, a crowd of phantoms waited on his pleasure, and he lived again, with new delight, the happy days before the Pecksniff era.' (Chapter V)

After reading this passage, we are not surprised to find that many of the fairy-tale passages in Dickens are notably pictorial. Concluding the description of Paul Dombey, Mrs Pipchin, and the cat sitting before the fire, he writes:

'The good old lady might have been—not to record it disrespectfully—a witch, and Paul and the cat her two familiars, as they all sat by the fire together. It would have been quite in keeping with the appearance of the party if they had all sprung up the chimney in a high wind one night, and never been heard of any more.' (Chapter VIII)

The use of fairy-tale motives was not, of course, something that Dickens needed to learn from the caricatures, but it should be noted that the imaginary worlds of caricature and fairy-tale illustration overlapped. The more fantastic caricatures make a free use of ogres and goblins, and it was in keeping that George Cruikshank, the last great caricaturist, found fairy-tales his most congenial subject in book-illustration.

An evening with the caricatures was an institution in the English home during Dickens's childhood. The editor of a reissue of Gillray, in 1818, observes that 'among the amusements at a winter evening party we know of none more interesting, or more rational than that of turning over a portfolio of well-selected caricatures'. Dickens had no need even to leave the house to gain his familiarity with the 'caricatures . . . of effeminate Exquisites' that he describes in *Bleak House* (Chapter XII). Thackeray also recalled the 'two or three old mottled portfolios, or great swollen scrap-books of bluepaper, full of the comic prints of grandpapa's time'. The 'great coloured prints' were not confined to the portfolios, but were also to be found 'in some other apartments of the house, where the caricatures used to be pasted in those days'.

ODD FISH

19. George Cruikshank, 'Odd Fish'.

It may be assumed then that the young Dickens, in his most impressionable years, could scarcely have escaped the impact of the caricatures; it remains a moot point whether one should say that his taste for the fantastic would have made him study them with special interest, or rather that the caricatures helped give him his taste for the fantastic. If in his mature years he frequently compares people to animals, as Reid notes, then it is hard not to relate this practice to the fact that the transformation of men into animals was far and away the most frequent strategy of Gillray and the lesser political caricaturists. Gillray's 'John Bull and his Dog Faithful' (8) is one example – but examples are countless. Outside the political context, Cruikshank showed a fondness for such changes in innumerable plates which must be represented here by 'Odd Fish' (19).

In Cruikshank's work, transformation into animals is simply one among many styles of metamorphosis, a variation of his habitual animism. But although with Cruikshank, as with Dickens, this vision seems so personal that one would not look for antecedents, metamorphosis – and animism especially – had a long ancestry in the satiric print. In the background were such plates as Gillray's 'French-Telegraph making Signals in the Dark' and Hogarth's 'Royalty, Episcopacy and Law', in which the king, bishop, and judge have for their heads a guinea, a jew's harp, and a mallet respectively, while the courtier is a mirror, the soldiers are fire-screens, and the courtly lady has a tea-pot for a head and a fan for her torso.

Satirical animism such as Hogarth's is clearly related to the traditional personifying habits of allegory; it was not of course invented by Hogarth and may already be seen in its full force and liveliness in Bruegel's 'The Battle of the Moneybags and the Strongboxes' (20); at one point Dickens associated his own animistic imagination with just such prints as this. Nicholas Nickleby and Smike are entering London:

'As they dashed by the quickly-changing and ever-varying objects, it was curious to observe in what a strange procession they passed before the eye. Emporiums of splendid dresses, the materials brought from every quarter of the world . . . vessels of burnished gold and silver . . . guns, swords, pistols, and patent engines of destruction; screws and irons for the crooked, clothes for the newly-born, drugs for the sick, coffins for the dead, churchyards for the buried – all these jumbled each with the other and flocking side by side, seemed to flit by in motley dance like the fantastic groups of the old Dutch painter, and with the same stern moral for the unheeding restless crowd.'[41]

It would also seem likely that a powerful memory of Bruegel contributed to Dickens's handling of another item in Reid's list, Hell. In *Bleak House*, the nightmarish slum Tom-All-Alone's is described as a 'pit' into which the protagonists have 'descended', and the inhabitants are 'a concourse of imprisoned demons'

Within the image: *P. Bruegel Inue.*, *Aux quatre Vents.*, *Æ.*

20. Pieter Bruegel the Elder, 'The Battle of the Moneybags and the Strongboxes'

(Chapter XXII). Mr Snagsby 'feels as if he were going, every moment deeper down, into the infernal gulf' while 'the crowd . . . hovers round the three visitors, like a dream of horrible faces'. Dickens accentuates the horror of his subject by superimposing on it a picture of Hell, and his image of Hell resembles that of Bruegel more than that of any other artist:

'As, on the ruined human wretch, vermin parasites appear, so, these ruined shelters have bred a crowd of foul existence that crawls in and out of gaps in walls and boards; and coils itself to sleep, in maggot numbers, where the rain drips in. . . .' (Chapter XVI)

The swarming 'maggot numbers' half-human and half-vermin, with the reptile suggestion of 'coiling', recall the crowds of stunted hybrid creatures crawling across many of Bruegel's works. These creatures inhabit distorted and broken human bodies and monstrous ruined heads, and such recollections would have facilitated Dickens's comparison of the 'ruined shelters' to the 'ruined human wretch' with 'vermin parasites'.

Tracing the image of Hell in Dickens's work, Reid refers also to the treatment of the industrial north in *The Old Curiosity Shop*, where factories 'now shone red-hot, with figures moving to and fro within their blazing jaws, and calling to one another with hoarse cries' (Chapter XLV). Although Reid stresses the general, archetypal character of such references, there is surely here a more specific recollection of the medieval paintings and carvings of Hell-mouth?

When he proceeds from Hell to the Devil, Reid suggests again that Dickens is harking back to archetypal fears. The fear may be there in the background, but in Dickens's writing the more ominous suggestions are mitigated by a constant play of humorous fancy. There is a sustained comparison of Fagin with the Devil in *Oliver Twist*,[42] but Fagin is a very sprightly Devil. Similarly, when Lammle is identified with the Devil in *Our Mutual Friend*, the treatment is humorously sinister. On the Shanklin sands, 'the gentleman has trailed his stick after him. As if he were of the Mephistopheles family indeed, and had walked with a drooping tail' (i, Chapter X). A darker shadow falls on Lammle when he 'has turned to a livid white, and ominous marks have come to light about his nose, as if the finger of the very devil himself had, within the last few moments, touched it here and there'. But the grimness dissipates when the marks fluctuate 'like white stops of a pipe on which the diabolical performer has played a tune'. Quilp, too, dances a 'demon-dance' (Chapter XXI), and the tormented Mrs Nubbles is driven to believe that he is the Devil (Chapter XLVIII). Chesterton said that 'Quilp is precisely the devil of the Middle Ages; he belongs to that amazingly healthy period when even the lost spirits were hilarious'.[43] It might equally be said that Dickens's Devil is precisely the Devil of the caricatures, for a boisterous, impish Devil recurs in graphic satire. Thackeray recalled how Gillray had presented the Broad-bottom Administration as 'demons . . . cursing the light (their atrocious ringleader Fox was represented with hairy cloven feet, and a tail and horns)'.[44] And the caricature-devil is, by direct continuity, the Devil of the Middle Ages; he came into caricature from the primitive wood-cuts that had kept him vigorously alive for several hundred years.

With the Devil, the caricatures inherited also the medieval Death. In 1815–1816 Rowlandson and Combe let the traditional skeleton rove through the world in which they lived, in *The English Dance of Death*. From caricature, the Dance of Death was passed on to book-illustration by uch sprints as the frontispiece by Robert Cruikshank for Pierce Egan's *Finish to the Adventures of Tom, Jerry, and Logic*. The items of traditional iconography are listed by Egan in his commentary.

'The *circle* of the frontispiece mournfully represents the OXONIAN *floored* at full length under the Table by the unwelcome Guest (the grim King of Terrors) over the "*last bottle*!" It also shows that CORINTHIAN TOM has not a single word to offer on the fascinating subject of *Life in London*; and JERRY must be viewed upon his last legs, as a perfect *dummy*, alarmed at the *defunct* state of his *pals*, endeavouring to avert the pointed dart of DEATH; and also to hide from his eyes the emblematical hint of the *hour-glass*, that the "TIME *must* come!"'

As Egan notes, at the bottom of the design 'the CHARLIES are reeling', and this dance of the link-men clearly recalls the Dance of Death itself, for the link-man on the right is a skeleton.

Dickens had read *The Finish to Tom and Jerry*, and he could scarcely have escaped seeing the Dance of Death in the caricatures of Rowlandson and others. He also owned a set of Holbein's *Dance of Death*, bought in 1841.[45] And he slips without difficulty into a medieval mode of visual imagining when, for instance, he describes Mrs Skewton 'in her finery leering and mincing at Death, and playing off her youthful tricks upon him as if he had been the Major' (Chapter XXXVII). The vision of the old moral prints was still alive in his imagination, fused with the world he saw about him.

The caricatures of the early 19th century, of Gillray, Rowlandson, and the Cruikshanks, are not merely caricatures. They perpetuate and revitalize an older vision of life, and this vision coincides surprisingly with that of Dickens. R. D. McMaster is unconsciously describing the print-world of Gillray and Cruikshank when he says 'the people and objects of Dickens' world seem caught by surprise in the midst of a universal metamorphosis. Objects behave like people; people verge on the inanimate; or they resemble animals, birds, fish, and other inhuman forms of life.'[46] The same description applies to Hogarth's predecessor, Bruegel; and to Bruegel's master, Bosch. The Dickensian 'vision' was not, then, a new creation; if not archetypal it runs back through ages, and Bruegel and Dickens are linked in one long continuity. But the vision was new in the novel, and in the novel it flourished, though it died out of satiric drawing. The total case gives a remarkable demonstration of a great imaginative mode moving out of one art and into another.

There were, none the less, disadvantages for the novel in the fact that the older vision was largely transmitted to Dickens through caricatures. One result of this mediation is that Dickens will elaborate a visionary idea for its humour as well as for its power, when sometimes the humour and the power do not agree. Yet in the caricatures themselves, the humour is, at its finest, a robust visual wit which, working on the percurrent tendency to metamorphosis, generates such powerful metaphors as the wooden leg of John Bull which is also his scraped bone. Dickens's own energy in metaphor is too well-known to need demonstration. It, too, is simply the sharpening and turning to purpose of the habitual metamorphosis and animism of his imagination. The full picture is complex, but it may at least be said that a full understanding of what Dickens absorbed from visual art can greatly help us to understand and appreciate the abilities that make him unique among novelists. It would not do, however, to suggest that these strengths were mainly confined to him, or that they ceased with his death. Among his contemporaries, one novelist especially knew both the caricaturists and Hogarth as well as he did, and independently shaped an art of fiction that grew out of graphic satire: this was Dickens's great competitor in the monthly parts, William Makepeace Thackeray.

4

'A Voice Concurrent or Prophetical':
The Illustrated Novels of
W. M. Thackeray

21. W. M. Thackeray, capital for *The Virginians*, II, Chapter II.

illiam Makepeace Thackeray is the one major English novelist who illustrated his own works; and as an artist he belongs in the English satiric habit running back to the early 18th century. He venerated Hogarth and Gillray, learnt etching from Cruikshank, and was himself a caricaturist. And it was an art of versatile visual irony, learnt from the caricatures, that he carried into his novels as illustration, and exercised in his innumerable etchings and woodcuts for *Vanity Fair*, *Pendennis*, and *The Virginians*.

His interest in art had shown itself long before his gift as a novelist. For his first attempt at a creative career, he studied art in Paris. When Dickens required an illustrator for *Pickwick* Thackeray applied for the post, and he later claimed that if his application had been successful, he might have been an illustrator all

[76]

his life.[1] His first published work was the series of lithographs *Flore et Zéphyr* (1836), a satire on the ballet that perhaps derives too much of its humour from the simple device of giving his ballet-dancers bony shoulders, spindle shanks, and splay feet – though the actual rendering of arms and legs is careful and precise, and the figures have a firmness that Thackeray does not seek in his later, more sketchy style. In 1840 he brought out *The Paris Sketch Book* with his own illustrations, and published his *Essay on the Genius of George Cruikshank*, who had been his teacher.[2] In 1839 and 1840, he was almost the only artist in *Fraser's Magazine*, providing the illustrations for his serial *Catherine*. He wrote for *Punch*, illustrating his work and also providing separate cartoons, and he included his illustrations when he brought out his contributions in book form, as in *The Book of Snobs* (1848). In 1846 came his first Christmas Book, *Mrs Perkins's Ball*, in which the text is no more than an extended caption to the series of full-page plates. In 1847 the first monthly numbers of *Vanity Fair* were issued, with etched plates, woodcuts set in the text, and capital letters with symbolic drawings in them, all by Thackeray.

This record might suggest that Thackeray was an expert draughtsman. But if his contemporaries thought so, standards had changed by 1880, when Russell Sturgis wrote in *Scribner's*:

'That he should make such designs at all, at the age of twenty-seven, seems to argue a less strong feeling for art than has generally been attributed to him, for one who feels the value of fine design must of necessity see something of the difference between it and feeble design, and realize the relative value of his own work. But that he should publish them is amazing!'[3]

Yet an artist who imagines clearly what he wants to draw may, when he looks at the finished work, still see what he wanted to draw, and not what he has drawn. And since Thackeray was not his own publisher, the real problems would be better expressed in the words: that someone else should publish them is amazing!

So one looks back to see what Thackeray's contemporaries did think, taking, as a test-case, a work in which the illustrations played a peculiarly important part, and which drew from Mr Sturgis his most severe comment:

'In that year there was one more Christmas book, "The Rose and the Ring," a fairy story; but Thackeray's better fun and better taste are both wanting to it, and the wood-cuts in particular are hideous.'

The December press of 1854 responded in a different tone:

'It is illustrated by the author with a profusion of comical pictures, which at a first glance appear to be somewhat too extravagant, but cease to seem so when

[77]

we have once caught the spirit of the jest. And so we say of the illustrations as of the comical exaggerations – nobody could have done them so well.'[4]

'The pictures, by the author, are very numerous; and they will add greatly to the amusement of the small children. They are broad of course, and of course the faces are old friends; but we had many a good laugh over them, and they have the first-rate excellence of being unmistakably stamped with meaning and character.'[5]

'But the cuts by which that tale is illustrated! How to give a sample of them! Oh that we had the power to present to our readers, as our author has to his, Prince Bulbo dressed for dinner, and the same prince making love to Betsinda, . . . [a list follows] – but we find we are writing a catalogue, instead of making a selection. It is of no use attempting to discriminate; every illustration appears the drollest and brimful of fun, till its successor appears and challenges for itself the same designation. We give up the invidious task therefore; we can only recommend our readers to get the book for themselves; and we can assure them that they will recur to its pages long after the festivities have passed of the season that called it forth.'[6]

The question of how well Thackeray draws is never raised, and any irregularities

22. W. M. Thackeray, Amelia in Russell Square.

are justified by 'the spirit of the jest'; the book was designed to give lasting pleasure to the Victorian family, but a simple pleasure, of which the keynote is 'but we had many a good laugh over them'.

One would not quarrel seriously with these generous appreciations of the pictures in a light and successful children's book like *The Rose and the Ring*. But Thackeray's contemporaries applied very similar criteria to the illustrations in his novels, and here we might be more demanding. Should we, for instance, wish to see the original illustrations in modern reissues of Thackeray? Professor Joan Stevens has argued that all the illustrations for *Vanity Fair* should be revived, since Thackeray had such clear intentions for them that the book is simply not the novel he wrote if the illustrations are absent or misplaced; and she makes a strong, and very necessary, plea that if one is going to reprint the illustrations, one should have them in the right place.[7] It is still arguable, however, that to reprint all the illustrations would be less of a kindness to Thackeray than she suggests. She says, for example, that the woodcut of Amelia sitting in Russell Square (22) helps 'to establish an emotional climax'. Yet in this illustration figure, posture, face, and costume are so inexpressive and banal, and the drawing itself is so non-committal, that it is hard to believe the picture could make a positive contribution to any kind of emotional climax. The situation, surely, is that the emotion generated in the text overflows into the illustration, when we know that this picture shows not just any woman but 'poor little silly Amelia' and when we know she is looking round in an anxiety to see the son who has been taken from her? Even so, the affected reader might feel that the pathos is dispersed rather than increased by so flat a representation. It is to Thackeray's credit that he attempted a poignant quietness of effect, rather than the energetic luxuriance of pathos expected by the Victorian reader; yet in this drawing the 'little delicate fiddle-playing' of which he was so proud is muted to the point of silence.[8]

The inadequacy of Thackeray's draughtsmanship frequently poses problems at just those places where an illustration is most appropriate. There is, for instance, the incident in which George Osborne decides to condescend to Becky:

'he walked up to Rebecca with a patronising, easy swagger. He was going to be kind to her and protect her. He would even shake hands with her, as a friend of Amelia's; and saying, "Ah, Miss Sharp! how-dy-doo?" held out his left hand towards her, expecting that she would be quite confounded at the honour.

Miss Sharp put out her right forefinger, — '

The dash introduces the cut (23), after which the text continues:

'and gave him a little nod, so cool and killing, that Rawdon Crawley, watching the operations from the other room, could hardly restrain his laughter as he saw the lieutenant's entire discomfiture; . . .' (Chapter XIV)

23. W. M. Thackeray, George Osborne and Becky.

The illustration comes at the point which would arrest a spectator, and which his surprised attention would record with special clarity. There is a place here for a brisk, economic picture which could be taken in quickly, and which would contribute to the timing and emphasis of the incident. Yet we should need to take in the illustration very quickly indeed not to notice Osborne's wooden body, and the grotesque heads on his and Becky's shoulders. It can happen in reading a novel that one feels a particular encounter is 'seen', that the author had a clear picture in his mind's eye of what he describes. Here the situation is rather the reverse: we have not merely a description but an actual drawing, yet when we look at the drawing we may feel the writer has not 'seen' the incident at all, but is merely making a kind of hesitant visual guess.

To say this is not, of course, to recommend a painstaking study of models carefully posed. A minutely solid drawing, suggesting a hard morning's work in the studio, would make too large an interruption in the text even if it were smaller than the present woodcut. A quick, free, sketchy drawing would be preferable, and sufficient; but the quickness and freedom would need to be those of an experienced observer, who can realize a body in a few strokes and touches because he

[80]

knows so thoroughly how the body acts and responds. The style of John Leech might be ideal for the present context. Leech was a friend and admirer of Thackeray, and a colleague on *Punch*, and his style of drawing resembles Thackeray's in its light, humorous sketchiness; yet Leech, who had less formal training than Thackeray, demonstrates in every line he draws a more seeing eye (24). He has

24. John Leech, 'The Romans walking off with the Sabine Women' (wood-engraving for Gilbert à Beckett's *Comic History of Rome*).

noticed how men tilt when moving and slump when sat, how they brace themselves, bend, and let themselves go; and he has noticed and noted innumerable faces and expressions. These atomic noticings, rapidly supervening on each other, have become cemented, transfused, and incorporated into an instinctive-seeming sense of the way the body would move and look in any given situation which he has perhaps not seen, but which he is required to imagine. Leech draws easily out of the great knowledge that accumulates with sustained sharp observation, while Thackeray draws casually out of a little knowledge. His drawings often suggest that in his actual seeing of life he was not less perfunctory and desultory than in his formal artistic studies.

Presumably any talent is at the initial stage chiefly a capacity for taking interest, a habit of seeing with an unusually alert and noticing eye; and there is little evidence that Thackeray felt this interest with the intensity that would justify a sense of vocation as artist. And yet the interest was there. A reader troubled by Thackeray's illustrations has to take into account Charlotte Brontë's tribute:

'You will not easily find a second Thackeray. How he can render, with a few black lines and dots, shades of expression so fine, so real; traits of character so minute, so subtle, so difficult to seize and fix, I cannot tell — I can only wonder and admire. Thackeray may not be a painter, but he is a wizard of a draughtsman; touched with his pencil, paper lives. And then his drawing is so refreshing; after the wooden limbs one is accustomed to see portrayed by commonplace illustrators, his shapes of bone and muscle clothed with flesh, correct in proportion and anatomy, are a real relief. All is true in Thackeray. If Truth were again a goddess, Thackeray should be her high priest.'[9]

Charlotte Brontë could speak from some experience: she had done enough drawing to damage her sight, and the passage comes from a letter in which she shows herself — in discussing her own work — sufficiently critical in the question of illustration. What she says can apply to only a very small proportion of Thackeray's graphic output, and is perhaps extravagant praise of even his best things, yet his drawing does at times show an unusual reality. In some of the inset cuts, such as the picture of Colonel Crawley visiting Captain Macmurdo, the figures have a naturalness and mobile solidity far beyond that of Becky and George in Figure 64, while the etching 'Venus preparing the armour of Mars' (25) is wholly a success in its delicately genial humanity.

There is, moreover, one type of illustration in which Thackeray consistently succeeds, and where his actual linework often seems apt and right: the pictorial capitals that start each chapter. A pictorial capital letter is a much more modest field for an artist than the full-page etchings or the large wood-engravings that interrupt the text; but it is in the nature of Thackeray's talents that consistent success should be sought only where his ambition is working within closely circumscribed limits. Having taken this drastic step, however, one is free to emphasize how well Thackeray drew his capitals, and how much meaning he put into them. The capitals are often large drawings in themselves — they increase in size from novel to novel as his interest in them grows — and he finds functions for them that extend far beyond those of the naturalistic illustrations. The convention of pictorial capitals encouraged what the other illustrations prohibited, an imaginative use of visual irony and analogy unhindered by any need to depict a 'real' scene; and Thackeray had learned from Hogarth and the caricaturists how to use poetic resources to their best advantage.[10] As a result his capitals frequently have the strength that a reviewer of *The Newcomes* saw in the pictorial

25. W. M. Thackeray, 'Venus preparing the armour of Mars'.

capitals of Richard Doyle (which were of course drawn from Thackeray's instructions):

'... in the symbolic drawings, which form round the initial letters of chapters, [Doyle] is wonderfully successful, and, as an artist should ever be, no faint echo of other men's thoughts, but a voice concurrent or prophetical, full of meaning; they are little sketches apt to be passed over in carelessness, but on examination found to be full of real art and poetical comprehension.'[11]

The first chapters of *Vanity Fair* show how quickly Thackeray realized the possibilities of the illuminated letter. At the very start he is feeling his way. Chapter I is neatly defined by a picture, in the capital, of a coach coming towards us (26); and by a vignette, at the end, of a coach driving away (27). The chapter begins with the two heroines awaiting the coach that will carry them from the shelter of the academy into the turmoil of Vanity Fair; and it concludes with Miss Jemima watching the coach depart. The second chapter has an initial 'W' supported by the head and shoulders of a satyr (28); it is a small rococo decoration of no significance. Chapter III shows Jos framed by a large capital 'A', so that there is a certain allusion to his figure (29). By the next chapter, Thackeray has decided how a pictorial capital can make a point, and direct attention to the centre of interest in the coming chapter. He has drawn a little girl holding out a fishing-rod for a very rotund fish, and thus refers with graceful irony to Becky's angling for Jos (30). Later capitals show Thackeray well-versed in using the capital to point the moral of his story. Chapter XIII begins with a picture of George admiring himself in a mirror, and a large egotistical 'I' appropriately cuts across the reflection (31).

Professor Stevens makes some brief but illuminating points about the capital letters. Their importance could be further brought out by noting the significant addition made by the pictorial capital to one of the effects that she describes. She is discussing the 'linking of Number to Number by means of word and picture':

'Figure 5 [32] shows the justly famous final page of Number 4, the end of Chapter 14. The woodcut is placed so as to create suspense for the eye, as an actor creates it for the ear with a pause before a good line. "Come back and be my wife ... I'll do everything reglar," offers Sir Pitt Crawley. What Victorian heroine could ask for more? Alas for Becky, who must confess, "Oh, Sir – I – I'm *married already*." Typographically, too, the block in this position makes a satisfying final page, a matter of great importance in Number issue.

'A month later, Number 5 begins with these words: "Every reader of a sentimental turn (and we desire no other) must have been pleased with the *tableau* with which the last act of our little drama concluded; for what can be prettier

[84]

26 27

28 29

30 31

26–31. W. M. Thackeray, capital and tailpiece for *Vanity Fair*, Chapter I, capitals for Chapters II, III, IV, and XIII.

than an image of Love on his knees before Beauty?" These words explicitly recall the final woodcut of the previous Number, and the dramatic moment to which it gave visible substance. There *was* such a tableau, there *was* such an image. This is satirically biting, for if Becky is Beauty, then that old satyr Sir Pitt must be Love, and we are indeed in "Vanity Fair". The word and figure combination has strengthened the ironic narrative control, while also serving to link the successive movements of part-issue.'[12]

has got muddled agin. You *must* come back. Do come back. Dear Becky, do come."

" Come—as what, Sir ?" Rebecca gasped out.

" Come as Lady Crawley, if you like," the baronet said, grasping his crape hat. " There ! will that zatusfy you ? Come back and be my wife. Your vit vort. Birth be hanged. You 're as good a lady as ever I see. You 've got more brains in your little vinger than any baronet's wife in the county. Will you come ? Yes or no ?"

" Oh, Sir Pitt !" Rebecca said, very much moved.

" Say yes, Becky," Sir Pitt continued. " I 'm an old man, but a good 'n. I 'm good for twenty years. I 'll make you happy, zee if I don't. You shall do what you like ; spend what you like ; and 'av it all your own way. I 'll make you a zettlement. I 'll do everything reglar. Look year !" and the old man fell down on his knees and leered at her like a satyr.

Rebecca started back a picture of consternation. In the course of this history we have never seen her lose her presence of mind ; but she did now, and wept some of the most genuine tears that ever fell from her eyes.

" Oh, Sir Pitt !" she said. " Oh, Sir—I—I 'm *married already*."

32. W. M. Thackeray, text

But not only was there such an image: for the reader of Chapter XV, there is such an image before him. For the capital 'E' shows a figure – apparently a boy in medieval costume – on his knees, with his face in his hands, before a sculptured figure on a pedestal. The picture is a delicate reminder that the idea of 'Love on his knees before Beauty' can have an unironical meaning as well as the ironic one. The irony is expressed in the malicious imp peering round behind the 'E', but he is clearly separated from the actual picture. That picture, in its firmness and clarity, gives an additional weight to Thackeray's opening sentence,

CHAPTER XV.

IN WHICH REBECCA'S HUSBAND APPEARS FOR A SHORT TIME.

VERY reader of a sentimental turn (and we desire no other) must have been pleased with the *tableau* with which the last act of our little drama concluded ; for what can be prettier than an image of Love on his knees before Beauty ?

But when Love heard that awful confession from Beauty that she was married already, he bounced up from his attitude of humility on the carpet, uttering exclamations which caused poor little Beauty to be more frightened than she was when she made her avowal. " Married ! you 're joking," the Baronet cried, after the first explosion of rage and wonder. " You 're making vun of me, Becky. Who 'd ever go to marry you without a shilling to your vortune ? "

" Married ! married ! " Rebecca said, in an agony of tears—her voice choking with emotion, her handkerchief up to her ready eyes, fainting against the mantel-piece—a figure of woe fit to melt the most obdurate heart. " O Sir Pitt, dear Sir Pitt, do not think me ungrateful for all your goodness to me. It is only your generosity that has extorted my secret."

" Generosity be hanged ! " Sir Pitt roared out. " Who is it tu, then, you 're married ? Where was it ? "

" Let me come back with you to the country, sir ! Let me watch over you as faithfully as ever ! Don't, don't separate me from dear Queen's Crawley ! "

" The feller has left you, has he ? " the Baronet said, beginning, as he fancied, to comprehend. " Well, Becky—come back if you like. You can't eat your cake and have it. Any ways I made you a vair offer. Coom back as governess—you shall have it all your own way." She held out one hand. She cried fit to break her heart ; her ringlets fell over her face, and over the marble mantel-piece where she laid it.

" So the rascal ran off, eh ? " Sir Pitt said, with a hideous attempt at consolation. " Never mind, Becky, *I'll* take care of 'ee."

" O Sir ! it would be the pride of my life to go back to Queen's Crawley, and take care of the children, and of you as formerly, when you said you were pleased with the services of your little Rebecca. When I

K

and picture in *Vanity Fair*.

[87]

and modifies the tone in which we should read it. It also gives the total contrast more symmetry, for now picture is opposed to picture and prose to prose; the contrast gaining when the Numbers are bound together in a volume, and the pictures face each other.

As the series of pictorial capitals advances, Thackeray builds up a cast of rich children, urchins, men in fool's costume, and couples in 18th-century finery, who perform in advance, in simple tableaux, the actions that the protagonists will presently perform with more complexity and pain. The men in fool's costume, especially, have the function of a Chorus.

Each monthly part of the novel had on the cover a picture of a Fool preaching to Fools, and by recurring to this picture in the text, Thackeray was able to project it over the action of the novel like a lantern-slide:

'And while the moralist, who is holding forth on the cover (an accurate portrait of your humble servant), professes to wear neither gown nor bands, but only the same long-eared livery in which his congregation is arrayed: yet, look you, one is bound to speak the truth as far as one knows it, whether one mounts a cap and bells or a shovel-hat.'

This comes from Chapter VIII; in Chapter XIX Thackeray cries: 'O brother wearers of motley! Are there not moments when one grows sick of grinning and tumbling, and the jingling of cap and bells?' There are further allusions to this picture in the pictorial capitals. They have the mixture of satire with sadness that marks Thackeray's melancholy irony in the text: a procession of Fools in mourning heads Chapter XL, in which Sir Pitt dies (33), and Chapter XLVI

33. W. M. Thackeray, capital for
Vanity Fair, Chapter XL.

begins with a Fool in tears. Since the unifying theme of the novel – 'vanitas vanitatum' – is very general and yet very simple, the repeated assertion of it could easily become monotonous and inert; some unobtrusive and easily varied reminder is necessary, and the Fools in the pictorial capitals (with the variant of the Clown in Chapters XXVII, XXXVII, XLIX) perform this function with an easy humour.

The use of the Fool suits so well the mood and burden of *Vanity Fair* that it might be taken for an invention of Thackeray's. Yet the Fool plays a similar part in one of Cruikshank's most famous etchings, 'The Folly of Crime' (34). In the centre is a lurid picture of a murderer in a fool's cap falling into an abyss, while each of the surrounding vignettes employs the fool allegorically in much the same way as Thackeray does in his capitals. One shows a fool looking behind him as he runs away with two bags of money, and not seeing that he is thrusting his foot into a man-trap. In the next picture, the Fool, left on a desolate shore by a parting ship, carries a coffin on his shoulders with the words 'For Life' on its side. He pauses to notice a skull set in the ground as he drags his way towards a freshly dug grave: his shadow runs to the edge of the grave, parallel to the shadowed underside of the coffin. A spade stands beside the grave, which has presumably just been dug by the Fool himself. The picture does not show merely the end of a career in crime: it sums up each stage in the course of that career, and brings home the way in which the life of crime is not passive but active self-destruction.

'The Folly of Crime' appeared in the March number of the short-lived magazine *George Cruikshank's Table-Book* (1845). Thackeray's 'Legend of the Rhine' was serialized there from June to December with illustrations by Cruikshank, and Thackeray could easily have seen the etching. He had already written some chapters of the novel that was to become *Vanity Fair* when 'The Folly of Crime' appeared, but it is unlikely that he had conceived the pictorial use of the Fool at that stage. The use of the Fool associates with the general theme expressed in the title, and it was only in the latter part of 1846 that the formula 'Vanity Fair' occurred to Thackeray, inspiring him to reorganize the novel; it would seem that before then the novel had no theme, and it is fair to assume that the idea of the Fool came with that unifying imaginative bouleversement.[13] It could well be, therefore, that in the genesis of the idea animating the novel, the inspirations of Bunyan and Cruikshank combined.

'The Folly of Crime' relates the Fool of *Vanity Fair* to traditional graphic satire; and there was in any case a substantial connection by way of *Punch*, for when the satiric print died, political caricature and the pictorial satire of manners survived in that magazine. *Punch* had many illuminated capitals, often involving the puppets from *Punch and Judy*; and the various scenes in which Mr Punch is shown contending with situations in the contemporary world, or simply in a contemporary character, may have suggested to Thackeray the uses to which a

34. George Cruikshank, 'The Folly of Crime'.

puppet-play could be put in a novel. The capitals in *Vanity Fair* bear out the insinuation in the text that the action of the novel is, after all, merely a puppet-show: '. . . come, children, let us shut up the box and the puppets, for our play is played out.' The small, comical figures, in their fanciful costumes, continually compromise the reality of the novel's cast. A similar diminution follows from such cuts as that to Chapter XX, which shows the proprietor of a peep-show encouraging children to watch. Thackeray felt he had strong points to make about the real world, and actual human nature, but a child's entertainment, which was a cross between a fairy-tale and a puppet-play although rendered locally with a wealth of naturalistic detail, provided the convention in which his imagination could work most comfortably.

Thackeray once said to his wood-engraver 'Ah, Swain! if it had not been for *Punch*, I wonder where I should be!'[14] If his artistic development is considered as a whole, the difference made by the years on *Punch* stands out clearly. In *Vanity Fair* Thackeray demonstrates a remarkable aptitude in integrating text and picture, yet at the start of his career he had shown no such skill. *Barry Lyndon* was not illustrated, and the illustrations for the earlier novel, *Catherine*, added little to the text. There were no inset cuts, and in the full-page plates the outline is insensitive and hard, and the small amount of hatching seems only to be there because the plate would look so empty without it. The outline manner was popular at the time, and was used elegantly by Flaxman and Retsch, but it was inappropriate for a satirical novel. The *Paris Sketch Book* (1840) shows a similar style, with a little more hatching, but Thackeray seems no nearer to his best manner in *Vanity Fair*.

In the following year, however, *Punch* started. Thackeray provided four illustrations for his first *Punch* article, 'The Legend of Jawbrahim-Heraudee'. Three of these were 'blackies' – a genre of small visual puns, drawn in silhouette, which *Punch* inherited from other comic papers; Thackeray's first experience of relating published word and picture in a single comic effect was of this simple kind. The fourth of these early drawings was the pictorial capital with which the article began. Pictorial capitals were a prominent feature of *Punch*, and Thackeray drew a number of them for his later contributions. He carried into the capitals of his novels both the style and a number of specific motifs from those in *Punch*. There are knights and dragons, and people on stilts making capital letters; and it was perhaps in the Shakespearean capitals in *Punch* (35) that Thackeray found the precedent for his own (36).

From the start *Punch* had many humorous woodcuts set in the text. At first these were chiefly 'blackies', but presently they were replaced by larger drawings which had to be set between two particular lines, so that a specific part of the text could serve as caption to them. Often the picture, with the one line of dramatic speech beneath it, could stand alone; and as this was realized, the modern cartoon developed. Thackeray quickly learned to tie a picture into its narrative context by setting beneath it a line of dialogue that served both as caption and as

35. Capital in *Punch* (27 Nov. 1841).

36. W. M. Thackeray, capital for
The Virginians, I, Chapter XI.

continuation of the text. The relationship between picture and dialogue is the
same in some of the cuts for the novels. '"Lor!" cried Miss Swartz, spinning
swiftly round on the music stool,' and before the sentence continues we are given
a clear brisk drawing that can be taken in at a glance (37) of Miss Swartz just

turning round on the stool, her face lighting up as she stares straight at us. The explanation for her joyous excitement is given in the words which follow, '"is it *my* Amelia? Amelia that was at Miss P.'s..."'. The drawing is not so assertive that the reader takes much notice of it before he comes to it in the text; but at the moment he does, he sees through George Osborne's eyes, and the imaginary world of the novel becomes visually precise in a moment of surprise, sudden movement, and spontaneous response.

A similar *Punch* device is the use of a drawing rather than a passage of narrative, to bridge a delay in the action of a story. In Chapter VI of 'The Natural History of Courtship' the protagonist is trying to write a love-letter and pausing at every word: '... then, at the end of another pause, "to express" – what, he is unable at the moment to make up his mind.'[15] Instead of reading a description of

37. W. M. Thackeray, Miss Swartz.

the man casting round, we dwell for a moment on the picture of him sitting frowning at his desk; then the text continues with the next phrase that occurs to him. In *Pendennis*, Arthur is having difficulty getting some verses written. '"And I'll go out to dinner," said Warrington, and left Mr. Pen in a brown study.' We are shown a cut of Pen frowning at his desk, and the text resumes with the next active development: 'When Warrington came home that night, at a very late hour, the verses were done.'

[93]

One of the principal artists in the early years of *Punch* was Richard Doyle, and when he left the magazine Thackeray promptly engaged him to illustrate *The Newcomes*. Doyle's connection with the earlier school of graphic satire was particularly strong, for Doyle's father 'H. B.' had been a famous political caricaturist in the time of Gillray, and he had trained his son in the manner of that school.

Thackeray did all he could to work Doyle's art as closely into his own as possible. Evidently he did not insist that Doyle's illustration should come at exact points in the text, for the manuscript of *The Newcomes* has none of the marks for illustrations that are to be found in the manuscripts of *Vanity Fair* and *Pendennis*;[16] but he introduces Doyle in the actual text of the novel as a collaborator and, as it were, 'touches up' the artist's pictures. In Chapter XXIV of *The Newcomes*, Volume I, he observes of Clive:

'For being absent with his family in Italy now, and not likely to see this biography for many many months, I may say that he is a much handsomer fellow than our designer has represented; and if that wayward artist should take this very scene for the purpose of illustration, he is requested to bear in mind that the Hero of this story will wish to have justice done to his person. There exists in Mr. Newcome's possession a charming little pencil drawing of Clive at this age; ...'

The narrator here is invisibly present at a specific scene, taking a study of the actual Clive – 'All the time we have been making this sketch Ethel is standing looking at Clive ...' – and having finished the gentleman, he turns to the lady:

'And now let the artist, if he has succeeded in drawing Clive to his liking, cut a fresh pencil, and give us a likeness of Ethel. She is seventeen years old, ...'

In a bound version of the first edition, Doyle's etching of the subject, 'A Family Party', would face the relevant passage of prose, so that it would be clear to the reader that Thackeray is thinking of an actual picture, and not merely using a figure of speech. He thus relates the illustration to his text in the most easy and natural way; he directs the reader to just those points that an illustration can make clear, and also fills out the picture with those details of behaviour and character (and colouring) that the etcher cannot show, moving in and out of the visual by easy gradations.

Reference to the artist is particularly appropriate in *The Newcomes*, for the visual arts have a prominent part to play in the story. The life of the art student is described in detail, and there is sharp observation of the English upper-class attitude to art. That attitude gets a special emphasis because it is voiced by the heroine: Ethel writes to Colonel Newcome: 'You will order Clive not to sell his pictures, won't you? I know it is not wrong, but your son might look higher than to be an artist' (i, Chapter XXVIII). Also, the visual arts are a constant source of imagery in the novel, and the theme of the Bought Bride is represented by the sale of pictures: 'Ethel appeared with a bright green ticket pinned in the front of her white muslin frock, and . . . said, "I am a *tableau-vivant*, papa, I am No. 46 in the Exhibition of the Gallery of Painters in Water-colours"' (i, Chapter XXVIII). The various references to art are all taken up in the figure of J. J. Ridley, whose career in art is offered as an ideal way of life, in contrast to the vocations followed by almost all the other characters; and J. J. Ridley has clear affinities with Doyle.

Apropos of the frontispiece for the first volume, 'J. J. in Dreamland' (38), Lewis Lusk remarked that 'Doyle could sympathise entirely with [J. J.]'.[17] Lusk noticed the profound similarity of character in J. J. and Doyle, and he recorded that in 'J. J. in Dreamland' Doyle 'very fitly has used his own face for that of J. J.'. He assumes the similarity was not intended by Thackeray, but was simply a happy coincidence. Yet there is reason to think that Thackeray had Doyle in mind in describing J. J. If J. J. wears Doyle's face in the frontispiece, that face is still precisely the face that Thackeray had described, 'with a great forehead, and waving black hair, and large melancholy eyes'. In imagination, J. J. inhabits a fairy-land that is peopled with Doyle's knights, princes, and comical banditti:

'knights in armour, with plume, and shield, and battleaxe; and splendid young noblemen with flowing ringlets, and bounteous plumes of feathers, and rapiers, and russet boots; and fierce banditti with crimson tights, doublets profusely illustrated with large brass buttons, and the dumpy basket-hilted claymores known to be the favourite weapon with which these whiskered ruffians do battle; wasp-waisted peasant girls, and young countesses with O such large eyes and cherry lips!' (i, Chapter XI)

Doyle's women are remarkable for their wasp-waists, ripe lips, and huge eyes. J. J.'s 'Dreamland', as Doyle depicts it in the frontispiece, is also Doyle's own favourite imaginative world of fairy-land. The production of fairy pictures was to become one of Doyle's main preoccupations in later life, but at the time of *The Newcomes* his interest in the fairy world was marked without, as yet, being morbidly intense. J. J.'s surname, 'Ridley', may itself be significant, since Doyle signed his works 'R.D.'.

The Newcomes had, then, strong ties with the old school of pictorial satire: that mode had passed into the magazine *Punch*, and out of *Punch* came both the novelist, who was also a *Punch* caricaturist, and the illustrator, who was both a caricaturist and the son of a caricaturist. To complete this picture of distinct streams of graphic satire converging in one novel, it need only be added that in *The Newcomes* Thackeray took his theme from Hogarth's *Marriage à-la-Mode*,

38. Richard Doyle, 'J. J. in Dreamland'.

and expected his readers to see he was doing this. Lecturing on Hogarth, he describes this series as 'the most important and highly wrought of the Hogarth comedies', and goes on to give a perceptive and detailed account of it.[18] At the end of the summary, he relaxes and sums up the 'moral' dismissively – 'The people are all naughty, and Bogey carries them all off,' – but the preceding account implies a more serious and thoughtful sympathy with the work. He observes: 'The care and method with which the moral grounds of these pictures are laid is as remarkable as the wit and skill of the observing and dexterous artist,' and he proceeds to show how the drama is enacted in communicative details. In his analysis of the first picture, he notes:

'The girl is pretty, but the painter, with a curious watchfulness, has taken care to give her a likeness to her father; . . . The pictures round the room are sly hints indicating the situation of the parties about to marry. . . . There is the ancestor of the house (in the picture it is the Earl himself as a young man), with a comet over his head, indicating that the career of the family is to be brilliant and brief. In the second picture, the old lord must be dead, for Madam has now the Countess's coronet over her bed and toilet-glass, and sits listening to that dangerous Counsellor Silvertongue, whose portrait now actually hangs up in her room. . . .'

Clearly Thackeray understood Hogarth's technique and valued it. His responsiveness to Hogarth's larger structures is shown in *Barry Lyndon*, a stern moral biography in which the hero follows the Rake's Progress through gaming, debauchery, and marriage for money, to final madness. Barry 'falling into a state of almost imbecility, was tended by his tough old parent as a baby almost . . .' (last chapter). His end recalls that of the Rake, although Barry's mother replaces the girl the Rake had ruined.

Localized in the long drama of Ethel's temptations is the principal theme of *The Newcomes* — marriage, and the damage done to it by fashionable life — which could not strike Thackeray's contemporaries as a new one:

'Too truly it is an old story; we have seen it elsewhere also: above all others, one is before me in all the memory of its painted horrors — Hogarth's Marriage à la Mode, which seems its painted counterpart.'[19]

The writer could be making the connection simply on his own initiative, but in fact, in the course of the novel, Thackeray had himself linked his 'fable' with Hogarth's:

'Have you taken your children to the National Gallery in London, and shown them the Marriage à la Mode? Was the artist exceeding the privilege of his calling in painting the catastrophe in which those guilty people all suffer? If this fable were not true, if many and many of your young men of pleasure had not acted it, and rued the moral, I would tear the page.' (i, Chapter XXXI)

At one point Thackeray poses the characters in a tableau from Hogarth's series, and tells us that this is what he is doing: 'In the cloak-room sits Lady Clara Newcome, with a gentleman bending over her, just in such an attitude as the bride is in Hogarth's Marriage à la Mode as the counsellor talks to her' (ii, Chapter XVI). Lady Clara, in love with another man, is the victim of an arranged marriage, and the moment is given a further, and specifically pictorial, emphasis by one of Doyle's etchings. One can understand how another contemporary of Thackeray's could assert so firmly (in the first sentence of his review): 'What Hogarth meant by his pictures entitled Marriage *à la mode* Mr Thackeray means by his novel of *The Newcomes*.'[20]

At this point it would be helpful to know whether the emphasizing illustration was introduced on Doyle's initiative, or on Thackeray's. Fortunately there is an indication that Thackeray planned such allusions himself in a letter he wrote to *The Times* in 1853. In the second chapter of *The Newcomes* he had referred to George Washington as 'heading the American rebels with a courage . . . worthy of a better cause', and he then found himself accused of casting aspersions on American Independence. In his letter to *The Times* he defended himself by insisting that the incriminating remark belonged to a historical context, which he defined by saying:

'I am speaking of a young apprentice coming to London between the years 1770–'80, and want to depict a few figures of the last century. (The illustrated head-letter of the chapter was intended to represent Hogarth's "Industrious Apprentice".)'[21]

In the same way, Thackeray himself alludes to Hogarth at a crucial point in *The Virginians*: the pictorial capital of Volume i, Chapter XXVII (39) is a copy

39. W. M. Thackeray, capital for *The Virginians*, I
Chapter XXVII.

of the third plate from *Industry and Idleness*. The capital makes more than a passing reference to the gambling of Harry Warrington. *The Virginians* is set in Hogarth's time, and London, here, is Hogarth's London:

'Quick, hackney-coach steeds, and bear George Warrington through Strand and Fleet Street to his imprisoned brother's rescue! Any one who remembers Hogarth's picture of a London hackney-coach and a London street road at that period, may fancy how weary the quick time was, and how long seemed the journey: – scarce any lights, save those carried by link-boys; badly hung coaches; bad pavements; great holes in the road, and vast quagmires of winter mud. . . .' (ii, Chapter I)

The novel describes the contrasted careers of two young men, of whom one is light, and bent on enjoying himself, and the other serious, and ambitious of a successful career. Harry may seem too engaging to be identified with Thomas Idle, but it is clear from Thackeray's description of Hogarth's series that he felt 'Tom' Idle was an engaging young man, and that he felt Hogarth was forcing the issue in suggesting that an easy-going nature necessarily turns to crime. He begins: 'Fair-haired Frank Goodchild smiles at his work, whilst naughty Tom Idle snores over his loom. Frank reads the edifying ballads of "Whittington" and the London 'Prentice; whilst that reprobate Tom Idle prefers Moll Flanders, and drinks hugely of beer.'[22] And while Harry Warrington does not come to a bad end, Thackeray thought Tom Idle deserved a better fate. Thackeray has 'unaffected pity' for Tom Idle sentenced to death, and concludes: 'There's more pity and kindness and a better chance for poor Tom's successors now than at that simpler period when Fielding hanged him and Hogarth drew him.' Harry has that 'better chance': but Thackeray goes so far as to like the two brothers almost equally, and the simple moral distinction – that had given tautness, shape, and direction to Hogarth's series – is not so much reversed, as obliterated altogether.

If *The Virginians* represents, in some sense, Thackeray's response to *Industry and Idleness*, there is no question of a close correspondence of purpose and episode comparable to that of *The Newcomes* with *Marriage à-la-Mode*. None the less, the Hogarth picture in Chapter XXVII is intended to make a point; it is as if, in a full-page illustration showing Harry in his dissipation, the Hogarth painting were prominently hung on the wall. Hogarth himself frequently used pictures in this way. The affinity between their techniques can be seen in the use they make of biblical scenes. Hogarth hangs a picture of Abraham and Isaac in the Harlot's room, in Plate III of *The Harlot's Progress*, when she is about to be suddenly arrested; similarly, Gillray ironically hangs a picture of Adam and Eve behind the Prince and Mrs Fitzherbert in 'Wife and No Wife' (3). In Thackeray's capitals, the Good Samaritan is introduced both in *The Newcomes* (ii, Chapter XXXIX) and *The Virginians* (21); the latter example is one of the largest capitals in the novel, and the evident seriousness of the subject has brought out an unusual strength of drawing in Thackeray.

The Good Samaritan was a common subject in illustrations. In Charles Lever's *The Knight of Gwynne* (1846–7) an ironic textual reference to Mr Dempsey's 'Samaritanism' (p. 431) is expressed pictorially by the painting of 'The Good Samaritan' hanging beside Mr Dempsey in Browne's plate 'Mr Dempsey finds out "something to his advantage"'. In Ainsworth's *The Miser's Daughter*, Abel Beechcroft has a similar painting on his wall:

'In the hasty glance cast by Hilda at the pictures on the wall, the most noticeable of which was a copy of Rembrandt's "Good Samaritan", and a fine painting on the subject of Timon of Athens, she thought she could read somewhat of the character of the owner of the house.'[23]

In his text, Ainsworth uses paintings in just the way Hogarth had done; and in Cruikshank's illustration of the scene, the general composition and the prominent hanging of the pictures recall Hogarth. Cruikshank also hung a Good Samaritan in a plate for *Oliver Twist*, with obvious relevance to Mr Brownlow's kindness.

Thackeray expected his pictorial capitals to be examined as a painting by Hogarth would be examined; they were to be borne in mind and pondered as the reader proceeded with the story. A capital in *The Virginians* shows Sinbad with the Old Man of the Sea on his shoulders. The meaning of it is not immediately clear, and Thackeray evidently intended the reader to think about it all through that section, for he does not elucidate it until the beginning of the following chapter:

'Hath the gracious reader understood the meaning of the mystic S with which the last chapter commences, and in which the designer has feebly endeavoured to depict the notorious Sinbad the Sailor surmounted by that odious old man of the sea? What if Harry Warrington should be that sailor, and his fate that choking, deadening, inevitable old man? What if for two days past he has felt those knees throttling him round the neck? If his fell aunt's purpose is answered, and if his late love is killed as dead by her poisonous communications as Fair Rosamond was by her royal and legitimate rival? . . .' (i, Chapter XXIII)

The manuscript version of this passage illustrates Thackeray's allegorical habit of mind, for he first wrote: 'Hath the kind reader understood the meaning of the mystic S with which the last chapter commences and which signifies . . .'[24] He then crossed out 'signifies', inserted 'in', and continued, as in the printed version, 'in which the designer. . . '. The picture of Sinbad was the visual equivalent of a poetic conceit, although Thackeray preferred a more graceful way of reading off significance to the crude 'which signifies . . .'.

John Loofbourow observed that Thackeray's prose 'must be read like witty poetry – a poetry expressed in delicate conceits and sustained allusions rather than in the traditional narrative rhetoric of his own time'.[25] The capitals are often witty conceits in which the imaginative habit of the prose has simply expressed itself in another form. In the capital for Chapter XXXVI of *The Virginians*, Volume i, (40) the stance of the highwayman identifies him with one half of the large

40. W. M. Thackeray, capital for *The Virginians*
Chapter XXXVI.

'T' above him, while the form of the other half is repeated in the gallows just below it: the letter 'T' is the equals sign in a poetic equation. This capital, also, requires pondering from the reader while he reads, for Mme Bernstein's reference to highwaymen later in the chapter proves to be a red herring. The actual robbery of Harry's pocket-book in the course of the chapter gives the highwayman his cue, but the reader has to work out for himself that the real subject of the cut is the plot to rob Harry of Maria. The capital's function in the novel, here as elsewhere, is to arouse apprehension, and to make the reader ask questions which he will repeat with increasing urgency as the hints in the prose accumulate.

The pictorial capitals provide a neat vehicle for Thackeray's imagery,[26] and help also in the constant process of distancing, sifting, and judging which is his principal activity as an artist. They are one of the many resources he used to transpose the local action of the novel into generality. He was accustomed to re-inforce his protagonists with a huge shadowy cast of figures from traditional story: mythical and legendary, classical and biblical, from folklore and Shakespeare. With this aid, he could people his crowds with individuals who were also perennial Types:

'Is it poor Prodigal yonder amongst the bad company, calling black and red and tossing the champagne; or brother Straightlace, that grudges his repentance? Is it downcast Hagar that slinks away with poor little Ishmael in her hand; or bitter old virtuous Sarah, who scowls at her from my demure Lord Abraham's arm?' (*The Newcomes*, i, Chapter XXVIII)

The general human representativeness of his principal characters is extended by passing them rapidly through a succession of classical and traditional embodiments. In *The Virginians* George Warrington apostrophizes his wife: 'But sweet Joan, beloved Baucis! . . . thy Darby is rather ashamed of having been testy so often; and . . . Philemon asks pardon for falling asleep so frequently after dinner' (ii, Chapter XXXVII). Similarly, in the pictorial capitals Harry Warrington is successively a Knight, a Hogarthian Apprentice, and a boy flying a kite.[27] Such incarnations often place an important emphasis: in Chapter XI of *The Virginians* (Volume i) George is gripped by a vindictive jealousy of Colonel Washington and plans to make unjust exactions from him. Thackeray makes sure we see the Hero's mood for the ugly thing it is (for, since he is the hero, it would be easy to sympathize with him) by starting the chapter with a picture of Shylock, holding his knife and a pair of scales (36). In context, the picture of Shylock stresses the degeneration of George more emphatically, for in the capital for Chapter VIII he had merely been Othello. Successive capitals can work together and work with the text in cumulative effects.[28]

The Virginians could be called a lavishly illustrated book by virtue of the capitals alone. Thackeray's interest in other kinds of illustration appears to have dropped away completely by this stage. Apart from the capitals, there are few inset woodcuts, and both in these and in the etchings the drawing is hesitant and careless, and the figures are unrealized. In the plate 'Whose voice is that?' the man who has just come downstairs is drawn as though he were climbing up, and his trailing leg ought in theory to pass through the staircase like the leg of a ghost. In the following novel, *Philip*, the full-page illustrations were executed by another artist, Frederick Walker; but Thackeray drew most of the pictorial capitals for *Philip*, and in general his interest in the capitals grew as his interest in the other illustrations declined. The pictorial capitals increased in size until they dominated the page; they left behind the comicality of the capitals for *Vanity Fair*, and became strong and full-bodied as drawings (21).

This development may seem surprising in a novelist with such strong inclinations to naturalism, but Thackeray's artistic inheritance predisposed him to follow the course he did: as an artist he followed after Hogarth and Gillray, who gave almost every detail of their work an allusive, metaphorical, or ironic significance. Moreover, he was not alone in this, for a similar line of growth was followed by Charles Dickens and Hablôt Browne.

5

Dickens and Browne:
Pickwick Papers to *Barnaby Rudge*

Hablôt Knight Browne, ('Phiz'), the artist who illustrated ten of Dickens's fifteen novels as they appeared serially, has an ambiguous position in the history of British illustration. Like the novels they illustrate, his plates have acquired the status of classics. Yet, unlike the novels, and unlike most classics, they have almost no reputation. In a 'Painting of the Month' talk on Cruikshank, Brian Robb expressed a general attitude to Browne when he said, 'Phiz's ham rhetoric and hack humour make by contrast an artificial, a flabby showing.'[1] It is usual for Browne to be disparaged by means of a comparison with Cruikshank:

'[Browne] was an indifferent draughtsman gifted with a certain charm and a light and easy humour. He is never dramatic. If his engravings are compared with those by Cruikshank for *Oliver Twist* the inferiority of "Phiz" is to be seen at the first glance.'

This criticism comes from Sacheverell Sitwell, quoted in the *Dickensian*.[2] The *Dickensian* contains a good deal of similar criticism of Browne, and the usual defence – that one should retain Browne's illustrations because one has grown up with them – hardly does Browne's reputation a real service.

No one would question the superior placing of Cruikshank, and the limit of one's claim for Browne could be made clear at the start by saying that he never showed the genius for the art that Cruikshank habitually showed. None the less, he deserves his institutional status as an illustrator. For he possessed a talent of real originality, sensitivity, and liveliness, which unfolds with remarkable rapidity and brilliance in the illustrations for the early novels of Dickens.

But there was a frailty in the talent. He produced his best work very early in

41. H. K. Browne, 'The Breakdown'.

his career, and having done so, he did not go on, as many artists do, to produce an impressive second-best for his remaining years: he went into a steady decline. And as it is natural to judge an artist by the general quality of the work he produces in his mature years, Browne's best work has been undervalued, and has passed almost unnoticed. A reader who judges Dickens's illustrations from a perusal of *Little Dorrit* will not expect much of Browne: so it may help to show that one is dealing with work of more artistic interest if one traces the graph of Browne's development, and shows how pronounced the curve is, both in its first sudden rise, and in its subsequent swoop. Browne's work is commonly taken to be all of a piece, but in fact it not only changes radically in quality, it passes – within this large shift – through a rapid series of metamorphoses. It is here that we see the positive side of the frailty: he had a remarkable imaginative dependence on the work he illustrated, and where that work was strong, he could be truly inspired by it; each of his metamorphoses comes as the direct result of a new inspiration provided by Dickens, who was himself changing rapidly. Browne illustrated the works of many other novelists, and he was the regular illustrator of Charles Lever's monthly parts, but no novelist other than Dickens provoked any comparable changes in his art.

Before Dickens and Browne met in the *Pickwick* partnership, Browne had already provided some small illustrations for Dickens's pamphlet, *Sunday under Three Heads*. The three plates are closely worked, and the massed figures give an impression of energy and movement; but taken individually they seem mean, stiff, and puppet-like. There is none of that confident flow of quick, characterizing line that marks his later work; but we could not say that Browne's style is at this time unformed, for the elaborate use of cross-hatching and twisting lines is in its own way sophisticated. It is not a hesitant attempt at something other than itself.

The first plates Browne did for *Pickwick* have the same character.[3] The third plate, 'The Breakdown' (41), is finely worked and sensitive, if one takes it simply as a piece of delicate texturing. But the faces are obscure, and the hands are vestigial. The intricate linework is liable to flatten the plate; it does not serve any developed sense of space. The artist does not seem to know what to do with all he draws, or how to give it life. The two horses take a prominent place in the foreground, but they are clearly just properties. The foreshortened white horse might be a piece of tarpaulin on a post.

Yet while *Pickwick* was being published, Browne's style changed rapidly. The full extent of the change can be demonstrated easily, for the demand for *Pickwick* increased so much during its serialization that when it was complete, and the publishers wanted to bring out the bound edition, the steel plates for the early numbers were quite worn out, and new ones had to be made. The large demand had meant that the later illustrations were etched in duplicate, and they survived sufficiently well to be used in the bound edition; but the first twenty-one plates were copied by Browne in new etchings.[4] The earlier plates are redrawn in a style that would make one think they were by a different artist.

In the first version of 'Mrs. Bardell faints in Mr. Pickwick's Arms' (42) the young Bardell is a cramped little knot of scratched lines, while in the later version (43) he is brought out from under Pickwick, and is a vivid and finished drawing in his own right. Pickwick's three friends are rigid in the first plate, wear similar expressions, and stand in similar poses (the attitudes of Tupman and Snod-

42. H. K. Browne, 'Mrs Bardell faints in Mr Pickwick's Arms', first version.

grass are almost identical). In the second they are humorously differentiated individuals; their legs are not interchangeable, no gesture is repeated, and there is expressive variation even in the tips of Winkle's fingers. The faces are done with more ease, but the simpler lines convey more, for here Browne has contrived to infuse their dismay with the other response that Dickens suggests:

'"Placed me in such an extremely awkward situation," continued Mr. Pickwick.

'"Very," was the reply of his followers, as they coughed slightly, and looked dubiously at each other.' (Chapter XII)

In the first plate Mrs Bardell might be a porcelain doll tipped against Mr Pickwick: in the second she is a very heavy woman voluptuously sagging against him.

43. H. K. Browne, 'Mrs Bardell faints in Mr Pickwick's Arms', second version.

The setting too, is better rendered. In (43), the dim recess behind the door is drawn with a true sense of space, while in (42), the shadow overflows its bounds so as to flatten what had been recession; the difference between the plates in spatial sense being symbolized by the door, which in (42) is a regular rectangle, running parallel to the wall behind it, while in (43) the door is at an angle, and comes out towards us.

The difference is more extreme, if we take the earlier plate 'First Appearance of Mr. Samuel Weller' (44, 45). In the later version the unformed and ambiguous faces of Sam and Pickwick have become clear and vital. The sketchy linework of the early version – it is almost stipple – is replaced by a brisk, clear outline. Perker is turned so as to be seen in profile, and his expression is suggested with a more economic sharpness (though the tight, nervous elegance of his stance, so well caught in the earlier plate, is lost). The dog at Pickwick's feet is turned from a scruffy bunch of fur to an excited animal that quite clearly *is* a dog; and the boots Sam is working on are shown clearly as boots, and the shoes as shoes, where

44. H. K. Browne, 'First Appearance of Mr. Samuel Weller', first version.

in the loose sketching of the earlier version, some seemed to be boots, some socks, and some hybrids between the two.

The change in technique involves a change in character. A new inspiration has come into Browne's art: the confused hatching and speckling of his earlier drawings give way to the expressive curves of a sharp and wiry line. The stiff puppet-like figures expand, and take, in exaggerated form, the curves and actions of living people. Faces acquire the clarity and uniqueness of caricature, while every detail of stance and gesture becomes a witty touch of expression; and things that

45. H. K. Browne, 'First Appearance of Mr. Samuel Weller', second version.

cannot be expressed wittily – such as extra horses, trees, and other properties in the early plates – are likely to be left out. All these characteristics have their equivalents in those features of Dickens's writing that were most conspicuously his own. If we said that Browne found himself in the *Pickwick* plates, we should have to add at once that the self he found was a particularly Dickensian self: there is a comic vitality akin to Dickens's own.

The *Pickwick* illustrations are uneven, but if one had to single out an illustration showing Browne both at his best and at his most Dickensian, one might choose 'The Trial' (46). The lawyers of *Bleak House* would require the penetrating satire of a Daumier to do them justice, but for the presentation of the law in

46. H. K. Browne, 'The Trial'.

47. Thomas Onwhyn, frontispiece for *Valentine Vox*.

Pickwick the lively variety of Browne's imagination is delightfully apt. To present so many figures, and to give each one a distinct personality and interest, with such spaciousness, and at the same time in such a lucid and unified composition, requires a fine sense of design. In looking at the plate, the eye is guided through a connected series of loops that start from, and come back to, the startled figure of Pickwick. One loop includes Serjeant Buzfuz, who seems, appropriately, to rise out of the Bardell group like a dark wave; his raised arms help to give him the appearance of surging upward motion. He is given additional yet ironic impetus by the parallel figure of the yawning lawyer, who relates him to the receding perspective of the plate, and who, in yawning, passes comment on the spontaneity of the Buzfuz eloquence.

Browne's achievement in *Pickwick* was sufficiently impressive for illustrators to imitate him as writers did Dickens. One may compare Onwhyn's frontispiece (47) for Cockton's novel *Valentine Vox* (published as a single volume in 1840, and serialized in monthly parts before then) with Browne's frontispiece for *Pickwick* (48). Both pictures are framed in a mixture of Gothic tracery and curtain, drawn in similar ways, and both have some ingenious goblin activity round the edges; while there is a curious intrusion of *chinoiserie* in the Oriental faces in the Browne plate, in the chinese hats in both, and in the chinaman on the screen in the Onwhyn plate. The domestic interior, the costumes, and especially the figure of a bald, plump, elderly man in an armchair, are executed in similar styles of drawing.

The plates for *Nicholas Nickleby* (1838–9) contain some undoubted successes, such as the Kenwigs girls in 'Nicholas engaged as Tutor in a Private Family' or the children and their tormentors at Dotheboys Hall, realized throughout with a horrifying intensity of meanness; but in general the drawing for this novel betrays a relaxation which foretells the later slackness of Browne's work. The figures in the *Pickwick* plates seem to be miniature people rather than full-size adults, with a fetching smallness and neatness in their oddity. These qualities were lost, with no compensating gain, in the *Nickleby* plates, and no work that Browne was illustrating at that time provided him with the inspiration and incentive he had felt while working on *Pickwick*. The drawing is equally casual in the plates for *Harry Lorrequer* (1838–9), and the gradual relaxation can be observed in three successive phases in the plates for the *Sketches of Young Ladies* (1838), *Young Gentlemen* (1838), and *Young Couples* (1840) by Dickens and 'Quiz'.

It is equally clear, however, that in *Nickleby*, Dickens himself was marking time rather than advancing. As Gissing notes, 'in writing *Nicholas Nickleby* [Dickens] was often overwearied, often compelled by haste to an improvisation which showed him at anything but his best. The book as a whole is unsatisfactory ...'.[5] When Dickens did break new ground, in *Master Humphrey's Clock*, Browne spontaneously developed new styles that suited the modes of those novels.

48. H. K. Browne, frontispiece for *Pickwick*.

He was encouraged to do this by the new attention to illustration that Dickens gave there. This is not to suggest that Dickens failed to provide for illustration in the text of his earlier novels: in the first number of *Pickwick* he began the passage which was to be the artist's first subject with the words, 'What a study for an artist did that exciting scene present!' and in *Nickleby* Dickens will accommodate his artist both by imagining a scene of strong visual interest and by insisting in the text that it makes a good picture.[6] But *Master Humphrey's Clock* shows a marked advance in integration.

The *Clock* came out once a week, and consisted, after the opening numbers, of the successive serializations of *The Old Curiosity Shop* and *Barnaby Rudge*. Dickens wanted the magazine to be lavishly illustrated, and he originally planned to employ a number of artists; but in practice the great majority of the illustrations were by Hablôt Browne, and Dickens's friend, George Cattermole. One must see the partnership of the three men as a whole in order to appreciate Browne's own development at this stage, for it was a special feature of Dickens's intentions for the *Clock* that word and picture should be bound together as closely as possible. In broaching the subject with Cattermole, he said that 'among other improvements' he had turned his 'attention to the illustrations, meaning to have woodcuts dropped into the text and no separate plates'.[7] He gave full, detailed, and enthusiastic instructions for the cuts;[8] and he made provision for them in his text.

49. H. K. Browne, Kit and Whisker.

The wood-engravings in the *Clock* are not merely inserted at the moment in the story to which they refer, but are often treated as distinct paragraphs of the narrative. The writing leads into the illustration, which then does certain work for the writing, before directing the reader back to the text. On his release from prison, Kit Nubbles is welcomed by the Garland family, and then visits the pony, Whisker. Dickens concludes the paragraph: 'It is the crowning circumstance of his earnest heartfelt reception, and Kit fairly puts his arm round Whisker's neck and hugs him' (Chapter LXVIII). This is a climax, a moment to dwell on; but the prose does not dwell on it. Instead, there is a picture of the scene (49) to be gazed at with pleasure. Taking it in, the reader presently notices that there is someone else in the stable, who has not so far been mentioned. Kit has his back to her and has not seen her yet. So the question arises 'But how comes Barbara to trip in there?' That is how Dickens begins the next paragraph, and he goes on to explain. The reading of the text flows naturally into a contemplation of the illustration, and flows as naturally back to a reading of the text. At the end of Chapter LXVIII of *Barnaby Rudge* the 'spectacle' that appals Barnaby is described in general terms rather than as a specific scene, and ends with a general comment by Dickens. A picture of the scene creates the particular individuals seen by Barnaby, enabling Dickens to begin the next paragraph: 'With all he saw in this last glance fixed indelibly upon his mind, Barnaby hurried from the city. . . .' The picture assists us to see through Barnaby's eyes, and helps fix the scene on our minds too.

In her article on *Master Humphrey's Clock*, Professor Stevens has noted the attention Dickens gave to the visual effect of the last page of a number:[9] perhaps the most striking use of illustration, as a part of the text, comes on the last page of *Shop*, Chapter LV. This was also the last page of the weekly issue, Number 35, and of the eighth monthly part, so the page was an especially important one.

In preceding pages the reader has accompanied Nell round the church, in the friendly village where she and the old man settle. The impression given is genial, mellow, quietly idyllic. But a new note is struck when the Sexton announces that he will show Nell the old well in the church. She lifts off the cover – and at this point the reader turns over and finds that by far the larger part of the final page of the number is occupied by a large and dramatically lighted wood-cut, set a little above centre (50). It comes at a precise moment in the text, following the exchange:

> '"A black and dreadful place!" exclaimed the child.
> "Look in," said the old man, pointing downward with his finger.
> The child complied, and gazed down into the pit.'

The text breaks off, and the eye drops to the well itself, enacting the pause during which Nell herself gazes into it. The motion downward mentioned in the text

" A black and dreadful place !" exclaimed the child.

" Look in," said the old man, pointing downward with his finger. The child complied, and gazed down into the pit.

" It looks like a grave, itself," said the old man.

" It does," replied the child.

" I have often had the fancy," said the sexton, " that it might have been dug at first to make the old place more gloomy, and the old monks more religious. It's to be closed up, and built over."

The child still stood, looking thoughtfully into the vault.

" We shall see," said the sexton, " on what gay heads other earth will have closed, when the light is shut out from here. God knows ! They'll close it up, next spring."

" The birds sing again in spring," thought the child, as she leant at her casement window, and gazed at the declining sun. " Spring ! a beautiful and happy time !"

50. Daniel Maclise, the well, with accompanying text.

('pointing downward', 'gazed down') is continued in the plate. The darker, heavier part of the archway framing Nell flows down to the winch, from which the massive posts, the handle, and the very taut rope plunge straight down. Almost parallel to these comes the old man's arms, with his brightly lit, pointing hand. He himself is a mass of unobtrusive downward movements: his crutch, with a line of light on it, runs to the outside edge of the well, across the heavier and darker movement in which the bellropes (which hang from the top of the picture, and are of just the same shade as the old man's coat) run into his elbow. The eye continues down forearm and thigh to his pointing hand, while his legs and coat dimly continue to the pit.

The cumulative effect of these details is to intensify the depths of darkness opening below Nell. The light on her own dress, and on both arms, slants down towards the pit. Nell herself glows; while the old man is contained by an area of heavy shadow, lit with stark gleams, she is framed by an archway that opens towards a brighter part of the church, and a window through which the sun streams. This strikes the note of the final detached paragraph, but the main burden of the page is given in the line that follows the illustration, and is, in effect, the caption to it: '"It looks like a grave, itself," said the old man.' The impact of this speech is increased by the break in the page, in which the reader takes in the picture, and it is to this line that all the downward movements of the illustration lead the eye. What follows in the text is very brief; without the cut it would lack point and fail to make a telling end to the chapter.

The picture gives the episode its force, author and artist having collaborated with an intimate understanding of each other's art. This illustration is not by either of the two regular artists on the magazine, George Cattermole and Hablôt Browne; it is by Dickens's close friend, Daniel Maclise, who had been mentioned as a likely illustrator in Dickens's initial letter to Cattermole.[10] The picture does not agree with the author's original intentions, for Dickens had first asked Maclise for 'a little design, embodying the bells above and the well below, and the old sexton and the child'.[11] Dickens made it clear, however, that he would write or re-write the relevant passage of the novel to suit the illustration when it came:

'. . . if you like to put any more people in, young or old, do so at your own discretion, and I'll take care to account for 'em. When you have done it, will you let *me* have it, that I may take care the text and it agree?'[12]

It is clear from the resulting picture that Dickens could afford to trust Maclise in this way. This was, however, Maclise's only drawing for the *Clock*; if he had done more, he would have disturbed the balance of complementary roles that was coming to characterize Dickens's use of his two resident illustrators in the magazine.

As it proceeds, *The Old Curiosity Shop* is divided more and more clearly into two distinct modes: the one, dominated by Quilp, is boisterous, comic, and fantastical, while the other, dominated by Nell, is subdued, solemn, and pathetic; the first becomes Browne's province, while the second is reserved for Cattermole. Dickens evidently found this specialization so much to his purpose that he ignored the principal advantages that accrued from the use of two artists: variety of effect, and ease of working under the pressures of weekly publication. Each artist executed the illustrations in several consecutive numbers, while the other was idle. Browne provides only one picture of Nell after her arrival at the country church;[13] apart from this he is confined to the plot involving Swiveller, Kit, the Brasses, and Quilp, while Cattermole does not provide a single illustration for the long stretch of the novel in which that plot is worked out (Chapters LVI to LXIX). With the return to Nell in Chapter LXX, Cattermole takes over, and Browne does no more illustrations. And in style, as in subject, there is the sharpest possible contrast between the two sets of pictures.

The solemn subjects associated with Nell's death went to Cattermole, in spite of the fact that he was chiefly an architectural and historical artist. He had been a pupil of the architectural draughtsman, John Britton, and from 1821 to 1824 his drawings had appeared in *Cathedral Antiquities of Great Britain*; his first painting for a Royal Academy Exhibition was a view of Peterborough Cathedral. His antiquarianism was relevant to the original conception of *Master Humphrey's Clock*, for Dickens made great play with furniture and architecture in establishing the dominant mood of sad, mellowed kindliness, which is focussed in the 'mis-shapen, deformed, old man', Master Humphrey, who has led 'a lonely, solitary life'.[14]

'I have a notion of this old file in the queer house, . . . and, among other peculiarities, of his affection for an old quaint queer-cased clock; showing how that when they have sat alone together in the long evenings, he has got accustomed to its voice, and come to consider it as the voice of a friend. . . .'[15]

Object and mood are united in the idea of 'quaintness'; Humphrey's clock is 'a quaint old thing in a huge oaken case curiously and richly carved' and the formula 'quaint old' becomes almost a refrain: 'You may be sure that in the time of King James the First, Windsor was a very quaint queer old town, and you may take it upon my authority that John Podgers was a very quaint queer old fellow; . . .'[16] Illustrations could make real the picturesque oddity in a way the prose could not, for words like 'quaint' lose their force with each repetition, and description in detail dissipates the overall charm. Detail does not matter, in any case, and in the illustrations the Clock itself is never the same clock twice: Cattermole's curling notation is masterly in suggesting a profusion of quaint details without any mood-dispelling precision. In later years, his work typified quaint fancifulness in architecture for Dickens – visiting an old *palazzo* Dickens found 'every room in it like the most quaint and fanciful of Cattermole's pictures'[17] – and it is to be supposed that Dickens had the same impression of Cattermole's work in 1840. Cattermole's first subject for Dickens was 'an old quaint room with antique Elizabethan furniture, and in the chimney-corner an extraordinary old clock'.[18]

Cattermole's experience in book-illustration had consisted chiefly in providing opulent costume-pieces for the historical works of Scott and Bulwer, and he was qualified to illustrate the historical fiction with which Dickens filled the early numbers of the *Clock*. In the second number, Cattermole had two subjects from a tale of romantic love and murder, set in Elizabethan times; in the third he had to compose his own subject from a tale of Charles II's reign.[19] In the fourth, he had the ancient armour and the picturesque relics of the Curiosity Shop.[20]

As the Curiosity Shop tale was protracted into a novel, however, Cattermole's services could easily have become redundant, for the *Shop* was not historical fiction. We find Dickens writing to Cattermole of 'a subject of an old Gateway which I had put in expressly with a view to your illustrious pencil';[21] but here Cattermole's relationship to the story is purely external, and it might be expected that as the novel progressed, Cattermole would have had less and less to contribute. Yet Dickens himself saw Cattermole's contribution in quite a different light:

'I cannot close this hasty note, my dear fellow, without saying that I have deeply felt your hearty and most invaluable co-operation in the beautiful illustrations you have made for the last story – that I look at them with a pleasure I cannot describe to you in words – and that it is impossible for me to say how sensible I am of your earnest and friendly aid. Believe me that this is *the very first time* any designs for what I have written have touched and moved me, and caused me to feel that they expressed the idea I had in my mind.'[22]

After reading this, it would be natural to look through the late illustrations to see if a new Cattermole had emerged, shedding antiquarian ornament and becoming expert in rendering pathos. Yet that series of late illustrations which Dickens consistently assigned to Cattermole shows no such change; the artist's chief interest is still in the buildings (51). It is the series as a whole that Dickens praises, rather than the single picture of 'the child lying dead in the little sleeping-room',[23] and it follows that the beauty which impresses and moves Dickens so greatly is largely that of the architectural drawing. But the aesthetic qualities of gothic architecture could hardly have aroused such an intense response, and the deeply-felt beauty must rather inhere in the associations of reverence and sanctity that gather round ancient religious buildings. The *Dictionary of National Biography* praised Cattermole for restoring the 'religious sentiment' of bygone times, and 'beauty' was, for Dickens, a word with powerful religious overtones: in 'Old

51. G. Cattermole, late sequence of illustrations for *The Old Curiosity Shop*.

Lamps for New Ones' he identified the 'idea of Beauty' with a 'power of etherealising, and exalting to the very Heaven of Heavens, what was most sublime and lovely in the expression of the human face divine on Earth'.[24] It was not by chance that Nell settled in the precincts of a church, and in the text Dickens stresses in every way he can that Nell's death was not merely a tragic event, but a holy one:

> '"It is not . . . on earth that Heaven's justice ends. Think what it is compared with the World to which her young spirit has winged its early flight, and say, if one deliberate wish expressed in solemn terms above this bed could call her back to life, which of us would utter it!"' (Chapter LXXI)

The ecclesiastical studies were agents in evoking the religious emotion with which Dickens wished to surround Nell's death, and they provide her with a visible shrine. Dickens's last request to Cattermole for this novel was for 'a little tail-piece . . . giving some notion of the etherealised spirit of the child'.[25]

52. H. K. Browne, Quilp at the window.

Browne, on the other hand, develops a style of striking intensity in grotesque effect. The picture of Quilp leaning out of the window (52) follows the text closely: the dwarf 'being swoln with suppressed laughter, . . . looked puffed and bloated into twice his usual breadth', and he 'saluted the party with a hideous and grotesque politeness' (Chapter LX). Browne's Quilp suits perfectly Dickens's characterization of the dwarf, which represents an innovation in his writing both in presenting such a joyous, energetic, and conscienceless villain, and in bearing out the idea quite openly with so many touches of violent brutality. Browne does not catch the new conception immediately, and at Quilp's first appearance the savage oddity appropriate to him is subdued by the general comic vision which is still that of the *Nickleby* plates; but Browne quickly acquires, and consistently maintains, an energy and harshness in rendering the grotesque which would have seemed forever out of reach to the mild and whimsical artist of *Pickwick*.

The difference between the work of the two artists is extreme, and Dickens's intentions for the illustrations could at first seem puzzling. The artistic difference emphasizes the difference in spirit between the two modes Dickens employs, and by confining each artist so rigorously to one field, Dickens achieved separation rather than integration. He seems to have aimed not for a final unity of mood, but for a special sharpness of contrast. In this connection it should be noted that Forster, reviewing the novel in *The Examiner*, described its progress as a steady expansion and deepening of the pregnant contrast presented at the start:

'from the image of little Nell asleep amid the quaint grotesque figures of the old curiosity warehouse, to that other final sleep she takes among the grim forms and carvings of the old church aisle; the main purpose is never put aside. . . . It was out of the more hideous lumber and rottenness that surrounded the child in her grandfather's home, that Quilp and his filthy gang had taken life. It was the practical human realization of that first still picture of her innocence in the midst of all strange and alien forms, that took the shape of her after wanderings; . . . And when at last she sits within the quiet village church, and gazes on those silent monumental groupes [*sic*] of warriors . . . it is as if the associations among which her life had opened were again crowding on the scene to witness its close –'[26]

As Professor Stevens has noted, discussing Forster's later version of this critique in the *Life*, his reference to 'that first still picture' suggests that he is thinking more of Samuel Williams's woodcut for the first number (53) than of Dickens's actual words. If it seems improbable that one illustration should have counted for so much in Forster's impression of the novel, his review may be compared with that by Thomas Hood, in the *Athenaeum*:

'To turn from the old loves to the new, we do not know where we have met, in fiction, with a more striking and picturesque combination of images than is presented by the simple, childish figure of little Nelly, amidst a chaos of such obsolete, grotesque, old-world commodities as form the stock in trade of the Old Curiosity Shop. Look at the Artist's picture of the Child, asleep in her little bed, surrounded, or rather mobbed, by ancient armour and arms, antique furniture, and relics sacred or profane, hideous or grotesque: – it is like an Allegory of the peace and innocence of Childhood in the midst of Violence, Superstition, and all the hateful or hurtful Passions of the world. How sweet and fresh the youthful figure! how much sweeter and fresher for the rusty, musty, fusty atmosphere of such accessories and their associations! How soothing the moral, that Gentleness, Purity, and Truth, sometimes dormant but never dead, have survived, and will outlive, Fraud and Force, though backed by gold and encased in steel!'[27]

53. Samuel Williams, Nell asleep.

Hood's review preceded Forster's, and there is reason to think that Forster was merely developing points that he had read in Hood's account.[28]

Not only Forster, but Dickens himself had been much impressed by Hood's review. Early in 1841 he wrote to Hood telling him how much he appreciated it; and in preparing the 1841 edition of the novel Dickens inserted four paragraphs immediately following the Williams engraving, which bring out the significance of the picture in just the way that Hood had done.[29] One would hardly expect a newspaper review to be numbered among the sources of the novel it reviewed, but there are several points of contact. Hood finds the picture by Williams 'like an Allegory', and in the inserted passage Dickens now says that the child seems to exist 'in a kind of allegory'. The particular idea that Nell's virtue had been made luminous and memorable by its contrast with the surrounding relics had been implicit in the *Clock* description; Hood makes it explicit: 'how much sweeter and fresher for the rusty, musty, fusty atmosphere of such accessories and their associations!' In the added passage Dickens perhaps labours the point:

'I am not sure I should have been so thoroughly possessed by this one subject, but for the heaps of fantastic things I had seen huddled together in the curiosity-dealer's warehouse ... I had her image, without any effort of imagination, surrounded and beset by everything that was foreign to its nature, and farthest removed from the sympathies of her sex and age. If these helps to my fancy had all been wanting, and I had been forced to imagine her in a common chamber ... it is very probable that I should have been less impressed with her strange and solitary state.'

Moreover, Hood's 'surrounded, or rather mobbed' presumably gave rise to Dickens's 'surrounded and beset'.

The treatment of the hostile grotesques surrounding and besetting Nell explains the side of the novel that runs to bizarre fantasy. Quilp and the Brasses are not introduced gratuitously: they are incarnations of the weird lumber in the shop. Forster said this explicitly in his review: 'It was out of the more hideous lumber and rottenness that surrounded the child in her grandfather's home, that Quilp and his filthy gang had taken life.' Re-writing the passage for the *Life*, he repeated the point in a more terse and downright way: 'The hideous lumber and rottenness that surround the child in her grandfather's home, take shape again in Quilp and his filthy gang.' In the inserted passage Dickens confirms this interpretation when he offers to 'place' the ensuing narrative as a 'curious speculation' involving 'a crowd of wild grotesque companions' clearly suggested by the 'heaps of fantastic things' in the shop; when, in the course of the novel, Quilp takes possession of the Curiosity Shop, and sets up house there, he is simply coming into his own.

There is no question of Hood imposing on Dickens a reading that conflicted with the latter's original inclinations, for a letter from Dickens to Williams, in which the author requests the artist to re-draw his first sketch, shows that Dickens attached great importance to the contrast that Hood brought out:

'The object being to show the child in the midst of a crowd of uncongenial and ancient things, Mr. Dickens scarcely *feels* the very pretty drawing inclosed, as carrying out his idea: the room being to all appearance an exceedingly comfortable one pair, and the sleeper being in a very enviable condition. If the composition would admit of a few grim, ugly articles seen through a doorway beyond, for instance, and giving a notion of great gloom outside the little room and surrounding the chamber, it would be much better.'[30]

The value of Hood's review for Dickens was, presumably, that it defined with clarity and emphasis a theme towards which he was feeling his way, through the slow progressive definition of his art. In endorsing Hood's review, Dickens confirmed the importance Hood had attached to Williams's 'first still picture', and with his reference to the 'curious speculation' he bore out Forster's suggestion that the subsequent course of the novel was a fanciful extension of the picture, with Nell 'holding her solitary way among a crowd of wild grotesque companions'. The central contrast of the novel is very much a visual one: on the one hand, a single figure of pure youthful beauty; on the other, a strange and fantastical crowd. And this contrast explains why Dickens encouraged his two artists to develop such opposed styles of illustration, and how it was that their pictures became an integral part of the novel.

Dickens's next story, *Barnaby Rudge*, was a historical novel, and offered a wealth of dramatic subjects for the historical artist. Dickens wrote to Cattermole:

'Here is a subject for the next number . . . the best opportunities of illustration are all coming off now, and we are in the thick of the story. . . . It is night, and the ruins are here and there flaming and smoking. I want — if you understand — to show one of the turrets laid open — the turret where the alarm-bell is, mentioned in Number 1; and among the ruins (at some height if possible) Mr. Haredale just clutching our friend, the mysterious file, who is passing over them like a spirit; Solomon Daisy, if you can introduce him, looking on from the ground below.'[31]

The instructions conclude, however, 'I think it will make a queer picturesque thing in your hands', and Cattermole's chief contribution to *Rudge* was not in depicting the swashbuckling action, but in realizing the picturesque setting and the queer buildings; the locksmith's house, 'The Boot', The Warren, Westminster Hall, and of course The Maypole (54). The setting had an active role and was not mere background. The Maypole resembles Bleak House, with its rambling zig-zag form in which it is easy to get lost, and its profusion of delights hidden away in odd nooks. The similarity is marked by verbal repetition in the relevant passages: the Maypole had 'more gable ends than a lazy man would care to count on a sunny day' (Chapter I), and Esther's room had 'an up-and-down roof, that had more corners in it than I ever counted afterwards' (Chapter VI). There is also a common warmth in the writing, suggesting that this free rambling growth was a quality Dickens particularly liked in Old English life. It would be natural for him to prefer the Tudor style, for it was in that period that English building rambled most freely, and ornament could multiply with abandon; and although *Rudge* is set in the 18th century, the Maypole itself 'was said to have been built in the days of King Henry the Eighth' (Chapter I). Bleak House is 'old-fashioned rather than old' (Chapter VI), but the fashion sounds Tudor or Jacobean.

Cattermole's architectural fancifulness was, of course, ideal for the Maypole, and Dickens was delighted with the drawing: 'I saw the old Inn this morning.

54. G. Cattermole, the Maypole.

Words cannot say how good it is.'[32] The Maypole sounds in the text like the perfect subject for Cattermole:

'Its windows were old diamond pane lattices, its floors were sunken and uneven, its ceilings blackened by the hand of time and heavy with massive beams. Over the doorway was an ancient porch, quaintly and grotesquely carved. . . .'

The drawings of the Maypole make real, as description could not, the way in which the actual architecture of the building expresses the richness, organized with a generous and necessary looseness, that Dickens saw in the normal human commerce of Old England.

For *Barnaby Rudge*, Cattermole was not required to use a style very different from that of the cuts in *The Old Curiosity Shop*. Hablôt Browne, however, developed once again a style of illustration which was quite new in his work, and which peculiarly suited the novel. He retained the grotesque vein evolved in the treatment of Quilp to do justice to Dennis and Gashford, and he naturally used his early humorous style for the Maypole cronies; but in the general run of illustrations he threw off both the grotesque manner of the *Shop* illustrations, and the comicality that had been so marked a characteristic of his work. A number of the illustrations are in a completely sober, naturalistic manner; the picture of Hugh dozing (55) would not be recognized as Browne's work if the signature were missing. This change of style in Browne's drawing corresponds remarkably to the change of style in Dickens's writing in this novel; for the prose of *Barnaby Rudge* is uncharacteristic of Dickens in its uniform levelness and restraint. In Gissing's phrase, the novel is written in 'good, plain, unimaginative English'.[33] Dickens certainly shows his customary force of imagination when, at the climax

55. H. K. Browne, Hugh dozing.

of the book, he is finally able to throw himself heart and soul into the looting and smashing and killing, the whole wild Dionysiac rampage, of the Gordon Riots. Yet although the prose describing the riots asks to be read in excited, appalled haste, it is, simply as prose, among the most monotonous that Dickens wrote; the Dickensian energy is diverted from the language and concentrated in the imagining of lurid incident. And for this writing too Browne develops the kind of illustration that is called for. He absorbs Dickens's excitement in the wild activity of the mob, and starts to produce designs which in their dense crowding, tumultuous movement, and variety of action, realize the violent ecstasy of the climax (56). The latter part of the novel is disturbing to read, especially when one recalls *A Tale of Two Cities* and reflects that Dickens never outgrew the revolutionary thrill of the Gordon Riots: but it may at least be said that author and artist are marvellously at one.

56. H. K. Browne, the mob.

With the end of *Barnaby Rudge*, however, came an end to the possibility of picture and text working so closely in harness. Dickens had found the unit of the weekly part increasingly irksome, and he resented having to divide up the extended dramatic crescendo of his climax into small pieces.[34] *Barnaby Rudge* concluded, he was glad to wind up *Master Humphrey's Clock* and return to his familiar monthly parts. The return to monthly parts meant a return to the use of two etchings per month, and he did not again have pictures set in the actual text of his novels. This return to the old form did not, however, imply any lessening of interest in the part that illustrations could play in fiction. On the contrary, his demands and expectations of the illustrations grew steadily in the succeeding decade. With the experiment of *Master Humphrey's Clock* behind him, he evidently felt, as Thackeray had felt, that although illustrations could make a large contribution to a story if they were worked so closely into the text that they belonged between two particular words, they could do still more if they were, so to speak, placed beside the text of the whole chapter, rather than tied to a precise point in it. If they were freed from an exact dramatic context they could express more of the whole drama; they could mean more.

6

Dickens and Browne:
Martin Chuzzlewit to *Bleak House*

Martin Chuzzlewit was the first novel that Dickens wrote after the demise of *Master Humphrey's Clock*. The interlude in wood-engraving had evidently been refreshing for his illustrator, for when Browne returns to etching for Dickens, his work is crisp and bright. His figures are full-size and solid, and while he retains the acuteness and economy of his caricatures, he seems concerned less with caricaturing people and more with drawing them well. The biting-in has produced an unusually clean line that shows Browne's etching at its most sensitive; the line takes delicate curves yet looks as though it has been slit in the paper with a razor.

The illustrations improved during the publication of *Chuzzlewit*, and the overall growth in Browne's talent since the days of *Pickwick* is striking, both in the crowded and dramatic set-pieces, and in the milder subjects. In 'Mr. Pinch is amazed by an unexpected apparition' (57) there is no lively, tumbling crowd of comic characters, no extravagant hypocrite to be lampooned, no scene of high drama; the plate simply demonstrates an unlaboured mastery of design, drawing, and the suggestion of space. It is again one of those plates that would scarcely be recognized to be by Browne if the signature were concealed; and it shows how mature, as an artist, he had become.

The preliminary sketches for this book, in the Dexter Collection, are among the most careful Browne produced. In many of his other pencil drawings, he lets the lead become blunt, but in those for Chuzzlewit he keeps a cutting point on the lead, as an etcher, who must execute the final work with a needle, naturally should. Every detail is decided, and nothing seems left to be extemporized on the plate. Even so, he introduces new precisions in the act of etching. In 'Mr Nadgett breathes, as usual, an atmosphere of mystery', one could imagine that the

57. H. K. Browne, 'Mr Pinch is amazed by an unexpected apparition'.

face of Mr Nadgett had been carefully reduced to this pointed economy in the pencil drawing; but there his face is concealed behind his shoulder. Similarly, in 'Mr Pinch is amazed by an unexpected apparition', the face of old Martin is clear in the etching, though it was concealed by the brim of his hat in the sketch.

The new sharpness and life in the *Chuzzlewit* drawings is due partly to Browne's discovery of Daumier. Thackeray had suggested in his article on French caricatures in *The London and Westminster Review* in 1839 that Browne could learn from the French artist:

'. . . if we might venture to give a word of advice to another humorous designer, whose works are extensively circulated – the illustrator of "Pickwick" and "Nicholas Nickleby" – it would be to study well these caricatures of Monsieur Daumier; . . .'[1]

In 1840 Browne illustrated Reynolds' novel *Robert Macaire in England*. Macaire, the principal character in a French farce, *L'Auberge des Adrets*, had been taken over by Daumier and made the protagonist in a long series of caricatures in the 1830s. Reynolds' hero is related only loosely to his French sources, and Browne could have illustrated the novel without turning up Daumier's series; yet his version of the arch-swindler Macaire and his assistant Bertrand is clearly based on Daumier's. In particular, he has taken over the very fine lines of facial expression that characterize Daumier's two rogues.

In the *Chuzzlewit* plates the influence of Daumier can be detected in a characteristic way of rendering eyelids and eyebrows, but the clearest proof of the connection is to be found in the studies of Sarah Gamp (58), who closely resembles Daumier's sick-nurse (59) of 1842. In both of Browne's etchings Sarah's head is seen from the same angle as the other nurse's, is drawn in the same style, and has the same features, down to the cleft chin. From Daumier, Browne

58. H. K. Browne, Mrs Gamp.

59. H. Daumier, 'La Garde-Malade' (*Le Charivari*, 22 May 1842).

acquired a new fertility and fineness in the witty touching in of faces; many of the *Chuzzlewit* plates are crowded, but each face in the crowd is an individual study. Earlier plates like 'The Trial' had been packed with comic individuals, but the

Chuzzlewit plates show a more generous sense of the range and substance of individuality. Browne never, of course, amounts to being a second Daumier, but it is a serious distinction of his art that he was able so adroitly to translate Daumier's style, evolved in terms of the lithographic crayon, into an appropriate style of etching. It is reasonable to assume that Browne's new, ample sense of human variety was absorbed from Dickens as well as Daumier, and rather than try to separate the influences, one might stress the common ground between the English author and the French artist that is indicated by Browne's response to both.

Daumier's sick-nurse is already characterized as a Sarah Gamp, and it may be that Dickens had seen the lithograph (perhaps at Browne's house) and found it a useful point of departure for the new comic creation. In 'Dickens and Daumier' Gordon McKenzie has drawn attention to the many parallels in theme, attitude, and character, in the work of Dickens and Daumier.[2] He does not posit, in either artist, any knowledge of the other's work; but, although such an inquiry is beyond the scope of the present study, the possibility that Dickens knew Daumier's work and found it suggestive is worth investigation. Like Tigg Montague, Macaire had started his career as a petty swindler: in the farce and the first caricatures, he is simply a down-at-heel, shabby-genteel rogue. He then reappears, suddenly, as the type of the successful swindler, enjoying the most opulent style of life; in some incarnations he is just such a company director as Tigg. He is also, like Pecksniff, an architect, and Daumier delights in showing his suavity and bland hypocrisy. It may then be that the work of Daumier combined with that of Molière in suggesting to Dickens the rich possibilities of an extreme hypocrite presented in energetic caricature.

Partly inspired by Daumier, the new sharpness and energy of Browne's drawing is a fit accompaniment to the new 'suggestiveness, compact and sure of stroke'[3] in Dickens's prose, and to Dickens's new sense of the way in which each visual detail can tell a story. In the following instructions for the plate 'The Thriving City of Eden as it Appeared in Fact' (60), Dickens is virtually moving the pencil himself: he imagines the plate in detail, and except for remembering that the river flows towards home, his details are not the psychic details one expects of a novelist, but the telling visual particulars of an artist like Hogarth. The picture he describes is a typical Hogarthian scene of tumbledown confusion, with its ironic written placards, and characterizing utensils that are not being used; the tools of men's trades, in and out of use, are always significant in Hogarth, as Dickens noted when describing *Gin Lane* – 'The best are pawning the commonest necessaries, and tools of their trades.'[4] The details are almost emblematic, and Dickens intends his reader to concentrate on each of them in turn and take its point:

'The first subject having shown the settlement of Eden on paper, the second shews it in reality. Martin and Mark are displayed as the tenants of a wretched

60. H. K. Browne, 'The Thriving City of Eden as it Appeared in Fact'.

log hut (for a pattern whereof see a vignette brought by Chapman & Hall) in a perfectly flat, swampy, wretched forest of stunted timber in every stage of decay, with a filthy river running before the door, and some other miserable log houses distributed among the trees, whereof the most ruinous and tumbledown of all is labelled Bank and National Credit Office. Outside their door, as the custom is, is a rough sort of form or dresser, on which are set forth their pot and kettle and so forth, all of the commonest kind. On the outside of the house, at one side of the door, is a written placard, Chuzzlewit and Co., Architects and Surveyors, and upon a stump of tree, like a butcher's block, before the cabin, are Martin's instruments – a pair of rusty compasses, &c. On a three-legged stool beside this block sits Martin in his shirt-sleeves, with long dishevelled hair, resting his head upon his hands – the picture of hopeless misery – watching the river and sadly remembering that it flows towards home. But Mr Tapley, up to his knees in filth and brushwood, & in the act of endeavouring to perform some impossibilities with a hatchet, looks towards him with a face of unimpaired good humour, and declares himself perfectly jolly. Mark, the only redeeming feature. Everything else dull, miserable, squalid, unhealthy, and utterly devoid of hope – diseased, starved and abject. The weather is intensely hot, and they are but partially clothed. . . .'[5]

The plot and meaning of *Barnaby Rudge* had been carefully planned, but in *Chuzzlewit* Dickens had a guiding principle of a more important kind: he had a single theme – the growth of selfishness from small beginnings – which could inform all aspects of a plot that could now, conversely, afford to be more flexible. A new and creative urgency of purpose shows in the writing, and extends to the instructions for illustrations. It must be said, however, that the finest, comic vitality of the writing often seems to have little relation to the moral preoccupation. The following novel, *Dombey and Son*, is the first in which Dickens truly gives himself up to his theme, and lets it organize his writing from within; and it is only when he does this that he makes his illustrations the expression of a coherent meaning.

The common note with *Dombey* is: 'The points for illustration, and the enormous care required, make me excessively anxious,' or again: 'The first subject which I am now going to give [for illustration] is very important to the book.'[6] His delight at good results and despair at bad ones are both extreme: he is 'really *distressed* by the illustration of Mrs. Pipchin and Paul'; on the other hand, 'The sketch is admirable – the women *quite perfect*' and, more importantly, he announces 'I think Mr Dombey admirable.'[7] The figure of Mr Dombey challenged Browne to achieve a sharp characterization while emancipating himself from the caricaturing tradition that had fostered his talent; and his emancipation can be seen in 'The Dombey Family' (61).

Here there is no facetiousness or exaggeration, although we might infer that the artist was an expert caricaturist from the very sharp sensitivity of the line that touches in Dombey's face. It is done with few strokes, but the Dombey of

the text is caught to the life: proud and handsome, but with his meanness showing in the contracted mouth, in the nose pinched in a fastidious sniff, and in the
tired eyes which wander uneasily and resentfully towards his daughter, while he
keeps his head turned away. It is Dombey, also, in the elegant clothing and in the
way he sits: he crosses his legs and sits back, as though relaxing a little, yet he
remains completely stiff. The line is delicate but strong: it looks as though the
needle ran through the wax quickly and easily, without hesitation or second
thoughts, but without any vagueness or neglect. The effect is of a fine and subtle
clarity.

One says this is the Dombey of the text, but the scene Browne depicts does
not occur in the novel. The 'List of Plates' required this illustration to face page
22 in the first edition, but there the position of the characters is different: 'When
little Florence timidly presented herself, Mr Dombey stopped in his pacing up

61. H. K. Browne, 'The Dombey Family'.

and down and looked towards her.' It is in a later scene, though on the next page, that we have Mr Dombey doing what he is shown doing here – sitting down at the table, and avoiding turning round to face Florence:

'The little altercation between them had attracted the notice of Mr Dombey, who inquired from the table where he was sitting at his wine, what the matter was.
"Miss Florence was afraid of interrupting, Sir, if she came in to say good-night," said Richards.
"It doesn't matter," returned Mr Dombey. "You can let her come and go without regarding me."'

The two scenes go together, and the discrepancy is of small account: it might be better Browne should be unfaithful to the immediate text, if it helps him to achieve a fidelity to the writing of a higher kind.[8] And the sitting Dombey does express better than a standing, staring Dombey would what Dickens says of him:

'His feeling about the child had been negative from her birth. He had never conceived an aversion to her; it had not been worth his while, or in his humour. She had never been a positively disagreeable object to him. But now he was ill at ease about her. She troubled his peace. He would have preferred to put her idea aside altogether, if he had known how. Perhaps – who shall decide on such mysteries! – he was afraid that he might come to hate her.'

Although Browne has been accused of 'ham rhetoric', he eschews the theatrical possibilities the text suggests – the pacing Dombey suddenly stopping in his tracks at the sight of his daughter – and prefers a still tableau, pregnant with suggestions of how the members of the 'Family' stand in relation to each other. Mrs Richards stands very much in attendance, though her eyes, sympathetic and uneasy, look towards Florence. She holds Dombey's child, who is, appropriately, a wizen little mite, and who sits upright in her arms, a little like his father. But while the father faces away from Florence and towards his favourite child, the child faces both father and neglected daughter. Father, child, and nurse are in a tight group, surrounded by various devices made from shadow and furniture, whereas Florence, neglected and isolated in the family, is outside that group.[9] Her timid hesitation is well caught in her way of bunching herself in. Although this detail is not in the text, it is the ideal visual expression of the conflict of impulses the text does record:

'Had he looked with greater interest and with a father's eye, he might have read in her keen glance the impulses and fears that made her waver; the passionate desire to run clinging to him, . . . the dread of a repulse; the fear of being too bold and of offending him; the pitiable need in which she stood of some assurance and encouragement; . . .'

[138]

Florence is not sentimentalized.

The large tear-like shape, hanging over Polly and the child, is not mention-ed in the text at this point, and one might wonder what it is doing there. But for the reader of the novel, it may recall a suggestion made a few pages earlier: 'Every chandelier or lustre, muffled in holland, looked like a monstrous tear de-pending from the ceiling's eye.' It hangs just over the new child.

Illustration in this plate is something very different from the precise visual-ization of what a moment in the dramatic action would have looked like: it in-volves searching for a tableau that will serve as a poignant epitome of what, most importantly, the text has to say. That Dickens desired illustrations to assist in communication as well as depiction we may conclude from this letter to Forster, concerning the Christmas books:

'I should like each part to have a general illustration to it at the beginning, shadowing out its drift and bearing: much as Browne goes at that kind of thing on Dombey covers. . . .'[10]

And the discrepancy mentioned above, in making Dombey sit, was not simply an initiative of Phiz, but a revision of the scene preferred by Dickens himself. Browne prepared two alternative designs for 'The Dombey Family': one with Dombey standing, the other with him sitting; and then he asked Dickens 'whether 'twere better to have him standing thus, stiff as a poker, with a kind of side glance at his daughter – or sitting, as in the other?'[11]

Where the illustrations do not have the deep suggestiveness of 'The Dom-bey Family', they still fit perfectly the text they illustrate. Where the text offers a noble sentimental drama of beautiful women, Browne adopts a sedate and digni-fied manner, with a majestic architectural backdrop and elegant properties, and we can see that the two beautiful women are playing parts ('Florence and Edith on the Staircase'). Where Dickens works up a climax of sonorous melodrama, in Edith's denunciation of Carker, Browne gets up a perfect *coup de theatre* ('Mr Carker in his hour of Triumph'). When Dickens gives us a caricature Major with a slight Mephistophelian suggestion, or when he attains a sober and serious truth in Dombey himself, Browne does likewise.

In the plate 'Coming home from Church' (62) we notice that while Dombey should be in the middle, the crowd has the middle position, and he and his wife are very much to one side. We are made to feel Dombey's serene indifference to low life: he holds aloof, turns his back on it, and takes a step above everyone else. He is literally a step up, for he has entered his massive doorway, a portico which Browne seems almost to have detached from the house, so as to make it seem very little a doorway and very much a frame or niche for Dombey. But though separate, framed, and aloof, Dombey does not impose, and he is here very clearly what Dickens also represents him as being: the inferior of the onlookers in vitality and

62. H. K. Browne, 'Coming home from Church'.

character. While Dombey holds his head high, Edith looks down, and her thoughtful, subdued look is more telling and ominous than a simple portrayal of the Proud Beauty would be. This small touch of reality reminds the reader that Browne wants him to regard the plate as a scene taking place before his eyes: the reader has a pavement to stand on and a place in the front row of an invisible nearside crowd; and he is invited to notice the rich variety of life, however scruffy and seedy, which is going on all round Dombey, and from which he is quite cut off. Further away there is the other marriage-tableau of a Punch and Judy show. In the far background a hearse, driving away, serves as an unobtrusive reminder of the two deaths on which this marriage is founded; but it has also a more immediate, severe, and thrilling purpose, for it associates with the wedding-party's coach and makes the point Blake made in his phrase 'marriage-hearse'. The effect is evidently calculated for the reader of novels who also 'read' pictures: the hearse is not likely to be noticed in the first glance at the plate, and the 'reader' was presumably intended to experience a shock of realization as the barb in the illustration suddenly pulled.

The two latter devices, commenting on the marriage, are what Browne's contemporaries would have called 'Hogarthian touches'; the hearse may be compared with the funeral procession in the background of 'Gin Lane' (15). Hogarth's regular practice of hanging on the walls pictures that make points about the action is used in the various pictures of Sol Gills's shop, where a portrait of a boy fades away and grows into prominence again as Walter travels away, is feared lost, and later returns; while, concurrently, a ship in another picture runs into bad weather, is battered by a tempest, and finds calm at last. When Mrs MacStinger invades the shop to do battle with Captain Cuttle, one picture on the wall shows two ships in battle, and another shows a man-of-war entitled 'The Medusa'. If such allusions sound like initiatives of Browne rather than of Dickens, it must be added that one might also credit Browne with the arrangement of 'Mr Dombey and his "confidential agent"' in which Dombey sits just under a large picture of a woman very like the haughty Edith – his hair almost touches the frame – while Carker sits opposite and takes in both with his gaze. Yet that picture is a decoration of Carker's room with which Dickens himself makes great play (in Chapter XLII).

Similarly, in the picture of the humiliated Dombey, 'Mr Dombey and the world', it might be thought that the way in which everything in the room has eyes that stare at Dombey is an invention of Browne's intended to express, visually, Dombey's painful self-consciousness and embarrassment. However, the text reads:

'The world. What the world thinks of him, how it looks at him, what it sees in him, and what it says – this is the haunting demon of his mind. It is everywhere where he is . . . .

'Mr Dombey receives them with his usual dignity, and stands erect, in his old attitude, before the fire. He feels that the world is looking at him out of their eyes. That it is in the stare of the pictures. That Mr Pitt, upon the book-case, represents it. That there are eyes in its own map, hanging on the wall.' (Chapter LI)

The animistic habit which (it was suggested earlier) Dickens absorbed from the caricatures here finds apt realization in the etching of an artist deriving from that school. The bust of Mr Pitt is a further detail given pointed use both by Dickens and by Browne: in most pictures of Dombey's home it is placed above him, reflecting his expression and projecting its stony nature onto him.

In *Dombey and Son*, author and artist work together with one inspiration, the illustrations taking their cue from the specifically visual liveliness of Dickens's imagination. The same close co-operation continues in the following novel, *David Copperfield*. A scene like that of Martha on the banks of the Thames, in Chapter CLVII, is not merely conceived with an accompanying illustration in view: it is actually imagined, in the narrative itself, as a 'picture'. Dickens first fills in the background in a strongly visual manner:

'. . . the ground was cumbered with rusty iron monsters of steam-boilers, wheels, cranks, pipes, furnaces, paddles, anchors, diving-bells, windmill-sails, and I know not what strange objects, . . . grovelling in the dust, underneath which – having sunk into the soil of their own weight in wet weather – they had the appearance of vainly trying to hide themselves. The clash and glare of sundry fiery Works upon the river side, arose by night to disturb everything except the heavy and unbroken smoke that poured out of their chimneys.'

He then touches in the centre of interest in explicitly pictorial terms: 'The girl we had followed strayed down to the river's brink, and stood in the midst of this night-picture, lonely and still, looking at the water.'

The chief feature of the *Copperfield* illustrations is the greatly extended use of the 'tableau'. In this novel Dickens will momentarily arrest his characters in a significant grouping which he describes as a 'picture' and which is evidently conceived with an illustration in mind. This pictorial technique had not occurred to Dickens at the start of the novel: in the first number a significant moment of this kind comes, and Dickens explicitly asserts its pictorial qualities, but there is no illustration (although the subject sounds more inviting than 'Our Pew at Church', one of the illustrations provided):

'She [Em'ly] started from my side, and ran along a jagged timber which protruded from the place we stood upon, and overhung the deep water at some height, without the least defence. The incident is so impressed on my remembrance, that if I were a draughtsman I could draw its form here, I dare say, accurately as it was that day, and little Em'ly springing forward to her destruction (as it appeared to me), with a look that I have never forgotten, directed far out to sea.' (Chapter III)

The resonance of this episode is amplified in the substantial paragraph that follows it, in the heavy reiteration of 'There have been times since. . . .' The insistence could have been spared had there been an illustration to isolate the scene and give it special stress.

This passage may be compared with the scene in which David and Steerforth arrive at Mr Peggotty's home (63). The problem of holding up the narrative

63. H. K. Browne, 'We arrive unexpectedly at Mr. Peggotty's fireside'.

while the picture is described is overcome by letting David come upon the scene from outside: since it is the first thing he sees, it is naturally described in some detail (it will be seen in the following examples how regularly this technique is used[12]):

'A murmer of voices had been audible on the outside, and, at the moment of our entrance, a clapping of hands: which latter noise, I was surprised to see, proceeded from the generally disconsolate Mrs. Gummidge. But Mrs. Gummidge was not the only person there, who was unusually excited. Mr. Peggotty, his face lighted up with uncommon satisfaction, and laughing with all his might, held his rough arms wide open, as if for little Em'ly to run into them; Ham, with a mixed expression in his face of admiration, exultation, and a lumbering sort of bashfulness that sat upon him very well, held little Em'ly by the hand, as if he were presenting her to Mr. Peggotty; little Em'ly herself . . . was stopped by our entrance (for she saw us first) in the very act of springing from Ham to nestle in Mr. Peggotty's embrace. In the first glimpse we had of them all, and at the moment of our passing from the dark cold night into the warm light room, this was the way in which they were all employed: Mrs. Gummidge in the back ground, clapping her hands like a madwoman.

'The little picture was so instantaneously dissolved by our going in, that one might have doubted whether it had ever been.' (Chapter XXI)

It might seem that there is some redundant detail here for a picture that is to melt at once, but the picture is significant. Dickens times David's arrival for the very moment that celebrates all those happy prospects for the Peggotty group, which the introduction of Steerforth will presently destroy (it is little Em'ly who sees the new arrivals first, and is stopped in her flight). So it is appropriate that with the coming of David and Steerforth, the 'little picture' should be 'instantaneously dissolved': the illustration allows Dickens both to erase it in the text, and to leave us with an indelible picture of it.

If a significant moment is preserved in a picture, both Dickens and the reader can easily return to it. In the sixth monthly part David comes upon Dr Strong and his wife and senses a world of unforeseen and still obscure possibilities:

'I went into the supper-room. . . . But a door of communication between that and the Doctor's study . . . being open, I passed on there. . . .

'The Doctor was sitting in his easy-chair by the fireside, and his young wife was on a stool at his feet. The Doctor, with a complacent smile, was reading aloud . . . and she was looking up at him. But, with such a face as I never saw. It was so beautiful in its form, it was so ashy pale, it was so fixed in its abstraction, it was so full of a wild, sleep-walking, dreamy horror of I don't know what.' (Chapter XVI)

The illustration of the episode, 'I return to the Doctor's after the party', cannot show all this, but it can serve as an index to what the text describes. In the last sentence of the chapter (three paragraphs later) Dickens suggests he may return to this scene: 'It made a great impression on me, and I remembered it a long time afterwards, as I shall have occasion to narrate when the time comes.' In the following monthly part, Dickens reminded the reader briefly of the scene, but five months passed before the scene was alluded to again (in Part Twelve), and an illustration, which could be turned up instantly, was a useful way of bringing back to consciousness a moment that many readers must almost have forgotten. In Part Twelve the characters were again posed as in the plate:

'When I left, ... she was kneeling on the ground at the Doctor's feet, putting on his shoes and gaiters for him. There was a softened shade upon her face, thrown from some green leaves overhanging the open window of the low room; and I thought all the way to Doctors' Commons, of the night when I had seen it looking at him as he read.' (Chapter XXXVI)

David's mother had similarly been the subject of a sudden and unexpected discovery, brief in the text, but picked out by an illustration (64):

'I believed, from the solitary and thoughtful way in which my mother murmured her song, that she was alone. And I went softly into the room. She was sitting by the fire, suckling an infant, whose tiny hand she held against her neck. Her eyes were looking down upon its face, and she sat singing to it. I was so far right, that she had no other companion.' (Chapter VIII)

This is one of the two emotional climaxes that come in the same number, in poignant juxtaposition, concerning David's mother: the one, the new child; the other, her own death. But her death could not have been shown in an illustration without giving the reader premature knowledge of it, while the illustration we do have helps the reader to keep clearly in his mind, in the painfulness of the second episode, the beauty of the first. The picture certainly signals a moment in David's life that stands out unique and is to be remembered through the subsequent narrative as providing an ideal standard. As with Em'ly on the breakwater, or the Peggotty group, the illustration comes at a momentary pause in the action, where one might feel 'If only things could always have been like this!' David the boy is taken into the group, and David the autobiographer reflects: 'I wish I had died. . . . I should have been more fit for heaven than I have ever been since.'

A vein of Christian sentiment runs through the novel and is expressed pictorially in the paintings of biblical scenes hanging suggestively in the background of various illustrations. In 'Changes at Home', David's return home and discovery of the new baby are expressed in two paintings, one labelled 'The Prodigal Son', and the other 'Moses. . .'. Such a use of biblical pictures harks back to Gillray's hanging of Adam and Eve in 'Wife and no Wife' (3) and to Hogarth's earlier practice. In a similar way, Dickens employs biblical pictures in his prose. In *Little Dorrit* 'a communication of great trap doors in the floor and roof with the workshop above and the workshop below, made a shaft of light in this perspective, which brought to Clennam's mind the child's old picture-book, where similar rays were the witnesses of Abel's murder' (i, Chapter

64. H. K. Browne, 'Changes at Home'.

XXIII). The religious note is perhaps the most difficult note of all to strike suc-
cessfully, and Dickens is notoriously not most successful when he is most in
earnest: yet it is where he most resembles Hogarth, in his use of a familiar religious picture to set sordid human decay against unsordid truth, that he particularly impresses the reader with the tender matter-of-factness of his handling:

'The room . . . is offensive to every sense; even the gross candle burns pale
and sickly in the polluted air. . . . Lying in the arms of the woman who has
spoken, is a very young child.

'"Why, what age do you call that little creature?" says Bucket. "It looks as if it was born yesterday." He is not at all rough about it; and as he turns his light gently on the infant, Mr. Snagsby is strangely reminded of another infant, encircled with light, that he has seen in pictures.' (*Bleak House*, Chapter XXII)

In context, the comparison is unexpected and very briefly made, and Dickens's fine reserve here compares favourably with Hogarth's down-to-earth sobriety in making such connections.

In *Copperfield*, the most powerful pictorial allusion to the Bible is made in the second tableau found by David in Yarmouth:

'The door opening immediately into it, I found myself among them, before I considered whither I was going.

The girl – the same I had seen upon the sands – was near the fire. She was sitting on the ground, with her head and one arm lying on a chair. I fancied, from the disposition of her figure, that Em'ly had but newly risen from the chair, and that the forlorn head might have perhaps been lying on her lap. . . .' (Chapter XXII)

In the illustration (65), a picture on the walls shows the Magdalen washing the feet of Christ;[13] Martha's pose, and the fall of her hair resemble those of the Magdalen. The picture also recalls the scene as it was the moment before David entered, for Emily has just left a position similar to Christ's.

This picture hangs both above Martha and between Martha and Emily, and one turns from it to the other picture in the room, which hangs above Emily and shows Eve being tempted by the serpent. It corresponds to the anxiety Emily feels about the bad things in her own nature: '"Oh, I am not as good a girl as I ought to be. I am not, I know!"' But Em'ly's own fall is in the future, and the painting is cut off from her by the half-open door, and is half-hidden in shadow.

For the original reader of Dickens her fall was two months in the future. The illustration belonged to Part Eight, and the reader did not know Em'ly had fallen in love with Steerforth and run away with him until the end of Part Ten. Part Eight came out at the beginning of December, while at the end of that month Dickens had still not begun Part Ten: on 29 December he wrote: 'I can't help pushing away the first page of Copperfield No. 10, now staring at me with what I may literally call a blank aspect, . . .'[14] Browne could have had no written text to tell him how the story would go. The available text gave only slight, ambiguous hints of what was to come; so presumably Dickens took Browne into his confidence with regard to Em'ly's intended fate, and gave instructions for the biblical hints. These pictures had more to do, of course, than merely intimate the plot. The painting of the Magdalen asserts the great authority for the Charity of Ham and Em'ly. In the text the biblical association shows in the phrasing and the

65. H. K. Browne, 'Martha'.

tone ('Then Martha arose . . .'), but it is not made explicit at any point – it is identified by the illustration. Browne, for his part, organizes the composition so as to make the pictorial allusion tell best. The faces of Peggotty, Em'ly, and Ham are arranged in a straight line upwards that ends (or begins) in the figure of Christ.

The *Copperfield* plate 'I make the acquaintance of Miss Mowcher' (66) shows that Dickens was prepared for future developments in the plot to be announced in the illustrations, although in this instance the prophesied development did not in fact occur. The dwarf on whom Miss Mowcher was partly

66. H. K. Browne, 'I make the acquaintance of Miss Mowcher'.

modelled, a Mrs Hill, was pained by the presentation; learning this, Dickens
wrote to her, saying 'that he had intended to employ the character in an un-
pleasant way, but he would, whatever the risk or inconvenience, change it all, so
that nothing but an agreeable impression should be left'.[15] John Butt and
Kathleen Tillotson concluded that Miss Mowcher 'was undoubtedly to serve
with Littimer as an agent of Steerforth's purpose',[16] and a clearer indication of
her original role is given in the plate, in the picture that hangs above and behind
her: it is included in the area of light surrounding Steerforth and Miss Mowcher,
and the frame just touches the ribbon of Miss Mowcher's hat. The picture
shows Faust and Gretchen in the garden, with Mephistopheles as a dark shape
just behind Faust.[17] Mephistopheles ought not to be there, of course, since his
function in the garden was to distract Gretchen's companion; but it is a fair
expression of his role in the episode to make him lurk behind Faust in this way.

67. H. K. Browne, 'Our Housekeeping'.

Miss Mowcher (on the table) looms above and behind Steerforth, and the feather on her hat asserts her relation to the figures in the painting. Steerforth has the seduction of Little Em'ly in view, as Faust had Gretchen's; and in *Faust* Mephistopheles played the part of a procurer. Dickens could thus use an illustration to convey Miss Mowcher's intended role unambiguously, when such a communication would have been a delicate matter in the actual text of a Victorian novel. The *Faust*-scene was, however, a late addition to the plate: unlike the biblical scenes in 'Martha', it is absent from Browne's sketch. Presumably, on inspecting the sketch, Dickens saw his opportunity to make clearer a suggestion that was fogged in the text, and he dictated the necessary amendment.[18]

It must be said, however, that the theme of the fallen woman belongs to one of the weaker strains in the novel. The sound part of the book is built round the pattern of growth by which the waif David, although gifted with a fine and growing consciousness, inevitably repeats the mistake in marriage that his father made. The whole process is beautifully done in all its essential stages, except for being vitiated at the end by the death of Dora, which is described with many false notes and seems far from inevitable. The plate 'Our Housekeeping' (67) epitomizes the marriage. In the top left-hand corner (the place one looks at first in reading a page) are the two love-birds in their cage. At the table, Dora looks on helpless while David does the work, and is tense with effort – the resistance of the uncooked mutton can be felt. In the middle of the table sits Dora's little dog, Jip. In the text, Dickens makes various uses of Jip in his characterization of Dora, and he finally equates Jip with Dora to the extent of presenting her death through the simultaneous and pathetic extinction of the dog. In the illustration, Browne shows his understanding of Dickens's art, for Jip's hair resembles Dora's in its glossy alternation of blackness and sheen, and Dora, facing the same direction as the dog, rests her arms on the table in the same way that Jip rests his paws (her limp left arm, with the slight droop of the hand, corresponds particularly to Jip's left paw). Jip, in the centre of table and picture, is the point from which all the havoc and mess radiates; and we may see that Browne has taken Dickens's point.

Browne's continuing readiness to renew his own art in response to new developments in Dickens's work shows in the series of plates he produced in 1850, *Home Pictures*. At first glance, however, these pictorial celebrations of the Victorian hearth might seem to have been most influenced not by Dickens but by Charles Lever, for they are executed in a technique similar to that which Browne had refined for Lever's novel *Roland Cashel* (1848–9). In this technique the etcher first uses a machine to draw, through the etching ground, a very close set of fine lines. When biting in he can take the plate out of the acid any number of times and cover certain parts with stopping-out varnish. When the process is completed, the areas bitten deeply will print a rich dark tone, while those bitten very lightly will print a pale grey; an infinite range of possible tones is available. White highlights can be added by covering parts of the plate with varnish before it ever goes into the acid; while with further drawing in the etching-ground, one can produce blacks as dark as one wishes. With this technique, the etcher can achieve an effect very similar to that of pen and wash, and many of the *Cashel* illustrations are like fine drawings in that medium.

Yet it is only in technique that *Home Pictures* shows any debt to Cashel. Although the purpose of *Home Pictures* is to provide a heart-warming hymn to the beauties of the Victorian home, there is little in *Cashel* that could have inspired this, while in *Copperfield*, domestic affection emerges as almost the greatest good in life. The statuesque but radiant figure of the wife and mother recalls the idealized figure of Agnes, while in 'The Dis-Jointed Nose' (68) the first child's jealousy of the new-born baby may well have been suggested by the *Copperfield* plate 'Changes at Home' (64), although David himself proves not to be jealous. Both plates show the same mother, wearing the same dress, although various small differences in pose and drapery suggest that the figure was copied from memory rather than from a first sketch.[19]

The technique evolved in *Cashel* is technically the same as that used for the 'dark plates' in *Bleak House*, although the latter have a different and sombre

68. H. K. Browne, 'The Dis-Jointed Nose'.

character. What would usually be background is now the centre of interest. Human figures, when present, are small and insignificant, while of the ten dark plates the first four and last two have no figures at all. Before the first dark plate in Part Twelve of *Bleak House*, Dickens had not given Browne 'atmospheric' subjects without figures; the change of style was radical and sudden. This development would not be surprising if, by this stage, Browne were choosing his own subjects, and were free to design a new kind of subject when a new technique occurred to him. Dickens's letter to Browne of 29 June 1853 shows, however, that at the end of the serial publication of *Bleak House*, author and artist were on the best of terms and that Dickens was still supervising the illustrations closely and specifying each subject:

'First. I beg to report myself, thank God, thoroughly well again. I was truly sensible of your hearty note, and of the right good will with which you fell to work at the plates under those discouraging circumstances.

'Secondly. I send the subjects for the next No: will you let me see the sketches here, by post.

'Thirdly, I am now ready with all four subjects for the concluding double No., and will post them to you tomorrow or next day!!!!!!!!!!!!!!!!!!!!!!!!!

'Fourthly. I wish you would so contrive your arrangements – if so dispoged – as to come and pay us a visit here. . . .'[20]

Of the six subjects Dickens mentions, four are dark plates. Yet the technical innovations involved in producing the dark plates, and the sudden change in subject-matter that went with this, make it seem very unlikely that Dickens himself should have conceived the new mode. The likelihood, then, is that Browne conceived it and suggested it to Dickens, who responded enthusiastically, and the new illustrations were the product of experiment and consultation. One credits Dickens with enthusiasm because, after the first dark plate, more illustrations were done in this style than in the old one. On Browne's part, the development of this mode shows the depth of his response to Dickens's writing at this time, for it is ideally suited to conveying the oppressive gatherings of fog and darkness in human affairs so powerfully presented in the novel. Browne's small fugitive figures reflect not only Lady Dedlock's situation, but also the novel's general intimation of the pitiable helplessness and isolation of hounded human beings.

On Dickens's part, an active concern with illustration is shown in the way he took up the new mode and used it to intensify effects of the narrative. The clearest case of this is 'The Morning' (69), which refers to the last page of the penultimate monthly part. D. C. Thomson praises it for its artistic qualities:

'Weirdness, horror, and loneliness are the characteristics of the design, which is one of the best Hablôt Browne ever did. It goes a long step further than the description in the letterpress, excellent though it be, and has done much more to realize the painful sentiment of the story.'[21]

But the plate is more closely related to the chapter as a whole than Thomson suggests. For the plates were bound in at the beginning of the monthly parts, and this plate must have been one of the first things that the reader would have

69. H. K. Browne, 'The Morning'.

seen in Part Eighteen. That number is devoted to the quest for Lady Dedlock: the first and last chapters give Esther's account of the pursuit, and the middle one the contingent troubles and anxieties at Chesney Wold; and the reader has with him, all the time, a picture of what the pursuers will find at last. Yet the picture tells him nothing that he wants to know. The Number has two dark plates, the other being 'The Night', and the reader at first assumes that the lone figure in both of them is Lady Dedlock. Then, when he realizes that the first plate does not in fact show Lady Dedlock, he must also wonder whether the second plate is similarly deceptive: whether it perhaps shows the other woman being tracked, Jenny. Esther believes she is finding Jenny when she comes upon the scene shown in the plate, and Dickens so elaborates Esther's mistake as to make the reader wonder whether, after all, it *is* Jenny. The reader's suspense is heightened, not resolved, by glances at the plate. The plate suggests, moreover, that the woman found is dead; and yet that is not clear: she may only be in a state of collapse, and one must read to the end.

The two plates, then, work together (their titles associate them: 'The Night' and 'The Morning') and play on the confusion Lady Dedlock causes by using Jenny to cover her tracks. The effect is to increase the tension in the reader's mind as he hurries through the number to the final discovery. With the last words of the chapter, 'it was my mother, cold and dead,' all the tensions are relaxed, and the plate ceases to be an ominous, ambiguous portent, playing off hope against fear; it remains with us now as a clear sad picture of Lady Dedlock's end.

A similar change of character occurs in the plate 'Sunset in the Long Drawing-room at Chesney Wold' as the reader proceeds through the text. In his description of the gradual onset of evening, Dickens refers at first to the golden light pouring in, 'rich, lavish, overflowing like the summer plenty in the land' (Chapter XL), and in his etching Browne has used the subtleties of the dark-plate technique to suggest the faint haze of warm light through which the further end of the room is seen.

'But the fire of the sun is dying. Even now the floor is dusky, and shadow slowly mounts the walls, bringing the Dedlocks down like age and death. And now, upon my lady's picture over the great chimney-piece, a weird shade falls from some old tree, that turns it pale, and flutters it, and looks as if a great arm held a veil or hood, watching an opportunity to draw it over her. . . .'

Looking back to the illustration, we find the portrait of Lady Dedlock in the top left-hand corner – it might not have been noticed before – with an ominous shadow rising to blot it out. What had been a neutral area of shadow becomes a threatening force, and a picture that had seemed simply mellow, dignified, and calm, now insinuates menace.

[155]

The chapter in question ends with Lady Dedlock listening in the darkening room while Tulkinghorn tells the story of her life, and a play of light and dark is one of Dickens's main resources in presenting Lady Dedlock; earlier in the novel, an effect of light and shadow on her portrait hints at her lapse:

'The cold clear sunlight . . . touches the ancestral portraits with bars and patches of brightness, never contemplated by the painters. Athwart the picture of my Lady, over the great chimney-piece, it throws a broad bend-sinister of light that strikes down crookedly into the earth, and seems to rend it.' (Chapter XII)

Lady Dedlock's portrait is only one example of the large part played in the novel by portraits and paintings. Almost every establishment visited in *Bleak House* has pictures on the walls that help to characterize it. Miss Flite's poverty is conveyed by her 'few old prints from books' (Chapter V), and Tony Jobling's noble taste by the 'Galaxy Gallery of British Beauty' that he takes everywhere with him. The prosperity and self-esteem of the Snagsbies and Guppies is reflected in their own portraits, while the pictures of Mrs Badger's two former husbands serve to show how the admirable Swosser and Dingo live on, almost as members of the household, in the reminiscences of Mrs Badger and the eulogies of her husband.

Most of these pictures are described with a cheerful amusement at artistic falsities, and even the Dedlock portraits, which have a weightier role in the novel, are described by Skimpole in satirical terms (in Chapter XXXVII).

Mr Tulkinghorn's Roman first appears in a similar character:

'. . . Allegory, in Roman helmet and celestial linen, sprawls among balustrades and pillars, flowers, clouds, and big-legged boys, and makes the head ache — as would seem to be Allegory's object always, more or less.' (Chapter X)

Allegory falls at once into a humorous relation with Mr Tulkinghorn, 'staring down at [Mr Tulkinghorn's] intrusion as if it meant to swoop upon him, and he cutting it dead'. But as the novel progresses, Allegory gradually becomes more imposing and more sinister: 'From the ceiling, foreshortened Allegory, . . . points . . . obtrusively towards the window. Why should Mr Tulkinghorn, for such no reason, look out of the window?' The ominous references accumulate, and little by little the reader realizes that Allegory is a serious allegory, and that what the Roman is in fact pointing to lies in the future, and is Mr Tulkinghorn's corpse.

The Dedlock portraits suffer 'lowness of spirits', 'doze in their picture-frames', and frown; they provide a comic chorus — 'A staring old Dedlock in a panel, . . . looks as if he didn't know what to make of it . . .' — and also a more serious one:

'Inside, his forefathers, looking on him from the walls, say, "Each of us was a passing reality here, and left this coloured shadow of himself, and melted into remembrance as dreamy as the distant voices of the rooks now lulling you to rest;" and bear their testimony to his greatness too.'[22]

Although the general tone in speaking of the portraits is light, Dickens has – in giving them a dramatic status in the novel – a point to make about Sir Leicester; it underlies Mr Bucket's appeal when he has some painful news to break:

'"If there's a blow to be inflicted on you, you naturally think of your family. You ask yourself, how would all them ancestors of yours, away to Julius Caesar – not to go beyond him at present – have borne that blow. . . ."' (Chapter LVI)

The ancestors in the portraits are given the status of live characters in the novel because they are alive for Sir Leicester: they live in him. The corollary to this is that Sir Leicester, at his grand moments, becomes a portrait:

'Sir Leicester's magnificence explodes. Calmly, but terribly.
'"Mr. Rouncewell," says Sir Leicester, with his right hand in the breast of his blue coat – the attitude of state in which he is painted in the gallery. . . .'
(Chapter XXVIII)

In his portrait of Sir Leicester, Dickens repeats the very simple characterization of a British aristocrat in Hogarth's *Marriage à-la-Mode*. In the first painting of that series (70) the monomania of lineage is expressed in the scattered coronets and the family tree held by the gout-ridden Earl. The Earl is very clearly drawing himself up into an 'attitude of state': he holds his right hand to his breast, and he resembles, moreover, the huge portrait above him.[23] Furthermore, a carved face on the wall looks with live eyes on the action. As a character, Sir Leicester belongs to 'the region of satire'[24] rather than to actual life, and he might well be seen as Hogarth's Earl stepped down from his picture-frame and given speech.

The treatment of Sir Leicester reflects Dickens's general intense interest in the pictorial, in all its aspects. His own imagination was brilliantly pictorial, and when he writes a narrative in the first person, he equips his protagonist – whether David, Esther, or Pip – with a lucid visual memory. When they recall an episode, they see it; and they see it whole, as a picture. There is, for instance, the passage at the end of the first chapter of *Great Expectations*, when Pip, released by the convict, looks back:

'The marshes were just a long black horizontal line then, as I stopped to look after him; and the river was just another horizontal line, not nearly so

70. William Hogarth, *Marriage à-la-Mode*, Plate I.

broad nor yet so black; and the sky was just a row of long angry red lines and dense black lines intermixed. On the edge of the river I could faintly make out the only two black things in all the prospect that seemed to be standing upright; one of these was the beacon by which the sailors steered – like an unhooped cask upon a pole – an ugly thing when you were near it; the other a gibbet, with some chains hanging to it which had once held a pirate. The man was limping on towards this latter, as if he were the pirate come to life, and come down, and going back to hook himself up again.'

The creative imagination of Dickens is very much a visual imagination. Few writers have shown such an energetic and noticing eye, and few have seen so sharply what they imagined. Indeed, although his genius is manifest above

[158]

all in his command of idiom, a particular visual metaphor will sometimes be the strong point in an encounter that is, in description and dialogue, artificial and histrionic. The confrontation between Mr Dombey and his wife, when he challenges her amid her cast-off and despised riches, is melodramatic in conception and speech; yet it has its poetic precisions:

'The very diamonds – a marriage gift – that rose and fell impatiently upon her bosom, seemed to pant to break the chain that clasped them round her neck, and roll down on the floor where she might tread upon them.' (Chapter XL)

The animistic metaphor comes easily and naturally because Dickens sees what he describes. He sees the diamonds moving sharply, their brilliant distinctness drawing the eye to themselves and making their movement so marked it seems independent. And when thus we can see the diamonds themselves as panting, we can appreciate the visual and more-than-visual image which so powerfully gives us the passional condition of Edith Dombey in the fused suggestions of something breathing and hot ('panting') and of something hard, glittering, and sharp (diamonds).

Dickens had from birth his acuteness of eye, and his magpie habit of hoarding innumerable observations; but there is reason to think that pictures he had seen directed his watchfulness, and put him on the alert for certain kinds of appearance. It was suggested in an earlier chapter that Hogarth and the caricaturists affected the way he saw life, and the way he imagined it when he wrote; and the text of his novels shows that this profound response to pictures was accompanied, more superficially, by an acute, amused interest in the pictures that people hung on their walls. Such pictures are not simply described and then left, for he had learned from Hogarth how they could be related to the action, and he frequently animates the painted figures and leads them down from their frames. The actual pictures in the novels, the illustrations, are merely one local activity of this thriving visual commerce. They were produced to Dickens's specifications, and as he matured, he found more and more ways of lifting them also from the inert paper, and involving them in the action. The various suggestive resources of visual irony and allusion lead the eye from the specific scene into the theme. The illustrations participate in a larger play of visual imagining which, in Dickens's writing, is inseparable from the total drama.

7

Illustration and the Mind's Eye

With the close of *Bleak House*, creative partnership is essentially finished for author and artist. The years from *Pickwick* to *Bleak House* had seen a sudden rise in Dickens's interest in illustration, and a corresponding rise in Browne's skill and resource, followed by a period of versatile and fruitful collaboration, in which, however, there are signs of Browne's impending decline. The illustrations to *Dombey* represent the high point in the partnership. There are some imaginative and successful new departures in the plates for *David Copperfield* and *Bleak House*, but Browne's drawing is never better than in the best plates for *Dombey*, and by *Bleak House* the drawing in the illustrations that are not dark plates has noticeably slackened. After *Bleak House*, there is no further creative advance to be recorded, although Browne went on to illustrate *Little Dorrit* and *A Tale of Two Cities*. The good illustrations in *Little Dorrit*, such as 'The Ferry' and 'Mr. F's Aunt is conducted into retirement', are few, and are no better than, and little different from, plates in the earlier novels. Browne has ceased to respond to what is new in Dickens's writing, and it would seem from the slipshod drawing that he has ceased to be interested. By *Little Dorrit* it is clear that writer and illustrator have diverged too widely for any collaboration to be productive, and that Browne has been left far behind.

From the time of *Little Dorrit* there follows a period of difficult personal relations between Dickens and Browne, the final result of which was that Browne ceased to be Dickens's regular illustrator. The monthly parts of *Our Mutual Friend* were illustrated by Marcus Stone, and those of *Edwin Drood* by Luke Fildes. This change of illustrator has an interest extending far beyond the immediate personal relations of Dickens and Browne, for both Stone and Fildes represent a new style in illustration which differed radically from that of Browne and Cruikshank. *Bleak House* (1852–3) had in fact been the last novel in which Browne could feel that his style of illustration was the style of the time, for 1855 is generally acknowledged as the year in which a new mode of illustration, represented pre-eminently by Millais, began its rapid and victorious invasion of the whole field of book-illustration. In that year, Allingham's *Music Master* came out, with illustrations by Millais, Rossetti, and Arthur Hughes, and in 1857 it was reinforced by Moxon's *Tennyson*, with thirty of the fifty-four illustrations coming from Millais, Rossetti, and Holman Hunt. By 1860 the new style was clearly dominant, and asserted its claims regularly in such lavishly illustrated periodicals as *Once a Week* and *Good Words*. Indeed, the Sixties are often treated as the Golden Age of English illustration; and, certainly, it was the age of Charles Keene.

The work of the new artists was not, of course, homogenous, and Forrest Reid rightly insists on its variety. But the 'marked individuality of method and vision'[1] that he notes rested on a basic agreement as to what art was – agreement on that deep level of tenacious presupposition, unquestioned and unquestionable, on which healthy and vigorous schools of art usually rely. In 1895, Joseph Pennell disposed of the early illustrators not so much through criticism, as through an appeal to the shared artistic instincts of the time: 'I suppose that among artists and people of any artistic appreciation, it is generally admitted by this time that the greatest bulk of the works of "Phiz", Cruickshank, Doyle, and even many of Leech's designs are simply rubbish.'[2] For admirers of the new mode, the work of the preceding generation had ceased even to be art. Gleeson White wrote:

'For certain qualities which are not remotely connected with art belong to them; but the beauty of truth, the knowledge born of academic accomplishment, or literal imitation of nature, were alike absolutely beyond their sympathy.'[3]

The three qualities are closely related: 'academic accomplishment' is the result of many hours' devotion to the 'literal imitation of nature' in the life class, gradually realizing the 'beauty of truth'. A heavy stress is laid on academic training, and the later illustrators were so trained. Fildes and Walker both graduated to the Royal Academy, from the South Kensington Schools and Leigh's Academy respectively; the polished technician, Millais, was also at the Academy, while Du Maurier served in the *ateliers* of Charles Gleyre at Paris, and N. de Keyser and J. Lerius in Antwerp. Of the early illustrators, on the other hand, Isaac, Robert and George Cruickshank, Leech, and Doyle, had not even been to an art-school, and Browne was trained as an engraver, not a draughtsman, and left Finden's well before he finished the course.

Yet the earlier artists were not untrained in hand or eye. Seymour, Cruickshank, Browne, and Leech had the technical skill of etching at their fingertips, and if their drawing did not have hours in the studio behind it, it did have hours of concentrated observation, and a special and strenuous training of the visual memory. This latter power was a positive pride to them: Browne 'owned that he never carried a sketch-book, and never made a memorandum from nature in his life'.[4] Cruikshank complained of Maclise's portrait that it 'represents me doing what I never did in the whole course of my life – that is *making a sketch of anyone*. All the characters which I have placed before the public are from the *brain* – after *studying and observing Nature*.'[5]

The early illustrators received, moreover, an education of a more important kind from graphic satire and the prints of Hogarth. On this account it might be asked whether, for all their advantages in other respects, the later illustrators were as well-equipped for the illustration of fiction as their predecessors had been. For the naturalism of the later mode was qualified by a marked tendency to idealize. Millais 'imparted . . . dignity to his men and women'[6] and the dignity imparted was that of a Greek statue: White complained that the work of Cruikshank, 'Phiz', Thackeray, and Leech was 'never infused by the perception of physical beauty that the Greeks embodied as their ideal, that ideal which the illustrators of *Once a Week*, especially Walker, revived soon after this date'.[7] The consequences of this predilection, given body by constant practice in drawing Greek statuary, or copies of it, show in the statuesque build and stance, and the noble profile, of their people. Resembling the ideal so often, these figures necessarily resemble each other also, and the tendency to a recurrent ideal sameness makes against the interest in character and the individual life that is so strong in a novelist like Dickens. Moreover, the concentration on accurate drawing left no place for the subtleties of allegorical and allusive by-play that occur in the corners of the earlier illustrations. The allegorical density of Rossetti's woodengravings shows how the later artists might still have produced illustrations that were 'read', but Rossetti was an isolated, and highly eccentric, case.

The difference in literary relevance shows clearly if Browne's original illustrations are compared with those in the Household Edition of Dickens's works. This edition actually appeared in the seventies, but, as White noted, 'it is illustrated almost entirely by men of the sixties, and was possibly in active preparation during that decade'.[8] The draughtsmanship is often sensitive, and the use of light and dark is frequently dramatic, but there is no attempt to communicate any meaning that cannot be expressed by a naturalistic study of character and setting, and a delicate communication of relationships like that in 'The Dombey Family' (61) is not to be looked for. The illustrations for a given novel do not reveal a distinctive spirit corresponding to the particular character of that novel, and as a result there is more uniformity of style in the work of the many Household artists than in the work of Browne alone.

It was inevitable that for this venture artists should be chosen who had a special gift for 'character', and Fred Barnard exercised this gift with conspicuous distinction; it is noticeable, however, that in creating characters the Household artists often rely on Browne, particularly with Micawber and

Pecksniff. Where the Household artists depart from the types created by Browne, they often lose vital qualities of Dickens's characterization which had been nicely expressed by Browne. Thus, in the Household Edition, Quilp is strikingly real as a brutal and deformed human being (71); but Dickens's Quilp is a figure of energetic fantasy, and his whimsical savagery is that of a fairy-tale ogre. The character is perfectly caught in Browne's illustrations, which were executed in a new style that he had developed especially for that novel.

71. C. Green, the Household Quilp.

However, the theme of the present book would be dissipated by a full investigation of the great change in illustration that occurred in the 19th century. A review of Dickens's relations with his illustrators after 1855 would properly belong in a separate study, which would take for its centre of interest the fact and significance of the large change, and the reasons for it. At the same time, it should be in order to note briefly, for the present argument, that there is no reason to adopt two assumptions that have very often been made: that Dickens expelled Browne either on a sudden whim, or because he wholeheartedly

[163]

preferred the new style of Stone and Fildes. The first assumption rests on a letter from Browne to Robert Young written when the decision on the illustration of *Our Mutual Friend* was pending. Browne complained:

'Marcus [Stone] is no doubt to do Dickens. *I* have been a 'good boy', I believe. The plates in hand are all in good time, so that I do not know what's 'up', any more than you. Dickens probably thinks a new hand would give his old puppets a fresh look, or perhaps he does not like my illustrating Trollope neck-and-neck with him – though, by Jingo, he need fear no rivalry *there*! Confound all authors and publishers, say I. There is no pleasing one or t'other. I wish I had never had anything to do with the lot.'[9]

The claims made in this letter have been taken on trust, but there is reason to suspect them. The situation of an artist awaiting confirmation that he has – as he fears – been sacked would not, in any case, encourage a balanced statement of the reason for dismissal. And the testimony of this letter must be weighed against that provided in another, in which Browne replies to a Dr Carpenter, who has evidently asked him to persuade Dickens to speak to a local 'Institution': 'I am sorry I can be of no use in catching Dickens for your Institution – as lately (Authors & Artists will *sometimes* squabble), I have not been on very good terms with him.' Both letters are undated, but the available evidence suggests that the letter to Carpenter came first.[10] In that case, Browne was being disingenuous in saying that he had no idea what was up. There had been a 'squabble' before the question of illustrating *Our Mutual Friend* arose, and there is reason to think that Browne had been the more fractious of the two. Traces of discontent show in the transactions relating to *Little Dorrit*,[11] and it is significant that none of the illustrations to that work and *A Tale of Two Cities* bear Browne's signature, and that Browne burned his correspondence with authors. To find the reasons for Browne's discontent after 1855, one would need to go outside the partnership with Dickens, and take account of a general change in illustrating conditions; but it is at least clear that for some years before the final break, the partnership of Dickens and Browne had become querulous and unproductive, and it would be reasonable to suggest that this was the principal cause of the change of illustrator.

The alternative assumption has been stated emphatically by Alice Meynell:

'Being essentially modern, Dickens was bound to be developed and modified by his times – to be as modern in 1870 as he had been in 1840, for his vitality never failed; and he could not be fitly illustrated by work which reverted to former ways of thought and observation.'[12]

When Dickens first engaged Marcus Stone, however, he expected him to produce illustrations in the manner of Browne,[13] and when he found that artist incapable of doing so, he took little interest in his work, and little interest in illustration generally. On most occasions in the past, Dickens had given very specific instructions for his plates, but in the case of *Our Mutual Friend* he let the artist take whatever subject he liked, and even neglected to inspect the sketches before the illustrations were engraved. Dickens had taken Marcus under his protection when the elder Stone died, and it is not surprising that he enthused casually and indiscriminately about the early illustrations; but his response was casual throughout the serialization of *Our Mutual Friend*, and suggests that he never took Stone seriously as a collaborator – as, at every stage, he had taken Browne.[14]

Dickens's opposition to the new school of art is reflected in a series of articles in his two magazines, *Household Words* and *All the Year Round*. In particular, a long article on book-illustration in *All the Year Round* deals explicitly with the large change in vision, and backs Cruikshank and Browne against their successors.[15] The article comes late (1869), but it exemplifies the general, long-standing view of the magazines that although art enjoyed unprecedented opportunities in their time, it was ceasing to express fancy and imagination, and was becoming merely a sophisticated trade.[16] Dickens supervised his magazines closely, and identified himself with what was published there.

Dickens's response to the changing character of visual art in his later years was, of course, complex – Millais, for instance, became his friend – and his own attitude should not simply be equated with that expressed in his magazines. The complexity needs pointing out, for it has sometimes been assumed that in questions of visual art, Dickens shared the most naïve philistinism of Victorian taste. He did, certainly, have a weakness for rising to any occasion with the appropriate rhetoric, and he instinctively suppressed his critical sense when called upon to pronounce publicly on the work of an artist-friend. But there are in his novels many asides about Victorian High Art which suggest that he viewed it with great suspicion; in *Little Dorrit*, for example, he notes how 'in the Royal Academy some evil old ruffian of a Dog-stealer will annually be found embodying all the cardinal virtues, on account of his eyelashes, or his chin, or his legs (thereby planting thorns of confusion in the breasts of the more observant students of nature)' (i, Chapter XIII). His public assertions about visual art (outside his novels) should be compared with what he wrote to Forster, when the juxtaposition of English and French painting at the Paris Art Exposition provoked him to some unusually sharp and decisive stock-taking of his country's art, and his own artist-friends:

'It is of no use disguising the fact that what we know to be wanting in the men is wanting in their works – character, fire, purpose, and the power of using the vehicle and the model as mere means to an end. ... Don't think it a part of my despondency about public affairs, and my fear that our national glory is on the decline, when I say that mere form and conventionalities usurp, in English art, as in English government and social relations, the place of living force and truth. I tried to resist the impression yesterday, and went to the English gallery first, and praised and admired with great diligence; but it was of no use. I could not make anything better of it than what I tell you. Of course this is between ourselves. Friendship is better than criticism, and I shall steadily hold my tongue.'[17]

Dickens relates the change that had occurred in English art in the middle of the 19th century (which is reflected in English illustration) to a general change in the national life – the change, or complex of changes, that provides one of his main themes in fiction. If we look back now, a hundred years later, and ask who at the end of the 19th century can be opposed to the great figures at the beginning – to, in their various fields, Turner, Constable, Girtin, Blake, and Bewick – we can see that Dickens was right. A radical dislocation occurred which involved, among other things, a disastrous substitition of form and conventionality for 'living force and truth'.

    This issue is, however, too large to pursue here. As far as illustrations are concerned, the likelihood is that up to the end Dickens wanted the kind of illustration that Browne had provided for *Dombey* and *Copperfield*, although this was no longer available either from Browne or from anyone else. Those earlier etchings fulfil, on their own level, several of the demands that Dickens makes of High Art. Hablôt Browne does not show fire, but he does show character when he draws Jip like a tress of Dora's hair; and most of his illustrations show 'purpose' and the power of using the vehicle as a means to an end. That being so, it is time to ask, in more general terms than have so far been invoked, what is the value of this purposive and literary kind of visual art that Dickens admired in Hogarth and encouraged in his illustrators. How does it compare with the other, very different kinds of illustration that have prevailed since? Does it give a more or less adequate answer to the question that underlies all uses of illustration: *can* visual art truly collaborate with literature in the form of illustration?

    The question is a serious one, for probably many people would say that illustrations can have no real function in a novel, though they may be decorative. Certainly novelists have said as much. Henry James was far from being impressed when it was suggested to him that a collected edition of his novels should be illustrated. In his preface to *The Golden Bowl* he noted the irony of a 'text putting forward illustrative claims (that is producing an effect of illustration) by its own intrinsic virtue and so finding itself elbowed, on that ground, by another and a competitive process'. He allowed that 'the essence of any representational work is of course to bristle with immediate images', but precisely because of that concluded:

'Anything that relieves responsible prose of the duty of being, while placed before us, good enough and, if the question be of picture, pictorial enough, above all *in itself*, does it the worst of services, and may well inspire in the lover of literature certain lively questions as to the future of that institution.'

James's argument – in so far as he is concerned to argue, rather than just to intimate a distaste for a certain kind of 'picture-book' – rests on the self-sufficiency of a given art. It would be a poor writer, he implies, who would delegate some of his essential work. And yet, conversely, if illustration *were* a genuine means to a novelist's end, it would hardly strengthen the novel, or say very much for the future of literature, if pictures had, for just this reason, to be excluded. The large question is whether illustration ever could assist in the essential work of a novel. To start with, a basic difficulty lies in the fact that the mind's eye sees, when reading, in a different way from that in which the actual eye sees, when looking at a picture.

This difficulty matters for the illustrator because, in James's phrase, the novel has so much eye. In it we are often told what people and places look like, and in a confrontation we may be told how the people move, and change colour, and what aura they have, to ensure that the encounter is seen, as well as being heard and felt. There are of course various novels where the imaginative eye is virtually shut; but when an attempt is made to give the feel of life, to convey the experience of being a live creature from within, visual details often abound, since seeing counts for more than three quarters of our perception. Even when visual details are scarce, people can feel they are 'seeing' what takes place in the novel, and after seeing a film version of it will say 'Oh, I had imagined so and so looking quite different' even if so and so is not described in the novel at all. Visual aid of this kind can easily run wild, but it is not to be wished away, for the visual imagination of the reader inevitably collaborates with that of the novelist. The novel is not simply a stretch of experience that is gradually pasted onto a blank space in the reader's consciousness; on the contrary, the reader recreates the novel imaginatively, and in doing so he draws on his experience and memory as the writer drew on his when writing. An adroit novelist spontaneously allows for this extra play; he stimulates it, checks it, and uses it.

The need for assistance from the reader partly explains why, in the novel, certain kinds of description do not work: for example, those which, in presenting a room, give an inventory of everything in it. If reading a novel meant exposing an empty canvas to the writer, who touched in detail after detail till every inch were covered, a full list would be the best means of realizing a scene. But the human imagination does not work in this mechanical, piecemeal way. It is not simply that the reader's imagination must have its licence, but that when we imagine a scene so that it is real for us, we do not see everything in it. We are more or less conscious of various items, but very much more or less, so that a seven-foot cupboard is only a shadow in the corner of the eye, while some slight object, a lit face or an expression, momentarily flares up in our consciousness, and lapses. The imagination moves in leaps and bounds as the live interest directs it, and it notices rather than sees: it notices this face, that hand, that spot of light on the panelling. Between noticings, it takes in a great deal of background fact, which is registered, is known to be there, but is there only hazily and irrelevantly. We often find an experienced novelist gives only the acute noticings, knowing that if he can provoke similar flashes in the reader's imagination, the latter will spontaneously supply the background. Vronsky surprises Anna Karenina in her garden:

'she was completely alone. . . . Dressed in a white gown, deeply embroidered, she was sitting in a corner of the terrace behind some flowers, and did not hear him. Bending her curly black head, she pressed her forehead against a cool watering-pot that stood on the parapet, and both her lovely hands, with the rings he knew so well, clasped the pot. The beauty of her whole figure, her head, her neck, her hands, struck Vronsky every time as something new and unexpected. He stood still, gazing at her in ecstasy. But, directly he would have made a step to come nearer to her, she was aware of his presence, pushed away the watering-pot, and turned her flushed face towards him.'[18]

Except for the motion at the end, this is, clearly, a picture. The point of view — in the literal sense — does not dart from character to character and vantage-point to vantage-point; we are looking through Vronsky's eyes the whole time, and the chief faculty involved is sight. But though the impression given is pictorial, the passage is visually indefinite. We do not know which way the terrace runs, or which way Anna faces. Tolstoy does not tell us these details because they do not matter to him and they should not matter to us. None the less, we need to see Anna a certain way round in order to see her at all, and if the mind did not immediately position her on its own initiative, we should not be able to feel we *were* looking through Vronsky's eyes. These small initiatives are not important in themselves, but they are necessary if the novel is to be real in our imagination. And in fact, in reading a novel, we take these small decisions all the time; we do it quite spontaneously, and almost without being aware of it.

The imagination does not, however, take these initiatives for their own sake; it takes them only when other qualities in the writing instil a strong conviction of reality. The solidity and substance that the characters are gradually accumulating through *Anna Karenina* makes the economy at this point feasible. Knowing so much about Vronsky's attraction to Anna, we do not need to have described the old-new beauties he notices; moreover, it is the fact of renewal, rather than the specific nature of the beauties, that matters here. More locally, the 'reality' is given by Anna's pressing her hot forehead on the watering-pot:

the sudden suggestion of contrasted coolness suggests a real person feeling the heat. We are, in fact, given only three pieces of precise visual information – that her dress is white, that she bends a 'curly black head', and that her face is flushed – but Tolstoy evidently felt (for this is his habitual method) that they were enough to make the reader fill in, with the appropriate sketchiness, the rest of the picture.

'Bending her curly black head, she pressed her forehead against a cool watering-pot that stood on the parapet, and both her lovely hands, with the rings he knew so well, clasped the pot.'

The phrase 'curly black head' adds little in itself, but it does put the reader into a habit of visualizing what he is told: because *that* comes at the start (as it does in the Russian), we also see her hands, her rings, and the watering-pot more clearly than we should otherwise. It ensures, moreover, that we are not inside Anna, feeling the delicious coolness, but outside her with Vronsky, watching her feel it. The 'curly black head' is a trigger to the visual imagination, engaging it more actively for the rest of the sentence. But our collaboration, which is so subtly invited and controlled by the novelist, only comes at all because, caught up in the interests and emotions of the story, and impressed by other details, we have a will to *give*, imaginatively.

A prospective illustrator, leafing through the book, might find his cue in this scene. Here, certainly, a picture is suggested; there is not much more than suggestion, but he can make it more. So, in a variety of different styles, he might go to work, and produce an admirable picture. And yet. . . . If the picture suggested by the text is hazy in large areas, it is not by default, but because we want to notice this, this, and this in sequence, and the whole picture as such does not matter. Extra visual information could easily displace or disperse the central interest in the episode. So one must question the illustration: does it tell us what, for the novel, we need to know – or what we don't need to know? Does the mind's eye *want* to see more than the signals in the text excite?

In a fine work of literary art there is a nice balance between the different kinds of information given, and an excess of visual information might be not merely redundant but positively limiting. In the method of characterization natural to Tolstoy, the characters need to be realized as individuals without losing their broad generic representativeness. In order to keep just proportions in individuation and in generalizing, Tolstoy is emphatic in referring time and again to certain features of his characters – such as Napoleon's white hands – while, about many other features of his characters, he preserves the necessary indefiniteness, and says nothing. The preservation of this balance in the writing is not of course a matter of subtle calculation, but of instinctive tact in the artist; and an illustration that tied down too many things would be a clumsiness, violating the local generality of the action.

Tolstoy's visual details provide his people with a representative individuality, but this is not, of course, all that they do. On the contrary, they remind us how deeply involved sight is with non-visual interests. Sight, we realize again, is very far from being a discreet and independent faculty. Even on the sensuous level, sight cannot be isolated. When it registers surface and texture, it is a way of taking our sense of touch further than the hand can reach, and sensitive drawing consists partly in using drawing as transposed touch. Our eyes have not evolved simply to enjoy light and colour, but chiefly to reconnoitre a world of material things and lives. We do not see everything, we notice this or that – and modify what we notice – because it affects us; and if the mind's eye sees patchily, it is because it sees with purpose. It is thus that visual details in a novel can be far from external in their significance. In *Anna Karenina*, when Anna sees her husband's hands looking clammily pale, with the swollen veins showing unpleasantly, the visual imaginations of both writer and reader work with some force. The effect is essentially visual, and would mean nothing to a blind man. But Anna's observations are acts in the drama in that while she is hemmed in by her marriage (which, we never forget, has been a real marriage), she can see only the unpleasantness of her husband, and her eye involuntarily intensifies the unpleasantness she sees. Anna's seeing is directed and coloured by her sense of being tied, and is thus part of her emotional life.

In such effects as this, the visual and the non-visual co-operate inextricably. And even the metaphorical strength of a novelist's prose may depend on a subtle but powerful play of visual suggestion:

'The last day of the appointed week touched the bars of the Marshalsea gate. Black, all night, since the gate had clashed upon Little Dorrit, its iron stripes were turned by the early-glowing sun into stripes of gold. For aslant across the city, over its jumbled roofs, and through the open tracery of its church towers, struck the long bright rays, bars of the prison of this lower world.' (*Little Dorrit*, ii, Chapter XXX)

The final comparison, of sunbeams to prison bars, is not a visual one in any simple way. The idea is difficult to take, and if we are to accept it as a strong expression of a dominating intuition in the novel, our minds need some preparation. And the preparation is primarily visual. When we see the iron panels across the gate transmuted to 'stripes of gold' – made immaterial and radiant – *then* we can imagine the sunbeams across the sky as irradiated steel. In particular, this Metaphysical yoking of sunbeams to iron bars draws its power from the reader's realization – which must be a visualization – of the way in which, if one looks up

[170]

at an 'open tracery' church-tower with a low sun behind it, the tracery divides the large flood of light into a cluster of close, round-seeming shafts.

Here, of course, we should not want an illustration, any more than we should want one showing Karenin's hands. A picture of sunrise over the Marshalsea would add nothing (though the rather hard sunbeams in some sunrise pictures may have been at the back of Dickens's mind, contributing to the full effect). But the passage does demonstrate the nature and possibility of visual metaphor, and it is only a short step from this to the reflection that metaphor is not something peculiar to literary art. If we grant that there is such a thing as the poetic imagination, a power of live and concrete characterization ready to open, with a wonder of discovery, into the familiar-foreign reality, we have no warrant to think it confined to formal poetry, to literature, or even to language. It is to the reassertion of just this point that the present book has constantly tended: that there is a kind of visual art which is, properly, self-sufficiently, and without being in any bad sense 'literary', the working of the poetic imagination. This fact gives illustrations their cue, provided that the illustrations are this kind of visual art. To make clear the nature of this form of art, however, one would not point to the illustrations themselves – they are too much a product and agent of literature. Nor would one point to such devices as emblem-books, for there the meaning has to be added on after the picture, and does not inhere in it. One might rather point to that massive school of popular and great art out of which, finally, such illustrators as Cruikshank developed: the art which, 300 years earlier, was the art of Bruegel, and Bosch.

Bosch's masterpiece 'The Garden of Earthly Delights' demonstrates the autonomy and strength of the school. The basis of the imagery in esoteric symbolisms and in popular adage is now obscure, but the significance of that imagery is still plain, direct, and powerful. We see at once on what intensities in love and sensuality the artist is drawing. This is not to say that the fantastic juxtapositions are merely dreamy (or nightmarish) emanations from the unconscious. We are aware rather of a remarkably energetic and clear-sighted consciousness at grips with its experience and striving to substantiate and define it; and the artist resorts to metaphor as the most direct and palpable means of definition. So we have the linking of human and animal life, the triple equation of flesh, marble, and fruit, and the wan couples sitting inside pink fruit which are, at the same time, luscious and brittle. Very clearly the artist's gift here is the gift of a poet, although the meaning lives in visual art with powerful and complete adequacy. The metaphors are partly metaphors of colour, and depend on the idiosyncratic use of glistening surfaces, and on the combination of olive green with the omnipresent, voluptuous pink of the Strawberry (so that the thrill to the eye is almost a thrill on the palate). Both the loveliness and the excess of the garden are felt in our own nerves.

Such pictures were very congenial to the young Bruegel, whose own early works were intricate exercises in the style of Bosch. But Bruegel was too lively and interested an observer of the actual world to confine himself to metaphors of the psyche, and he employed Bosch's poetic techniques in compositions which were as crowded, mobile, and rhythmic as those of Bosch, but which recorded the daily life of his own Flanders. It was likely, in any case, that a truly creative talent, schooled in the mode of Bosch, would be unable to rest in that art. The momentous originality of Bosch could result only from an extreme concentration of vision, and a vision so concentrated had to be limited. His fantasy has a pronounced morbid side which shows, for instance, in the obsessive interest in deformity. Fantastic juxtapositions seem also to have been an obsessive habit which, when there was little profound inspiration, would still proliferate in whimsical oddity; it is in this sense that Bosch is a precursor of the Surrealists. He was patently not interested in an abundant variety and wholeness of human living. Bruegel, by contrast, is a great artist because he dedicated his visual artist's genius – which, after Bosch, was a poetic genius – to a continuing attempt to see life whole. Of course he is not comprehensive, but his *œuvre* embodies and composes a wisdom about life. This wisdom is partly born of, and stays close to, popular tradition and proverb; but when Bruegel takes a handful of common proverbs as a starting-point, he seems to move at once through or behind the proverb into the range of deep-rooted, shared experience that the proverbs epitomize.

The well-known 'Dulle Griet', with its jostling demons and its intricate allegory, shows how Bruegel perpetuated the art of Bosch; a later work, such as 'The Peasant and the Birdnester' (72), shows how he changed that art and made it his own. Here there is no hectic and apocalyptic violence. His starting-point is the proverb, 'He who knows where the nest is, has the knowledge, he who robs it has the nest;' but in his painting he counteracts and complicates this practical cynicism. The extremely maladroit robber has dropped his basket in reaching the nest, so that he has a small chance of keeping the eggs. The peasant who knows where the nest is but does not steal it is amused by this, and does not see that he is himself just stepping into a stream. Bruegel's meaning is subtler than that of the proverb, but is still close to the genial irony of rural wisdom. In the visual characterization of the two figures, however, the irony proves peculiarly positive and rich. The thief is tiny, frantic, and laughable, cramped up tight under the top of the picture, while the peasant is almost poignantly large, solid, and warm. His body, in its graceful swing of motion, takes a curve parallel to that of the tree the thief is climbing; he has the roundness and weight of the tree, while his clothes have the brown and green that belong both to the tree and to the surrounding countryside. So solidly real as a live, amused human body – and one that is going to stumble – he is, none the less, at one with the surrounding countryside; in the visual wisdom of the picture, he is part of a harmony in which the agitation of the thief is the sole disturbance.

72. Pieter Bruegel the Elder, *The Peasant and the Birdnester*.

Unlike Bosch, Bruegel was an engraver on a vast scale. He put his vision into European currency through his engravings, and thus made it available to the English, and above all to Hogarth. Hogarth was far from insular, and drew on many Continental artists – he knew Bosch as well as Bruegel – but it was Bruegel who showed him how to make a crowded, vigorous, genre scene (for which there were many precedents) significant throughout in terms of a controlling theme; in Bruegel the theme was often a Vice, in Hogarth it is the suicidal effect of prostitution, dissipation, idleness. But Hogarth's wisdom, unlike Bruegel's, could not have found adequate embodiment in the traditional life of the peasantry. He was a Citizen, and though he shared Bruegel's sense of human ugliness and animality, and was a severe satirist, his work shows everywhere his proud trust in the worth of the Augustan civilization that his London had achieved. His attentive painting of posture, costume, and decor shows his appreciation of sophistication and grace in manners, and strength and beauty in art, architecture, and ornament. Responsive to the teeming diversity of City life he shows a finer sense than Bruegel of human individuality; his faces have more 'character' and a greater variety of inner life. At the same time, no figure by Hogarth compares with Bruegel's peasant in 'The Peasant and the Birdnester' in realizing what Lawrence called 'the warm procreative body' inside the clothes. Bruegel's drawing and brushwork insist on the roundness and firmness of the peasant, and make him massive without being heavy-footed, and warm with coursing blood; and though there is sufficient vitality and fire in Hogarth's painting, no figure of his seems, in motion, so collected, or gives off such a steady and inextinguishable glow.

Hogarth's wisdom is largely the 18th-century Common Sense of a prosperous London craftsman, and though he relates human activity to rigorous moral principle, he does not – as Bruegel does – relate both the activity and the principle to an intuition of Great Creating Nature. The plainest consequence of this difference in outlook is the difference in colour; Bruegel's sense of Creating Nature shows in many things, and particularly in the marvellous beauty of his colouring, in his later works especially. Hogarth's vision has little place for such beauty. The clarity and definiteness of his artistry reflect the clarity and definiteness that the issues of life had for him. His observation was ranging and acute, his sympathies were generous, his sense of irony was sharp and moral, so that, all in all, his art expresses a broad, tough humanity. But we gather from the Progresses that his sense of the inexorabilities of life was extremely simple and certain; and a robust combination of drama and allegory was sufficient for his purpose. Unlike Bruegel and Bosch, he seldom used the subtler poetic resources, such as metaphor; he had no need of them.

Metaphor returns to vigorous life in the work of Gillray, and with the restoration of poetic life returns much of the wilder imagining that Hogarth, in his 18th-century daylight, had excluded. Etched caricature was, of course, no adequate vehicle for the powers shown by Gillray; his true gift, one might imagine, was to have been an English Goya. But his talent was irrepressible, and though working in a genre that thwarted his better ambitions, he still worked with force, wit, and poetic felicity. With Hogarth's example before him, he responded to his profession with a positive sense of vocation, with the 18th-century conviction that there were vital rules in life which it was the worthy responsibility of the satirist to enforce. There is evidence in his work of irritation and frustration, but none of stunted or retarded sensibility, such as one associates with the 'born caricaturist'. Certainly one side of him found caricature a congenial art; but caricature does not necessarily express a will to spoil and distort. On the contrary, it can reflect an unusual acumen in picking out the essential characteristic, and be a proof of vitality and alertness. The caricature of Gillray – like the caricature of Dickens – is of this kind.

Gillray practised in satire a kind of visual art that expressed the poetic imagination; and his art was, at the same time, in closer contact with formal poetry than that of his predecessors – his work shows extensive reading of Shakespeare, Milton, and Pope. This was the art that Cruikshank inherited, with a full comprehension of its power, and which he both employed, and handed on, to illustrate the novel; it was an art with fine qualifications for a true collaboration with literature. There was, however, a concomitant difficulty. The visual satirist in the English print-tradition had a right to be proud of his autonomy and independence as a creator, and had little readiness to submit his imagination to that of another man; so that while one may wish that Cruikshank had illustrated Dickens always, it is doubtful whether the combination could have been sufficiently harmonious to be fruitful. The great advantage of the actual illustrator, Hablôt Browne, was his unformedness and transparency: he was ready to let Dickens's imagination work through him. But a man so transparent is not likely to be strong, and though Browne, working in this way, produced many sensitive and functional illustrations, he is obviously not the equal either of Dickens or of Cruikshank in creative power. His own psyche had little to offer or add, and if he produces, at his best, illustrations with life and poetic strength, it is both because he inherited an art of such suitability from Cruikshank and *his* ancestors, and because Dickens himself had absorbed so much from that visual tradition: part of him belongs in it.

Dickens, of course, received and transformed many 'influences', and was also robustly independent and original. But it is noteworthy that some of the most conspicuous characteristics of what is called his 'vision' – particularly his animism – coincided with marked interests that the caricaturists shared with Bruegel. At the same time, Dickens's more pictorial writing is often reminiscent of Hogarth. The profound response of a writer should not, however, be sought only where the writing is obviously pictorial. In a more radical lesson, Dickens learned from Hogarth (as Thackeray did also) what Hogarth had learnt from

Bruegel, a certain principle of organization. In his mature work, he, like the painter, creates a spreading, polycentric diversity of life, yet aligns this activity to the expression of a single, definite cluster of themes. In the scene, as in the whole novel, these themes are repeated, explored, intensified, and tested in an intricate, directed play of analogy and contrast.

Although the poetic mode of visual art did not survive for long in illustration, the infiltration of this mode into the novel, first visible in Fielding's work, achieved in Dickens's time the magnitude of an invasion, and certain imaginative habits were permanently incorporated. In Gissing, Conrad, and James we see individual developments of that unusually vigorous evocation of physical character which, in Dickens, was stimulated both by Hogarth, who placed special stress on material and visible personality, and by the caricaturists, who identified their politicians with certain physical features.

It may, however, seem strange to suggest that novelists needed to have their eyes opened by Dickens or by anyone. The born novelist is, presumably, ardently observant, and should not need the precedent of another author to have his own vivid sense of how the world looks. And earlier in this chapter it was suggested that the visual imagination is so active in the novel as to mark it off from other forms: the visual life can be constant and strong, and can relate closely to the inward evolution of feeling and character, in a way that makes it seem an essential characteristic of the novel. But it is only after 1800 that we could get this impression. The 18th-century novel had not been remarkable for 'eye'. It is true that Sterne will sometimes go into pages of detail specifying the exact posture of one of his characters. And there was a custom, in the picaresque novel, of occasionally describing at length someone whose appearance was extravagantly grotesque. Although Smollett normally says very little about his characters' looks, he will interrupt *Roderick Random* for such a set-piece of physical description as the account of Captain Weazel:

'But how was I surprised, when I beheld the formidable captain in the shape of a little thin creature, about the age of forty, with a long withered visage, very much resembling that of a baboon, through the upper part of which, two little grey eyes peeped: he wore his own hair in a queue that reached to his rump, which immoderate length, I suppose, was the occasion of a baldness that appeared on the crown of his head, when he deigned to take off his hat, which was very much of the size and cock of Pistol's. Having laid aside his great coat, I could not help admiring the extraordinary make of this man of war: he was about five feet and three inches high, sixteen inches of which went to his face and long scraggy neck; his thighs were about six inches in length, his legs resembling spindles or drumsticks, two feet and a half, and his body, which put me in mind of extension without substance, engrossed the remainder; – so that on the whole he appeared like a spider or grasshopper erect, – and was almost a *vox & preterea nihil*.' (Chapter XI)

Though the passage is striking, the fact that Smollett chooses to emphasize the oddity with a tape-measure – rather than with vivid visual comparisons, such as Dickens uses – means that the description is very little a visualization: the exaggerations are more for the ear than for the eye. Such realization as exists here is, moreover, uncommon in the 18th century, and where it does occur it is, almost invariably, facetious. And in the work of Fielding and Smollett such descriptions are often announced, explicitly, as borrowings from Hogarth.

The usual scarcity of visual detail in the 18th-century novel was not purely a negative matter of not seeing or not realizing what might be done, however. The serious novel had its own discipline of relevance as to the information which it was the business of the novelist to provide, and a conscientious practitioner might well have disapproved of the lengths to which his successors went in describing what the reader should see. Although she wrote in the 19th century, Jane Austen may serve to demonstrate the attitude to appearances that had largely prevailed in the English novel before Dickens. In *Pride and Prejudice* we learn from Mr Darcy that Jane Bennett is 'the handsomest girl in the room' and that Elizabeth is merely 'tolerable', but no precise physical differentiation between the sisters is attempted – though we do hear, a little later of Elizabeth's 'dark eyes'. This sparseness of information is not, however, a sign of neglect. The robust and assured society surrounding Jane Austen had its own clear, positive criteria for appearance and physique, and although Jane Austen did not always agree with them, she always visualized her characters in relation to them, and had little time for features or details which were, by these standards, irrelevant. As a result, she does not describe a person's appearance, she assesses it. In *Emma*, the heroine is annoyed to find that her protegée, Harriet Smith, has fallen in love with a young farmer, and when she and Harriet meet him, while out walking, she is interested to see how he looks:

'Emma was not sorry to have such an opportunity of survey; and walking a few yards forward, while they talked together, soon made her quick eye sufficiently acquainted with Mr. Robert Martin. His appearance was very neat, and he looked like a sensible young man, but his person had no other advantage; and when he came to be contrasted with gentlemen, she thought he must lose all the ground he had gained in Harriet's inclination. Harriet was not insensible of manner; she had voluntarily noticed her father's gentleness with admiration as well as wonder. Mr. Martin looked as if he did not know what manner was.' (Chapter IV)

The decisive last sentence reflects Jane Austen's confidence that she had said all that needed saying.

After Jane Austen, however, came Dickens. He was more interested in the individuality of people as such, and less interested in their grading on a social scale which, though inescapable for Jane Austen, meant almost nothing to him. Having immensely more imaginative energy than her, and being, at the start, accustomed to hold the reins very slack, he visualized fully what his characters looked like, and brilliantly described all he saw. His habitual and electric realization of the human body – a power that shows chiefly as keenness of eye – caused a permanent alteration in the descriptive economy of the English novel. His was the original genius responsible for the pronounced and consistent vigour with which later English novelists gave their characters body – and not only English novelists. Tolstoy, who called Dickens 'the greatest novel writer of the 19th century', spoke of his 'tremendous influence' on him, and indeed there are countless Dickensian touches of physical character in his works.[19]

But Tolstoy's relation to Dickens has too often been presented in terms of the Dickensian details sprinkled through Tolstoy's œuvre, and it needs to be said that Dickens was for Tolstoy far more than a repertoire of 'touches'. We see Tolstoy learning the greater, anterior lesson when we find him turning from Thackeray to Dickens, because Dickens 'loves' his characters: Tolstoy insists that this love is just what any novelist should feel towards his people. 'Love', here, is a shorthand term for the generous but critical attentiveness to others, however unsympathetic, to which the true artist gives himself. In their concern with other lives, however, Dickens and Tolstoy did not attend only to the spirit, but to the body also – as had the great visual satirists whom Dickens admired. The popular moral print was produced to inculcate lessons that applied to every human soul, whatever the body; but when a Bruegel or a Hogarth came to the actual pictorial embodiment of the lesson, when he came to realize it by evoking live, individual people, his art inevitably did a great deal to complicate and contradict the moralist's working assumption that the soul could be cleanly and distinctly marked off from the body it inhabited. Dickens, too, identifies physique and spirit, so that it is hard to separate the physical from the spiritual radiance of Sissy Jupe in *Hard Times*, or the physical from the spiritual unhealthiness of Uriah Heep (these cases are the clearest, rather than the subtlest, that Dickens's art affords). We should have a very similar difficulty in dividing off body from spirit in Anna Karenina and her husband. Professor Christian could be describing Dickens's method when he says of Tolstoy:

'No one can fail to notice how the essence of a Tolstoyan character is distilled into a mannerism, a gesture, a physical feature, an outward and visible sign which recurs continually and is the permanent property of that character.'[20]

Dickens's vivid treatment of externals frequently expresses, moreover, an interest in the way the physical idiosyncrasies of one person can work deeply in the consciousness of another, often in that of a child. More generally, we could relate the life in the writing of both Dickens and Tolstoy to a capacity to keep alive in the adult mind the freshness of vision, the readiness to notice new things, of a child. In Tolstoy's case, this could be borne out by noting how closely his mature, independent vision as impersonal narrator is related to the vision of the child-hero of his first book, *Childhood*; and it is a well-attested fact that in the presentation of a child's vision of life, in *Childhood*, Tolstoy drew heavily on *David Copperfield*. But in any case it should not need hard argument to show that Dickens's use of 'externals' is at its best a demonstration of the emotional and spiritual relevance of body – as with Uriah Heep, who is described by David with the threat to Agnes at the back of his mind – and that this was something new in fiction; or that the quality of Tolstoy's dealings with the body lies not in the mystique of 'the seer of the flesh' – which seems, as some critics present it, to boil down too much to Vronsky's glow and delight in the springy firmness of his calves – but in the Dickensian sense of the body's importance that we find, for instance, when Karenin approaches Anna very soon after the deathbed scene of reconciliation, forgiveness, and love; husband and wife have only good intentions, and the brief scene (an essential stage in the tragic progression) makes painful reading:

'[Karenin] advanced and would have taken her hand.
Her first impulse was to jerk back her hand from the damp hand with big swollen veins that sought hers, but with an obvious effort to control herself she pressed his hand.' (Part iv, Chapter XIX)

Mention of the foreign novel should recall, however, that Dickens was not the only writer responsible for new visual life in fiction. The French had their own independent inspirations in Balzac and Hugo, though the lessons Balzac learned from Raphael were very different from those that Dickens learned from Bruegel, Holbein, Hogarth, and the caricaturists. Both within Dickens and outside him a cultural change was manifest, giving new importance to the eye. This change is too complex to be analysed here; an account of it would need to go back to the new priorities that emerged in the Romantic Movement, and to what Romanticism meant for the visual arts as well as for literature. The result, for fiction, was that in the process of gradually and fully finding, in words, the reality of his subject, the writer was making a more active and intimate use of his mind's eye; and this was the circumstance that made it possible for actual illustrations to help – provided that they were, genuinely, a further means of discovery. A carefully drawn naturalistic representation of a given scene, if it is only that, may not add anything of interest to the novelist. But the marriage-hearse point in the *Dombey* illustration is a live artistic 'finding' germane to the themes of the novel, a vital oscillating atom in the extended and charged molecular connectedness of the book. Again, a visual tableau that finely epitomizes the assertions and interdependences of a tight group of people, and sums up, in a moment, what in the novel takes a chapter, is also a creative finding. In a simpler and clearer way, the savagely grotesque picture of Quilp leaning out of the window in *The Old Curiosity Shop* is a pictorial capture of Quilp's character. It brings clearly into the open the intensely harsh grotesqueness, in this novel, of Dickens's mixing of the everyday and the fairytale. The illustration justifies itself in the surprise and shock we feel when we first see it. Is *this* the Dickens of the Little Nell novel? we might wonder. Looking back through the novel, we see that it is, and that 'Phiz' has not changed or distorted his subject; he has merely sharpened our sense of Dickens's own creation. An author could have no justification for wishing away such illustrations as improper intrusions in his art, or as evasions of his own responsibility.

One would not, of course, recommend the Dickens illustrations *en masse*; indeed, one would be hard put to it to find even one novel in which the illustrations invariably make a creative contribution. But they do show how, in speaking for the large part illustrations can play in a novel, one is not speaking merely for an easy-going accommodation of passengers. Illustrations can have point, and it would be a false economy in writer or reader to rule them out when they do.

It would not be fair, on the other hand, to suggest that illustrations should regularly be grafted onto the novel. The success achieved in the case of Dickens depended very much on the unusual situation in which the illustrations arose. The novelist wrote in collaboration with an artist he had worked with often before; he wrote knowing he must have illustrations, and designed them at the same time that he was writing his monthly part – sometimes before; he thought naturally in pictorial terms, partly because he was deeply influenced by certain artists; and his illustrators belonged to the school of just those artists, and inherited the same pictorial idiom as himself. Novels are not normally written in such circumstances, and the rarity of these conditions could be taken to imply the rarity with which illustrations are likely to be truly functional in the novel. None the less, it should still be worthwhile to maintain a sense of the available resources. William Blake is not the only example of an author who drew and an artist who wrote. George Du Maurier, for instance, though a small figure, was a distinguished draughtsman and illustrator, and had a talent for creating character, situation, and dialogue: it shows best in his cartoons for *Punch*. He illustrated his own novels lavishly, and we might expect him to outstrip Dickens in the co-operation of text and picture. But his illustrations add nothing that the novel needs to have; they are simply respectable drawings of people who look just as the characters are described, posed as the scene requires: they are just such illustrations as the later 19th century tended to produce. Yet Du Maurier greatly admired Hogarth, Dickens, and Thackeray, and if we ask how it was that he learned so little from them of visual metaphor and analogy, the answer can only be that he was a well-trained draughtsman of his time, and the whole habit of illustration in which his talent was formed to expertness ignored the mode.[21] So clear and impressive a routine was laid down for the artist that he never asked whether some radically different visual art could better extend the novel's life; it was not simply that he had no incentive to think of such things, but that he had, positively, too many other things to do. And though drawing schools teach different habits now, a modern illustrator, or a novelist who draws, is just as likely to not know, through his own expertness, how his talents could best assist the writing. Because the mind's eye sees so energetically in the novel, it matters to keep alive a full sense of the visual possibilities. In respect of illustration the modern novel has a withered limb, and while with many novelists it may just as well be withered, since they have no need of it, one cannot say who might have used it with the strength, suppleness, and sensitivity of a hand.

APPENDIX I

Conditions of Illustration in Serial Fiction

Most of the illustrations that have been discussed are basically either etchings or wood-engravings – 'basically' because even in first editions, some of the etchings were reproduced by lithography. Cruikshank, Seymour, and Browne were etchers because metal was the medium to use, and etching the quickest means to the end (as against engraving), rather than because etching was then regarded as a fine technique for an artist. Etching, in the 18th century, had been little more than a short cut. A line could easily be bitten into the metal with acid, and then given an engraved look with a few strokes of the burin. It took many years for etching to win respect as an independent technique, and when it was recognized Browne and Cruikshank were largely ignored (Ruskin was exceptional in his admiration for Cruikshank as an *etcher*).

Even the great caricaturists, Gillray and Rowlandson, were seldom referred to as etchers. Gillray was called an engraver, Rowlandson an aquatint-artist. Yet Gillray etched his designs, and in many of Rowlandson's aquatints the etching of the outlines was the only part of the process that Rowlandson himself did. And as late as 1878 a biographer of Cruikshank could still speak as though etching were simply engraving with a needle: 'Indeed, the simplest illustration must consist of thousands of little lines slowly and laboriously scratched on copper with an etching needle.'[1]

Gillray and the young Cruikshank etched on copper, and Hamilton relates that 'when Cruikshank was in his prime, copper was the only material used for etching',[2] but the only illustrations on copper, for Dickens and his fellow monthly-part novelists, were the small plates by Cruikshank for Dickens's first book, *Sketches by Boz*. These were on copper, afterwards coated with steel.[3] When Cruikshank copied these on larger plates for the part issue of the *Sketches* from 1837–9, he used steel, and all the etchings for the novels were on steel. In the Bentley Papers we find Bentley commissioning etchings on steel for various works, but the only case in which he refers to 'copperplate etchings' is that of *Oddities of London Life*.[4]

The original steel plates for the novels of Dickens remained in the possession of Chapman and Hall until they were distributed, one to a set, with the Nonesuch Dickens in 1937. A Nonesuch steel does not give quite a fair impression of the plate in its original state, however, for the plates have been cut down to a uniform size of approximately 5 in. by $8\frac{1}{8}$ in. They had originally been more than twice this size, for one steel plate would be used for two illustrations. They would be printed together and divided afterwards, and for this reason there is no plate-mark on the paper. The steel was, on the whole, of good quality. The first of Seymour's plates for *Pickwick* were on such poor steel that they broke down after a few hundred impressions and had to be etched again, but this was an isolated occurrence.[5] One steel plate (for two etchings) might cost 14s.[6]

In preparing an etching, a tracing of the artist's original sketch would be laid pencil side down on the etching ground which covered the steel plate. With a sheet of damp paper on top, it would be passed through the press so that the pencil marks were transferred to the ground (there is no evidence for Thomson's claim that artists simply copied their drawings straight onto the plate, reversing as they went).[7] The artist then drew on the plate with his needle, exposing the steel so that the acid could bite the lines to the required depth.

In making his drawing, the etcher could use the rich vocabulary of linear and textural effects that came down to him from the engravers of the previous century. In their local working, Cruikshank's plates often show great skill in integrating the many varieties of notation that were available. In the portrait of Arthur O'Leary used as the frontispiece for Lever's novel, much of the face is modelled with clusters of tiny dots (73). The effect is of stipple-engraving, and although Cruikshank seldom used this technique, it is clear that he had mastered its power to suggest the soft gradations of shadow and colour in the human face. Further inspection shows, however, a number of tiny lines among the dots, and areas of minute hatching. Arthur's coat is drawn in the dot-and-lozenge manner of the copperplate engravers; but for the shadowed arm-rest of the chair, he has drawn the lozenge-pattern, and then simply run over it with the roulette, so that it gives an effect of dot-and-lozenge if not inspected too closely. The roulette – the only mechanical aid Cruikshank used – appears a great deal in this plate, but almost always in an area that is already hatched and cross-hatched, as an unobtrusive deepening of the shadows.

Cruikshank takes from Gillray the use of short slightly curved strokes running in winding columns, and uses them for foliage – as in the background of the *Arthur O'Leary* plate – and also for shading areas of dirty wall in a style more interesting to look at than simple cross-hatching. He also uses the technique developed by copperplate engravers, and more minutely by steel-engravers, for

73. George Cruikshank, frontispiece for *Arthur O'Leary*.

suggesting the surface of rock and masonry with small snaky lines that surge and whirl round in a minute perturbation.

Although belonging primarily to the caricature-tradition, Cruikshank fully *possessed* the range of techniques for giving shadow and texture that came down to him from the 18th century, and he was able to use them whenever they would help; to take liberties with them when that would help; and to develop new techniques from them.

Hablôt Browne has not the same technical range. In the early plates he uses short strokes and cross-hatching in a small, pinched manner. With experience he comes to use a larger and more energetic style, though his resources are never so rich as those of Cruikshank. He relies a great deal on the roulette, and in his late etchings he uses a few slack runs of the roulette to fill in large areas of floor or wall: when there is no protective cross-hatching, the latterday casualness of his work is painfully clear. His great talent as an etcher shows in his power to capture a living human face in a few quick, deft lines, and his ingenuity as a technician shows in the use he made of the ruling machine and stopping-out varnish.

Varnish was, of course, in general use among etchers. Cruikshank's stopping out is very delicate and unobtrusive. He uses it for special effects of light: for instance, in the *Arthur O'Leary* plate 'A New Way to reckon without one's Host' the folds of the table-cloth that catch the light interrupt vertical lines that were clearly drawn in single strokes.

In the *Frank Fairlegh* illustration 'Mad Bess' the varnish has twice been used in similar ways. Some of the bright areas on the cliff-face have never been bitten, others have been bitten very lightly. This plate may have been experimental: the varnish has, in places, an unfortunate splashed look, and was rarely used by Cruikshank so obtrusively. In another plate for this novel, 'A Striking Position', there is a subtle transition along the bark of a tree, the lower part of which is only lightly bitten, while the upper part is strong. Since, however, the effects of stopping out tend to be lost in reproduction, these etchings are not shown here.

In his plates for *Pickwick* Seymour also showed skill in stopping out. The first plate is unfortunate, in that though the background is appropriately veiled, there is less reason why the objects on the table should be, and no reason at all why the head of the man at the far right-hand corner of the table should be so conspicuously faint. However, in the plate 'Winkle Soothes the Refractory Mare', the adroit use of stopping out varnish gives the country landscape a deep recession. The figures and the tree in the foreground are strongly bitten, while in the receding row of trees down the left side of the lane there is a gradual increase of stopping out, so that the last tree is faint.

His successor, Hablôt Browne, goes to work like a modern draughtsman for a line-block, and though he sometimes uses stopping-out varnish, few of his felicitous effects depend on it. Where he does use the varnish to some effect, he is far more ambitious. In his 'dark plates', innumerable layers of varnish are added during the biting in, so as to give an almost infinite gradation of tones to the one set of ruled lines that has been mechanically laid across the whole plate. He first develops this resource with any fullness in the plates for Lever's *Roland Cashel*. The frontispiece and 'The Game at Monte' are magnificent paintings in tone, with a rich effect of darkness and evanescent glimmering. And it is in the darker scenes that his use of this resource is strongest. For though Browne had a lively sense of outline, and a natural instinct for design and the attractive distribution of tones, he had little sense of the power of tone to model the figure, and in those plates showing brightly lit scenes, he scarcely attempts any modelling. Instead, he picks out and highlights faces and other points of interest, and darkens other areas as best suits the design. The effect is agreeable, but the scene is imperfectly realized. In some of the plates, the stopping out is minimal, and the ruled lines simply provide a general background tone, making the illustration resemble a drawing on tinted paper. And in some of the strongest uses of tone in the plates for this novel – as in 'The Fisherman's Hut' – the deep shadow, and the faint light that picks out prominent parts of the figures, are obtained by means of close and sensitive line-drawing. It is, however, in *Bleak House* that Browne uses the resources of ruling machine and varnish to the full, in each plate where he uses them at all; for he is using them expressively, and not simply as an experiment.

If one says that Browne drew often like a modern artist working for a line-block, one should add that etching required, in addition to the skills of draughts-manship, a great deal of technical skill, and a great deal of time; and the rewards were not proportionately greater. Etchers were very poorly paid, by modern standards. For the first work of Leech mentioned in the Bentley Papers, he was paid five guineas a plate. This was in 1838, when he had barely started on his career; and it is clear that he started well, for other etchers commanded much lower sums. In the same year, Bentley agreed to pay the etcher T. C. Wilson two guineas a plate (for illustrating *Oddities of London Life*).[8]

Leech's pay as illustrator was never very high. In 1841, Bentley advanced him £90 and drew up an Agreement that states the normal fees Leech was to receive:

'for a full square subject similar in size and style to those now in progress for the story of "Richard Savage", the sum of seven pounds – and for vignette subjects, similar to those executed for the "Porcelain Tower" – the sum of six pounds each; and of drawings on wood 25½/- each.'[9]

At this figure his pay rested. At the close of the following year, he agreed to illustrate Albert Smith's *The Wassail Bowl* 'at the price usually paid me by Mr Bentley – viz. £6 for vignettes or £7 for square subjects'.[10]

In 1843, Leech offered to illustrate Surtees for six guineas a plate: this was the lowest he would go, and even this was too high for Surtees's publisher. The low quality of illustration at this time is partly explained by the parsimonious attitude of the publishers. Colburn wrote to Surtees:

'I applied to Mr Leech, a very distinguished artist, but he will not execute them for less than £6, 6s. each, an expense which would detract very considerably from the profits. I next applied to Mr Tattersall, who is illustrating your present work in the 'New Sporting Magazine'. He required £5, 5s. each plate, and at least two months to execute them in. I have lately heard of another artist, Mr Standfast, who has been executing some plates for the 'Sporting Magazine'. He will, I believe, be satisfied with a very moderate price, possibly £3, 3s. each plate.'[11]

Conditions had been very severe for the artist. When Buss attempted to illustrate *Pickwick* he was offered 10s. a plate.[12] Seymour had received only 35s. for each subject,[13] and he had been accustomed to receive even less. His famous 'Humorous Sketches' were sold to their first publisher (Richard Carlisle) at 15s. for each lithographic stone.[14] Turning to see what Browne normally received, we apparently make the large jump from shillings to guineas. Thomson says:

'He was paid no more for the "Knight of Gwynne" or "Dombey" than he was for "Lorrequer" and "Pickwick". Fifteen guineas was his price at first for an etching, and though – as in the Smedley plates – he often took less, he never seems to have asked more.'[15]

Thomson is astonished that Browne accepted so low a figure – 'Hablôt Browne was in every sense of the word a bad business man' – but Thomson's figure is itself astonishingly high.

In 1836, when Browne's career may be said to begin, the better-known artist Hervieu was offered between £4 10s. 0d. and £7 for an etching;[16] and it is hardly likely Browne should receive more than him, and more even than George Cruikshank, who was then at the height of his fame. When *Bentley's Miscellany* started, Bentley agreed to pay Cruikshank twelve guineas a plate, plus fifty pounds 'it being understood that such payment of Fifty Pounds is for the value and use of the name of the said George Cruikshank Esq.'.[17] For this remuneration the artist was also ready to bind himself not to illustrate 'The Humourist' or any publication of Henry Colburn, under a penalty of £100 (the agreement was at first so phrased that if Bentley decided not to use Cruikshank's plates, or if he closed down his magazine, Cruikshank would still have to pay £100 if he sought work from Colburn).

A more likely figure for Browne's payment is given by Dickens in a letter to Bentley of 28 January 1837:

'I have spoken to my Pickwick artist. He is delighted at the prospect of doing an etching for the Miscellany. His demand is £5. I suppose it is not too much, considering all things.'[18]

Dickens's tone suggests that £5 may have been slightly more than Browne was receiving for the *Pickwick* plates. Some pages of the accounts of Chapman and Hall in the Widener Collection record a payment to Browne on 8 December 1836, of £8; presumably this was payment for two etchings – £4 would be a likely figure at the *Pickwick* stage. In a letter of 1841, Browne says that 'the amount of "damage" for the steel plate is 10s. making £5. 10 – due at yr. convenience',[19] so his charge for the actual etching was still, in that year, only £5.

The Accounts of Bradbury and Evans in the Forster Collection state that, for *Dombey*, Browne was given £25. 4s. 0d. for 'Etching No. 1 in duplicate' and £6 for 'Biting in Plates'. This totals £31. 4s. 0d., and Thomson may have derived his opulent figure of fifteen guineas by dividing in half this payment for etching 'in duplicate', making £15. 12s. 0d. But for 'No. 1' (which has the date 30 Sept. 1846, and clearly refers to the monthly part, and not the plate) *two* designs were etched in duplicate. Browne's payment is really for four etchings, and as the payment for biting in was passed on, presumably, to his lifelong assistant, Robert Young, it would appear that Browne received, per etching, a quarter of £25. 4s. 0d., or six guineas. His payment rose to seven guineas for *Copperfield* (the entry for the first number reads 'Etching, 2 sets, Browne . . . 29/8/-'), and rose again to £11. 8s. 6d. in *Bleak House* and *Little Dorrit*. The latter rise was offset, however, by the fact that with the development of lithography, his ordinary plates no longer needed to be etched in duplicate, so that for the first numbers of *Bleak House* and *Little Dorrit* he received only £22. 17s. 0d., as against the £29. 8s. 0d. of *Copperfield*. The 'dark plates' *did* need to be duplicated, and for the duplication Browne received a further seventeen guineas; even so it is a poor reward for one of the most popular illustrators of the time.

The way in which the artist *could* prosper was by becoming a partner in a serial venture. This did not happen with novels published in volume form, but if a novel was treated as a magazine of limited life which, on the evidence of former works, was bound to succeed, then author and artist could demand a position of more personal and financial force. In the agreement 'for the publication of a new monthly periodical to be entitled "The Tower of London"' Ainsworth and Cruikshank were the two partners, and the publisher, Bentley, had not even that status, although he was to receive a third of the profits.[20] A third of the profits proved to be £517. 16s. 7d. This was an unusual arrangement.

Poorly paid, etching was also a time-consuming art. Working under pressure, Browne allowed five days to etch (twice) a single design, as we may see in the schedule he prepared for his publishers. He worked to a deadline, and had no opportunity to repeat a plate that went badly:

'A DIARY

Friday evening, 11th Jan.	Received portion of copy containing Subject No. 1.
Sunday	Posted sketch to Dickens.
Monday evening, 14th Jan.	Received back sketch of Subject No. 1 from Dickens, enclosing a subject for No. 2.
Tuesday, 15th Jan.	Forwarded sketch of Subject 2 to Dickens.
Wednesday, 16th Jan.	Received back ditto.
Sunday	

Tuesday, 22nd Jan.   First plate finished.
Saturday, 26th Jan.   Second ditto finished. . . .
I make ten days to etch and finish four etchings. . . .'[21]

The wages an etcher received, combined with the time it took to produce an etching, explain why these artists were very busy men. They had to be practical in the way they organized their time. Cruikshank settled early into his lifelong regimen of a nine-hour day, divided into three sets of three hours' work:

'He breakfasted punctually at eight o'clock, after which he smoked a pipe, and went to work at nine. When biting up plates, he would smoke more in the course of the morning to drive away the fumes of the acid. At twelve he lunched, and then resumed work until three o'clock, when he dined. After dinner he sat, with a jug of porter before him, enjoying his pipe, and talking with any friend who dropped in. His visitors were many. At five he drank tea, and then worked again from six o'clock till nine, when supper concluded the labour of the day, and was the preliminary to pipes and grog.'[22]

Browne spent his mornings working, and in the afternoons and evenings he read or worked;[23] and he did not even bite in his own plates.

Being seriously overworked, the illustrators had often to postpone the commissions they had accepted. Browne kept putting off his etchings for Surtees, and in the end he abandoned the commission; and Surtees's regular illustrator, John Leech, behaved in the same way. During the monthly publication of *Handley Cross* the publishers had cause to complain on several occasions: 'Leech is again failing us with the illustrations, so that No. 14 cannot appear.' When *Plain or Ringlets* was in progress, the publishers complained again: 'Two or three days before publishing day I received a note from Mr. Leech that it was impossible for him to do it this month.' It may be imagined how damaging it was for a monthly-part novel to miss publication several times during its run. Yet, notwithstanding the harm to the novel's sales caused by these delays, Leech was asked to illustrate the novel that was to be Surtees's last, *Mr Facey Romford's Hounds*. Leech replied:

'I owe you many apologies for not writing to you sooner. The truth is I have been so overwhelmed with work that I have not been able yet to come to any positive decision as to when I can take up the new story. I hope, however, to be able to commence in the course of January.'

He was unable to approach the task before the summer. The proofs were sent to him on 22 July 1862; and in March 1863 Surtees wrote to Leech, evidently with flagging hopes, 'Re "Romford", as the lawyers say, I have been in hopes of hearing from you relative to the above distinguished individual, . . .' The publishers consulted Leech, and the task was postponed until January 1864, when Leech wrote:

'I . . . long to put on the red coat with you. I had fully intended commencing in February, but found it impossible. However, I will have a shy at it for March if you do not think that it is too late.'

Fortunately the first number came out in March – fortunately, for Surtees died on 16 March; Leech himself died on 29 October, overworked to the end, and the illustrations were finished by Surtees's first illustrator, Hablôt Browne.[24]

Poorly paid for the artist, etching was also inconvenient for the publisher. Unlike wood-engravings, etchings could not be printed in the same way as the letterpress. They required more elaborate and delicate treatment (the description is a contemporary one):

'The copper or steel-plate is placed above a charcoal fire, and warmed before the ink is rubbed into the hollowed lines by a woollen ball. When enough of ink is thus put into the lines, the surface of the plate is wiped with a rag, and cleaned and polished with the palm of the hand lightly touched with whiting. The paper is then laid on the plate, and the engraving is obtained by pressing the paper into the inked lines.'[25]

It was a slow process, and involved a good deal of wear (of which the human hand was the most serious cause), and the inevitable consequence was that etching was replaced by wood-engraving, even when the author-editor favoured etching:

'And when Thackeray projected the *Cornhill Magazine*, he found to his great disappointment that a circulation of 80,000 copies would not permit of the illustrations being printed apart from the type, and he was compelled to abandon his favourite copper and steel plates for the rough-and-ready wood blocks.'[26]

The contemporary article on engraving, quoted above, claimed that:

'A plate of metal is useless after a few thousand impressions have been taken from it, while a wood-block will yield sometimes two or three hundred thousand impressions: and thus the expenses – and it costs much less to produce a first rate wood-cut than it does to produce a first rate copper-plate – are divided among nearly a hundred times as many purchasers.'[27]

The more popular the work, the less chance etching stood.

Before wood-engraving triumphed, however, a number of other expedients were tried. A design could be transferred to several steel plates, and then etched. Browne soon acquired the habit of etching two, three, or even four steels simultaneously. This was a laborious process, however, and the next device tried was the transference of the etched design to lithographic stone; a single stone could cope with the largest Victorian print order without any serious loss of quality. Nor was there any great loss of quality in the making of the lithographs, and – printing conditions being what they were – it is often very difficult to tell whether a given plate is a lithograph or an etching.

It has been thought that this multiplication of plates, in steel and stone, arose because a single plate would have worn down before an average Dickensian print-order (of twenty or thirty thousand) could be completed. Metal was relatively short-lived, as the writer quoted above claimed, but he was perhaps thinking more of copper than of steel. He gives the figure of 2,000 or 3,000, and Hamilton relates that when Cruikshank was using copper,

'An impression of two, or, at the most, three thousand, wore a plate completely out. The artist tells us himself that in consequence of the prodigious demand for his celebrated etching of "Jack Ketch's Promissory Note" (a Bank Note *not* to be imitated) he was obliged to sit up a whole night to engrave a second plate, the first one being exhausted.'[28]

But steel was tougher, and after the first edition, the original steels were used to print the illustrations in the Library Edition, the Gadshill Edition, the National Edition, and the Nonesuch Dickens, and even so it is hard to discover in the plates issued with the Nonesuch Dickens any grave signs of wear. The Nonesuch plates are little different from those in first editions, and though such things as the small dots made by the roulette faded in some printings, very careful inking and printing could restore them. In the Nonesuch plates, there are some smudges in the *Pickwick* series that suggest the steel was deteriorating, but these were the only blemishes to be found. Professor Johannsen claimed that 'as the plates wore down, they were repeatedly touched up and strengthened by cross-hatching or recutting'.[29] But in his catalogue of all the variant plates he cites extremely few examples, and he perhaps exaggerates the effect of wear.[30] As one can see, if one compares certain plates he reproduces with the impressions in the Nonesuch Dickens, he does sometimes attribute to wear effects produced by under- or over-inking and careless printing.

Even when the use of stone became regular practice, the steel plates were still etched first, and no record survives of Cruikshank or Browne having anything to do with the making of the lithographs. Nor were the lithographs ever announced as such, and as no attempt was made for any of the characteristic effects of lithography, it is safe to assume that lithography was simply an economic device adopted by publishers who still wanted the public to think that all the illustrations came from genuine steel plates. Thomson suggests that 'Browne's first idea in using the [ruling] machine was probably to prevent any transference of his etchings to the lithographic stone, . . .'[31] This would imply a marked division of attitudes, concerning the use of lithography, between artist and publisher.

Lithography had been practised in England for some years. One finds a lively, experimental interest in it sweeping the country in the 1820s. In 1823 the *Newcastle Magazine*, which had previously published steel-engravings, announced:

'This portrait is a lithographic sketch – we believe the first specimen of stone-printing in connexion with the fine arts that has been executed in Newcastle. . . . We have ourselves taken up the art of lithography, and we trust we shall speedily make such an advancement in the knowledge of its various branches as will enable us, for facility of workmanship and clearness and style of execution, to be of material service to the arts in the north of England.'[32]

There were difficulties in mastering the process, shown in announcements of 'Embellishments' that did not appear, and some of the experiments were far from successful; but the publishers mastered the technique in the end, and printed a superior version of a drawing they had printed some months before:

'A specimen of art which we flatter ourselves will prove generally acceptable. Those who were subscribers to the Magazine in October last, will have the goodness to cancel the portrait they then received (which was imperfect as a likeness, and a failure in point of execution), and insert this in its place.'[33]

Unfortunately, the drawing is clearly by a copperplate engraver who cannot get away from his usual manipulations, and the portrait seems only a blurred version of an engraving. There is no sense of what lithography as such could provide. This defect remained, though publishers acquired great sophistication in transferring designs from steel to stone – and *vice versa*: Seymour's 'Humorous Sketches' were drawings on stone before Henry Wallis 'transferred the drawings very skilfully to steel'.[34] Seymour's drawing on the stone was altogether in the style of his etchings.

A brilliant example was being set in France at this time, and the English public was reminded of this. In 1839 a writer in *The London and Westminster Review* complained:

'With ourselves, among whom money is plenty, enterprise so great, and everything matter of commercial speculation, Lithography has not been so much practised as wood or steel-engraving, which, by the aid of great original capital and spread of sale, are able more than to compete with the art of drawing on stone . . . the state of art amongst the people in France and Germany, where publishers are not so wealthy or enterprising as with us, and where Lithography is more practised, is infinitely higher than in England, and the appreciation more correct.'[35]

But none of the English serial illustrators took to lithography as an art in its own right. The lithographs of work by Cruikshank, Browne, and Leech are only translated etchings, that have lost the sharpness of the etched line. One should perhaps make an exception for Clarkson Stanfield. Dickens wrote to his publishers:

'Mr Stanfield will draw the packet-ship for the frontispiece to the American Notes. He says "lithography is better than wood for that kind of subject." Please to let me know immediately whether it will suit us to lithograph it.'[36]

A subsequent letter shows that the publishers, who provided the stone, were not then used to such artists: 'Mr Stanfield wonders you didn't send him a paving-stone to draw upon, as soon as a block in this unprepared state.'[37] It is not surprising that wood-engraving speedily gained ground, and was not seriously opposed by lithography.

Wood-engraving, the most popular process of illustration in the 19th century, took several decades to establish itself, however. Bewick revived the art of engraving on the end-grain of the wood with an engraver's tools, rather than cutting into the plank with a knife, by the turn of the century. Yet in 1838 it was still possible to complain that 'few of our best draughtsmen have yet condescended to design for wood'.[38] By way of establishing the respectability of wood-engraving, the writer recommended wood-engraving to 'educated gentlewomen of the middle classes' as 'an honourable, elegant and lucrative employment, easily acquired, and every way becoming their sex and habits'.[39] In the sixties, however, a young illustrator inevitably studied drawing for wood (the classic wood-engraving of Germany then enjoyed a fashion), although older artists, such as Cruikshank, Browne, and Leech, continued to etch.

By the time Dickens was writing, the disadvantageous division of tasks between draughtsman and wood-engraver was common. Only one illustration to Dickens was engraved by its artist: the picture of Nell asleep, on Page 46 of *Master Humphrey's Clock* (Volume i), which was drawn and cut by S. Williams. Wood-engraving had not then reached the stage when it was monopolized by large firms, and the drawings by Cattermole and Browne for *Master Humphrey's Clock* were cut by a variety of hands. Hatton and Cleaver report that the inset wood-engravings were 'engraved by E. Landells (86); C. Gray (74); S. Williams (5); and Vasey (5).'[40] But even this list does not exhaust the number of engravers involved, for Hatton and Cleaver err in supposing that the engravings bearing Landells' name were necessarily cut by him. The Dalziels stated that

'it was for [Landells] that we engraved the prospectus block for *Punch*, also the covers for that journal . . . as well as the "H. K. B." drawings every week for "Master Humphrey's Clock".'[41]

The subjects in question may be identified from a scrap-book in the British Museum headed 'India-Proofs of Wood-Engravings by the Brothers Dalziel. General Work: Various: 1839–47.' There is an inscription stating that 'this Book was made up at the time the engravings shown in it were done' and it includes the following illustrations for *Master Humphrey's Clock*:

No. in the Scrap-Book	Vol. &	Page in M.H.C.
124	i	12
151		60
153		49
160		94
184		172
185		168
198		226
199		237
201		198
219		276
220	ii	61
226		124
230		142
231		155
233		158
234		175
244		233
249	i	306
251	ii	11
253		15
268		276
278	iii	35
288		68
298		118
302		137
303		131

Each of these engravings bears the name 'Landells' in the published version, but in each case, except the first, the version in the scrap-book has a solid black bar where the 'engraver's' name is later to be cut. The first illustration in the list has the name 'E. Landells' in both versions, but it is executed in an italic style quite different from that of Landells' usual signatures, and it is presumably for this reason that the Dalziels were not trusted, in the subsequent cuts, to sign Landells' name; he evidently did this himself, intending that the public should believe that the entire work was from his hand. The Brothers Dalziel do not appear to have resented this; on the contrary, they speak as though such farming out were common practice. (Hatton's attribution of the drawings to their artists in the Nonesuch Prospectus also appears to be at fault; I have assisted in preparing the new analysis given in Volume ii of the Pilgrim Edition of Dickens's Letters.)

By the time Dickens wrote *Our Mutual Friend*, the Dalziels had established themselves as one of the principal wood-engraving firms in the country, and the plates for that novel were all cut either by them or by T. Green. The plates for *Edwin Drood* would all have been cut by the Dalziels, if Fildes had not expressly asked for another engraver. Dickens wrote to his publishers:

'Mr Fildes has been with me this morning, and without complaining of – or expressing himself otherwise than as being obliged to him for his care of No. 1, represents that there is a brother-student of his, a wood-engraver, perfectly acquainted with his style and well understanding his meaning, who would render him better.'[42]

When the Household Edition of Dickens came out between 1871 and 1879, the Dalziels executed all the cuts, and the position is clearly very different from that of, say, the Christmas Books, which might employ six different firms at a time.

In the letter about Fildes just quoted, Dickens continues:

'I have replied to him that there can be no doubt that he has a claim beyond dispute to our employing whomsoever he knows will present him in his best aspect. Therefore, we must make the change; the rather because the fellow-student in question has engraved Mr Fildes' most successful drawings hitherto.'

It is clear that even at this late date, the division between artist and engraver was not absolute: truly collaborative effects could still be achieved. Again, an artist might try to find a wood-engraver who specialized in his own subject: 'Mr Stanfield wishes to know who are the best engravers on wood of landscape and architectural subjects, with small figures.'[43]

The technicalities of wood-engraving at this time are given in the 1838 article on engraving that has already been mentioned. The writer discusses the ink (which must be 'impalpably smooth and equally mixed'), the paper ('India paper from China, which until lately was supplied from the lining of tea-chests and wrappers of silk, is decidedly the best'), and the wood ('the box and pear-tree'). The Dickens artists favoured box, to judge from Dickens's comment on Landseer's illustration of the dog Boxer (in *The Cricket on the Hearth*), 'Here is Boxer on Box'.[44] The article also makes it clear that some Dickens illustrations were cut by the best engravers of the day: 'Though great merits belong to others, there are two families who may be said to be at this moment at the head of this art – the Williamses and the Thompsons. . . .'[45] There are both Williamses and Thompsons among the engravers for the Christmas Books, and Samuel Williams, who is praised for his 'versatility of talent and great variety of touch', engraved several of the designs in *Master Humphrey's Clock*. These considerations scarcely begin, however, to lessen one's inevitable regret that the 19th century saw no second Bewick, who could have done for Dickens in wood-engraving what Browne and Cruikshank had done for him in etching.

In conclusion, a brief survey may be offered of the later history of the original illustrations to Dickens. In the early collected editions, the illustrations were reduced to one per volume and were new ones, though still executed by Browne. The Cheap Edition, issued from 1847, had a wood-engraved frontispiece and the Library Edition (1858–9) a vignette on the title-page, engraved on steel in a style unusually elegant for Browne. The publishers evidently intended to produce the novels in a format suited to the more weighty prestige that Dickens now possessed. But whatever the public may have thought of the elegance and the prestige, the original plates were still desired: in 1861 a new Library Edition came out with all the original plates. Impressions of this edition were still being issued in the 1880s. The Charles Dickens Edition of 1867–75 had 'a selection of the plates of the Library Edition': a single volume would have perhaps eight plates, certainly not printed from the original steels. But between 1871 and 1879, Chapman and Hall issued the monumental Household Edition, with a completely new set of illustrations by a number of hands, engraved on wood. Browne prepared a new series of drawings for *Pickwick*; the new illustrations were weak, and his contribution ended there.

However, if there was an attempt to make the Household plates the classic illustrations for later editions of Dickens, it did not succeed. The next edition was Macmillan's Reprint of the First Edition (1892), with Browne's plates, followed in 1897 by Chapman and Hall's Gadshill Edition, in which the illustrations were printed from the original steels with a beautiful clarity and sensitivity. Other illustrators tried their hand at the turn of the century, and achieved a more complete emancipation from the visualizations of Browne. John A. Bacon, who illustrated Nelson's New Century Library Edition (1899) and The Imperial Edition (1901–3), and W. Cubitt Cooke, who illustrated the Temple Edition (1898–1903), owe nothing to Browne. But no artist was able to oust Browne from the editions that followed. The Biographical Edition (1902–3), the Autograph Edition (with the limited St Dunstan Edition and Bibliophiles' Edition, 1908), The Fireside Dickens (1903–7), the Authentic Edition (1901–1906), the National Edition (1906–8), the Nonesuch Dickens (1937), and various later editions, all use Browne's plates.

The plates are not always reproduced very well, mainly because it is easier to make line-blocks from the reproductions in another edition than to use the original steels or an especially fine first edition. This procedure is easily detected, since Browne etched most of his plates in duplicate: in first editions the plates were mixed in any combination that came to hand, but subsequently Chapman and Hall separated the plates into distinct alternative series so as to prolong their life. Both the Gadshill Edition of 1897 and the Library Edition of 1861 use the original steel plates, but, where possible, every plate in the Gadshill series comes in a different version from that in the Library Edition. However, the Charles Dickens Edition of 1867 reproduces, poorly, plates from the 1861 series; and although the Macmillan Reprint of 1892 claims to be a 'reprint of the first edition with the illustrations', it is evidently a reprint of the 1861 edition as far as the illustrations go: it adheres to that series, and the reduced reproductions are obscure. Thomas Nelson, also, used the 1861 edition for the New Dickens. On the other hand, the Gadshill series was reproduced by the Caxton Publishing Company in the London Edition (1901–2) with an inevitable loss of quality. Chapman and Hall also used surface reproductions of this series for their own later editions. This reproductive regress must go a long way towards explaining the popular picture of Browne's etchings as smudged obscurities, for in the various processes of reproduction and reduction, half the etched lines are lost, and the remainder swollen.

The special interest of the Caxton Company's London Edition is that it is almost the only edition to apply colour to the illustrations of Browne. There are eight coloured plates in each volume, and the colouring is, in most cases, infelicitous. Chapman and Hall used colour in the frontispieces for the Authentic Edition (1901–6), although the pictures coloured were not the original Browne plates, but outline copies of them. Colour was used more interestingly in the Temple Edition, though the illustrations there were not by Browne.

If the editions popularly available have tended to reproduce the plates in a poor form, there have been various limited editions that have used the original steels and tried to produce perfect prints of the etchings. It would be hard to choose between the Gadshill Edition, the National Edition, and the Nonesuch Dickens. Unfortunately a set of any of these editions is likely to be prohibitively expensive. A set of the Nonesuch Dickens recently on sale in Cambridge fetched £385. The high price might be attributed in part to the fact that the set included the original steel plate for Cruikshank's etching 'Fagin in the Condemned Cell'; yet another copy of the Nonesuch Dickens, with a small wood-engraving by Leech, fetched £340.

With the Nonesuch Dickens, the set of steels preserved by Chapman and Hall for so long was broken up, one being given away with each copy. To judge from editions that have appeared since 1937, this shameful distribution of the steels had no symbolic finality for the illustrations as illustrations, and it is more than likely that Browne's plates will still be printed in editions of Dickens one or two centuries from now.

APPENDIX II

Cruikshank and *Oliver Twist*

In his later years, when his fame and popularity had receded, George Cruikshank was accustomed to claim that he had originated many of the works he had illustrated; the trait was well-known to his contemporaries. In what he says of Ainsworth's novels he was very far from being deluded, but in other cases the question is more complex. A discrimination between the different claims Cruikshank made for *Oliver Twist* shows the involved and divided state of mind into which the Hogarthian artist was driven when he refused to compromise his independence mentally, although it was compromised in fact. There is a bizarre mixture of minor claims that have some justification, honest mistakes that are at the same time surprisingly large mistakes, and falsifications of evidence.

The intricate history of his assertions is succinctly resumed by Professor Tillotson:

'[Cruikshank's claim to *Oliver Twist*] was first brought forward in an article in an American periodical, by Dr. Robert Shelton MacKenzie, quoted in J. C. Hotten's *Charles Dickens: the story of his life* (1870), and repeated with additions in MacKenzie's *Life of Charles Dickens* (1870); it was emphatically denied by Forster in the first volume of his *Life* (1871); defended by MacKenzie in the *Philadelphia Press* (19 December 1871) and independently by Cruikshank in a letter to *The Times* (30 December 1871); denied again by Forster in his second volume (1872); and defended by Cruikshank in his pamphlet *The Artist and the Author* (1872). He adds no further evidence, but claims to have told MacKenzie that he was the originator 'at the time *Oliver Twist* was in progress', whereas MacKenzie in his *Life* had given the date of the conversation as 1847. It must have been earlier than 1852, when MacKenzie left England for good, and is therefore not simply a delusion of Cruikshank's old age.'[1]

The central document is Cruikshank's letter to *The Times*, since it is his own public statement of his claims (he added little to it in *The Artist and The Author*), and since he there jettisoned the central episode in Mackenzie's account: 'Dr. Mackenzie confused some circumstances with respect to Mr. Dickens looking over some drawings and sketches in my studio. . . .'

In this letter Cruikshank made five specific claims: that he suggested to Dickens the broad outlines of the plot, although Dickens only partly followed his suggestion; that he 'suggested that the poor boy should fall among thieves' and supplied Dickens with a detailed knowledge of the underworld; that he and Dickens disagreed about Oliver's appearance, and that Cruikshank's will prevailed; that he described to Dickens a particular Jewish receiver he knew, on whom Fagin was modelled; and that he was responsible for the climactic episode of the condemned cell.

First of all, Cruikshank says that he gave Dickens his 'subject':

'. . . in a conversation with him as to what the subject should be . . . I suggested to Mr. Dickens that he should write the life of a London boy. . . . My idea was to raise a boy from a most humble position up to a high and respectable one – in fact, to illustrate one of those cases of common occurrence, where men of humble origin by natural ability, industry, honest and honourable conduct, raise themselves to first-class positions in society.'

It is at least clear from this that Cruikshank cannot be accused of tailoring his 'suggestion' to fit the actual novel, for the story he gives is *not Oliver Twist*: Oliver is not a London boy, and the novel ends at the beginning of Cruikshank's story, for Oliver scarcely begins a career in which his 'natural ability, industry, honest and honourable conduct' could raise him to a 'first-class position in society'. Moreover, there is an inherent probability in an artist of Cruikshank's background suggesting this particular story to Dickens, for in every detail that Cruikshank gives here, he merely repeats the career of Hogarth's Industrious Apprentice. Similarly, a further claim that Cruikshank made, in the final paragraph of his letter, also rings true (the Industrious Apprentice's name was Frank Goodchild): 'I wanted the boy to have a very different name, such as Frank Foundling or Frank Steadfast.' It would at least seem likely, then, that Cruikshank did suggest to Dickens the story he says he suggested; it was not the story that Dickens wrote, and Cruikshank registered this: 'I was much disappointed by Mr Dickens not fully carrying out my first suggestion.'

The episode of the thieves, which Cruikshank mentions in his second claim, was not an essential part of the plot he describes, and was introduced to make a separate point:

'And as I wished particularly to bring the habits and manners of the thieves of

London before the public (and this for a most important purpose, which I shall explain one of these days), I suggested that the poor boy should fall among thieves, but that his honesty and natural good disposition should enable him to pass through this ordeal without contamination, and after I had fully described the full-grown thieves (the "Bill Sikes") and their female companions, also the young thieves (the "Artful Dodgers") and the receivers of stolen goods, Mr. Dickens agreed to act upon my suggestion. . . .'

Cruikshank never did explain what the 'most important purpose' was, and there is no evidence that he did first suggest the fall among thieves (although the Idle Apprentice fell among thieves, and Oliver's immunity to 'contamination' suits the 'Frank Steadfast' conception); but the illustrator of *Tom and Jerry*, who had spent a longer life than Dickens among 'the lower classes, workmen, small tradesmen, rascalry of all sorts, the drinkers, and comedians of the inferior theatres',[2] presumably knew the seamy side of London life more intimately and extensively than Dickens. It is clear both from the testimony of Ainsworth and Dickens, and from Cruikshank's letters, that he constantly plied his authors with suggestions, and it is very likely that he acquainted Dickens with certain details of criminal life which were useful as local colour; Professor Tillotson grants that Cruikshank suggested the use of Field Lane.[3] The kind of suggestion he may be assumed to have made may be seen in a letter he wrote to Ainsworth, accompanying his sketch for the *Jack Sheppard* plate 'Jonathan Wild throwing Sir Rowland Trenchard down the well-hole':

'Mr Wild has in his hand a short club stick, which he might be supposed to use instead of the common hand *staff* upon occasion of a scuffle – a Pocket Companion – a Sort of *Pet* and a favorite for part services – a short handle with a large *heavy* knob – which if not *quite* up to *your taste*, you can load with lead.'[4]

Cruikshank gives a diagram of the bludgeon, and further suggests: 'try to give the stick some odd name – what do you think of Knobblelybob? but something of a *soft* and *endearing character* would be better – ' How much Dickens used such suggestions, assuming he received them, can only be a matter for speculation; and originating such details is, of course, very different from originating the novel proper.

With the third claim a more detailed investigation can be made. Cruikshank says:

'. . . we differed as to what sort of boy the hero should be. Mr. Dickens wanted rather a queer kind of chap, and although this was contrary to my original idea I complied with his request, feeling that it would not be right to dictate too much to the writer of the story, and then appeared 'Oliver Asking for More'; but it so happened just about this time that an inquiry was being made in the parish of

St. James's, Westminster, as to the cause of the death of some of the workhouse children who had been 'farmed out', and in which inquiry my late friend Joseph Pettigrew (surgeon to the Dukes of Kent and Sussex) came forward on the part of the poor children, and by his interference was mainly the cause of saving the lives of many of these poor little creatures. I called the attention of Mr. Dickens to this inquiry, and said if he took up this matter, his doing so might help to save many a poor child from injury and death; and I earnestly begged of him to let me make Oliver a nice pretty little boy; and if we so represented him, the public – and particularly the ladies – would be sure to take a greater interest in him, and the work would then be a certain success. Mr. Dickens agreed to that request, and I need not add here that my prophecy was fulfilled; and if any one will take the trouble to look at my representations of 'Oliver', they will see that the appearance of the boy is altered after the two first illustrations, and, by a reference to the records of St. James's parish, and to the date of the publication of the *Miscellany*, they will see that both the dates tally, and therefore support my statement.'

Oliver's appearance does change as Cruikshank says: the plates for February and March ('Oliver asking for more' and 'Oliver escapes being bound apprentice to the Sweep') show Dickens's 'queer kind of chap', while, in the April plate ('Oliver plucks up a spirit') and afterwards, Oliver is good-looking, fair-haired, and classical.

    Moreover, the inquiry Cruikshank mentions was made at St James's, Westminster; and Joseph Pettigrew was involved in it; and it belongs to a March and an April. But Cruikshank gives the wrong year, for although *Oliver Twist* began in 1837, the inquiry took place in 1836. As Pettigrew records in his pamphlet on this issue, he wrote to Lord John Russell on 2 March 1836, complaining about the condition of the pauper children at St James's, and on the 12th he made the question public in a letter to the *Morning Chronicle*. The vestry clerk of St James's replied on the 14th, stating that the Poor Law Commissioners had investigated the subject and were perfectly satisfied. On the same day Pettigrew wrote again to Russell asking for a copy of the Commissioners' report. This was refused him, and on the 15th Russell said in the House of Commons, in reply to a question on the subject, that Pettigrew's statements were unreliable. The two rebuffs from Russell provoked Pettigrew to issue his pamphlet *The Pauper Farming System. A Letter to the Right Hon. Lord John Russell, ... on the Condition of the Pauper Children of St. James's, Westminster*, which is dated 19 April 1836. Pettigrew's public contribution to the cause appears to have ended here, although his obituary in *The Gentleman's Magazine* records that 'although at first his efforts were not received by the highest officers of the Poor-Law Board in the benevolent spirit which originated them, yet in the end the whole of the children were removed',[5] and Warren R. Dawson notes that certain grateful members of the St James's parish board presented Pettigrew with a silver tea-kettle.[6]

As far as Pettigrew is concerned little truth can be salvaged from Cruikshank's claim. The question of farming out may well have remained a topic of conversation between Pettigrew and Cruikshank until 1837. But Cruikshank implies that he changed Oliver's appearance at the time when Pettigrew came forward, and the facts are otherwise. Presumably Cruikshank was not being dishonest, for if so he would have been absurdly brave in insisting that the dates tally when they do not. But if he was not dishonest, we have to assume that the case of St James's came into his story many years later, when his memory was failing. Possibly, in a careless perusal of Pettigrew's pamphlet, he noticed how the months agreed and found this fact so much to his purpose that he never checked the years (it is possible there was a prior association in his mind between the name 'Pettigrew' and April 1837, since in that month Pettigrew's son, Thomas Lettsom, died; the death was a terrible shock to the father,[7] while Cruikshank's knowledge of the boy may be inferred from the fact that, four years before, he had illustrated Thomas Lettsom's novel *Lucien Greville*).

A further point, also damaging to Cruikshank's case, is that in the first episode of the novel, Dickens had attacked not merely the parish system in general, but the specific practice of farming out:

'... the parish authorities magnanimously and humanely resolved, that Oliver should be "farmed", or, in other words, that he should be despatched to a branch-workhouse some three miles off, where twenty or thirty other juvenile offenders against the poor-laws rolled about the floor all day, without the inconvenience of too much food, or too much clothing. . . .'[8]

The Pettigrew case was a recent and well-publicized exposure of the evils of farming out; moreover, Pettigrew attributed most of the appalling disease and deformity he found to the pitifully inadequate feeding, and Dickens's emphasis falls on 'the tortures of slow starvation'[9] with the pathetic pointing of Oliver's well-known request 'Please, sir, I want some more.'[10] It would therefore seem more than likely that Dickens already knew of Pettigrew's work when Cruikshank, as he claims, mentioned it as the third episode fell due; and if Pettigrew's name was mentioned in conversation, it would seem, on the available evidence, as likely to have been introduced by Dickens as by Cruikshank. The fact that Pettigrew was a personal friend of Cruikshank's may, in retrospect, have enlarged Cruikshank's sense of his own role.

As to the change in Oliver's appearance, there is no reason to think that this involved any change of plan on Dickens's part. Although Oliver is (after infancy) first presented as 'a pale, thin child, somewhat diminutive in stature, and decidedly small in circumference'[11] there is no discrepancy between this and the fact that Oliver seemed to Sowerberry 'a very good-looking boy'.[12] If

Oliver were not good-looking, he would not have been chosen for a mute; and if he were not a mute, he would not have seen the pauper funeral, which was a real event, actually observed by Dickens,[13] and which was, presumably, the *raison d'être* of the Sowerberry section. And that section was evidently planned before the end of the second (March) number, when Bumble entrusted Oliver to Sowerberry.

Cruikshank argued that Dickens's original conception of Oliver's physique is conveyed in his surname; but Dickens, unlike the proposer of 'Frank Steadfast', could use names ironically (as with 'Bleak House'), and there is no suggestion in the first number that Oliver had any worse physical drawback than thinness and smallness. The only remaining evidence is the fact that Cruikshank himself did draw two different Olivers; but there is no clear reason why this change should not have been made at Dickens's insistence. It may perhaps be felt that Cruikshank, having a much simpler conception of art than Dickens, would have been unlikely to make his 'Steadfast' hero a 'queer kind of chap' on his own initiative; and it is not impossible, or even improbable, that Dickens should first have desiderated the 'queer kind of chap' that Cruikshank speaks of, and then, seeing this figure in the illustrations, have decided that 'a nice pretty little boy' would have won the novel a larger success; if Dickens did change his mind on this point, it must have been at an earlier stage than Cruikshank suggested, although Cruikshank's hostility to the 'queer kind of chap' may have contributed to the change. The case for Cruikshank does not deserve any stronger statement than this very qualified allowance.

With the fourth claim it would seem likely that Cruikshank is simply telling the truth when he says:

'I had, a long time previously to this, directed Mr. Dickens's attention to Field Lane, Holborn Hill, wherein resided many thieves and receivers of stolen goods, and it was suggested that one of these receivers, a Jew, should be introduced into the story; and upon one occasion Mr. Dickens and Mr. Harrison Ainsworth called upon me, and in course of conversation I then and there described and performed the character of one of these Jew receivers, who I had long had my eye upon; – and this was the origin of Fagan' [*sic*].

Although Dickens was dead, Ainsworth was still alive, and if this were a fabrication, Cruikshank would hardly have introduced Ainsworth, of all people, as the witness; and as Cruikshank noted,[14] neither at this time, nor in the subsequent controversy, did Ainsworth deny this episode (it ought perhaps to be added here that, in one account, Cruikshank copied his own face when he drew *Fagin in the Condemned Cell*: uncertain about Fagin's expression, he 'saw his face in a cheval glass' and exclaimed 'That's it! . . . That's just the expression I want!'[15]).

The fifth claim Cruikshank states thus:

[204]

'Long before *Oliver Twist* was ever thought of, I had, by permission of the City authorities, made a sketch of one of the condemned cells in Newgate prison; as I had a great object in letting the public see what sort of place these cells were, and how they were furnished, and also to show a wretched condemned criminal therein, I thought it desirable to introduce such a subject into this work; but I had the greatest difficulty to get Mr Dickens to allow me to carry out my wishes in this respect, but I said I must have either what is called a Christian or what is called a Jew in a condemned cell, and therefore it must be "Bill Sikes" or "Fagan," [*sic*] at length he allowed me to exhibit the latter.'

The most relevant document in this case is a drawing in the British Museum entitled 'Bill Sikes in the Condemned Cell' (74). The title implies that it must have been made before Sikes's death by misadventure was agreed upon; and this suggests that Cruikshank had conceived a climactic episode in a condemned cell before Dickens himself wrote his Newgate *tour de force* ('He cowered down upon his stone bed, and thought of the past'). Kitton mentions in passing the possibility that this claim is proved by the drawing,[16] but he does not pursue the point, while Professor Tillotson assumes that the sketch was made in response to Dickens's earliest intentions for Sikes: she says 'the existence of several studies for an illustration showing Sikes in the condemned cell indicates at least one change of plan'.[17] The drawing has received no other discussion.

The position is complicated by the existence of another sketch, titled 'First idea and sketch for Fagin in the Condemned Cell', reproduced by Kitton. While the Sikes sketch shows the same cell, seen from exactly the same point as the finished plate, the 'first idea' shows the cell from a different angle — we are facing Fagin — and Fagin's posture is quite different from that of the final Fagin and that of Sikes. On this evidence, the Sikes sketch comes between the 'first idea' (with Fagin) and the final plate (again with Fagin); the resulting sequence would imply a curious oscillation in Dickens's planning, if Cruikshank were following his instructions in each case. If Cruikshank were not following Dickens's instructions, then to draw Sikes in the cell, after Fagin had been decided upon, is peculiarly pointless.

The 'first idea', however, is probably not what it claims to be, and what Kitton took it for.[18] The sketches of Fagin are all small, and one of them has the ornamental surrounds of an elegant vignette; and there is a very similar Fagin on the cover of the monthly-part reissue of 1846. There are no ornamental surrounds like those in the sketch, but that sketch has under it the word 'Woodcut', and the cover was a woodcut while all the earlier illustrations had been etchings. The same sheet also has three small drawings with the captions 'Monks, Bumble, and wife', 'Rose and Nancy', and 'Noah and Fagin' respectively, and while these subjects do not occur in the woodcut cover, they do have the air of preliminary possibilities being considered for the cover. But if this drawing belongs to the cover of 1846, it follows that the present title arose either because Cruikshank had forgotten the original order of things, or because he was content to put things in a misleading way. The title is in black ink, while most of the drawing and the word 'woodcut' are in pencil or brown ink, so it is safe to conclude that where Cruikshank added titles to his drawings in a different medium, those titles are not reliable.[19]

The title of the Sikes sketch is also an addition in black ink to a pencil drawing, and at this stage it might be asked whether, after all, the condemned man *is* Sikes. For the man in the cell has a thin aquiline nose, while Sikes's nose is broken and flattened, and the man in the cell has short hair and a fringe, while Sikes has rough hair and two long dark wings of hair waving down his cheeks (75). These wings are his most striking characteristic in the etchings, and it is

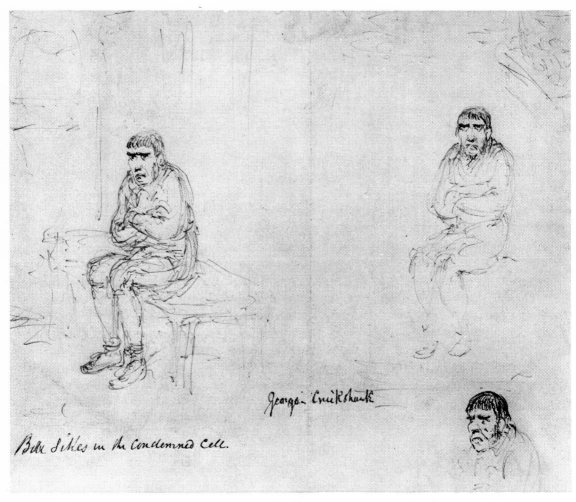

74. George Cruikshank, 'Bill Sikes in the Condemned Cell'.

[206]

curious that they should be missing from the condemned man. The man in the cell is not the Sikes of the other illustrations, and this fact raises the delicate question of Cruikshank's honesty, for the title of the drawing is plainly in Cruikshank's hand. Some kind of scruple, however, does inform Cruikshank's procedure, for if he really wished us to believe he had drawn Sikes in the cell

75. George Cruikshank, Bill Sikes.

before Dickens put Fagin there, he could easily have drawn a more plausible Sikes in that position. Evidently he drew the line at a deception that must have seemed, to his own mind, such a frank deception. A great artist's conscience would be most active in the art itself.

The corollary is that while Cruikshank's titles are compromised, the drawings themselves are authentic sketches belonging to the period when *Oliver Twist* was either being written, or being reissued. Presumably, therefore, the Sikes drawing was made before Fagin was sentenced; but this does not explain the identity of the condemned 'Sikes', who is clearly in the same cell that Fagin later entered. The difficulty could be resolved, however, by allowing that Cruikshank was telling the truth when he said that he had 'a great object in letting the public see what sort of places these cells were, and how they were furnished, and also to show a wretched condemned criminal therein'; and if it is also granted that Cruikshank had, as he claimed, already 'made a sketch of one of the condemned cells in Newgate prison' – this much may be inferred partly from the detail in the final plate. The Sikes drawing could then be placed as an early study of the 'wretched condemned criminal', made at a time when Cruikshank had no specific criminal in mind, with the lightly sketched but precise details of the cell taken from the original Newgate sketch. The similarity of arrangement suggests that Cruikshank consulted this drawing in preparing the Fagin design, although a further sketch also reproduced by Kitton (titled 'Fagin in the Condemned Cell'), shows that Cruikshank had experimented with a slightly different arrangement, closer to that used in the small study on the cover.[20]

If Cruikshank were meditating a Condemned Cell study before he started work on *Oliver Twist*, the subject-matter of the novel would have inclined him strongly to force it on Dickens's attention. Dickens did not need any introduction to the theme, for he had already, in *Sketches by Boz*, described an Old Bailey trial and condemnation (in 'Criminal Courts'), and the last night of a condemned man (in 'A Visit to Newgate'). Against this might be set the bad law by which Fagin is condemned. Dickens so manages the trial itself that we have no idea of the specific proceedings, and the only explanation offered is that of Kags:

76. George Cruikshank, 'Fagin in the Condemned Cell'.

'"The sessions are on ... if they get the inquest over; if Bolter turns King's evidence, as of course he will from what he's said already – and they can prove Fagin an accessory before the fact, and get the trial on on Friday, he'll swing in six days from this, by G – !"'[21]

As a contemporary reviewer noted,[22] if Bolter told all, he could only report that Fagin urged caution: '"You won't be – too – violent, Bill?"' (although 'there was a fire in the eyes of both which could not be mistaken').[23] Fagin could not be hanged for his words, and the fire in his eyes is scarcely admissible evidence. Professor Collins observes that 'Dickens's knowledge of the law was never at all professional',[24] but in Fagin's case the legal aberration sounds the result rather of bad planning than of ignorance. Professor Collins's book shows that Dickens had an intense and lifelong interest in the law; if, all through the novel, Dickens had intended Fagin for the condemned cell, we would expect him to have provided Fagin with some more substantial crime. Professor Tillotson notes that Dickens was very late in working out the details of the novel's conclusion, and she assumes the hanging of Fagin could have been a late decision.[25]

In fairness to Cruikshank, it ought therefore to be allowed that he may well have wanted and suggested the Condemned Cell climax on his own account, and also that Dickens may well have decided on Fagin's form of death only at a late stage in writing the novel. There is not the slightest evidence, however, that if Dickens did revise his plans in this way, he was at all influenced by Cruikshank. It perhaps speaks for Cruikshank that he etched the Condemned Cell plate with the finest intensity of his art, while no other illustration in the novel engaged his genius to the same extent; and it may be that this subject allowed Cruikshank to express finally and consummately a theme that had been burning hotter within him over a period of time. Equally, however, this theme was burning in Dickens's mind, for not only had he devoted his own intensity to it in 'A Visit to Newgate', but he had also paid a second visit to that prison in April 1837, and the condemned forger whom he saw on this occasion, Thomas Wainewright, haunted him strongly enough to colour the portrayal of Julius Slinkton in *Hunted Down* and Rigaud in *Little Dorrit*.[26] Dickens did not need Cruikshank's suggestions, and there is no likelihood that he heeded them. If, however, Cruikshank *had* suggested such a climax, he may well have believed quite genuinely that he had some responsibility for Fagin's form of death, and the mis-titling of the drawings might then have seemed to him a slight illicit emphasis rather than a lie. The whole episode illustrates the futile complexities into which a determined ego may drive itself when it tries, after the event, to reshape reality so as to make an injury that has been hard to bear emerge, somehow, as a secret triumph, and to impose conviction not so much on the world, as on itself; to call this delusion is to oversimplify.

It is not on this note, however, that one should conclude a discussion of

Dickens's relationship with Cruikshank. Both men were so rich in character that it is easy, in discussing their partnership, to be drawn aside into various issues of personality. But it is the illustrations that matter, and they matter not as historical documents, but as pictures that can collaborate profoundly with a text. The *Twist* illustrations have suffered too much from Chesterton's comment on what he believed to be pinched and morbid drawing. He said of 'Fagin in the condemned Cell' (76) that 'it is not drawn with the free lines of a free man; it has the half-witted secrecies of a hunted thief. It does not look merely like a picture of Fagin; it looks like a picture by Fagin.'[27] To bear Chesterton out, all that could be said of the actual linework is that the cross-hatching is very close. But it needs to be close to give the shadows in the cell their proper depth; the actual drawing of the lines proves, on inspection, to be not scratched, furtive, or niggling, but, on the contrary, rapid, confident, and firm. The relative tones in the cell are beautifully controlled, with a sensitivity which, while common in Cruikshank's work, could scarcely be found among 'the half-witted secrecies of a hunted thief'. The cell is, for a condemned cell, unexpectedly light and spacious, and the furniture is solid and clear. Fagin certainly has his intensity as a doubled-up, shrunken figure, aghast; but that intensity comes partly from the contrast between Fagin, in his hunched smallness and darkness, and the calm, firm cell. The character of the linework in which Fagin is drawn does not differ noticeably from that of the cell, though, since Fagin is darker, the hatching is more dense; and in any case, it is the whole picture, with its ordered contrasts, that expresses the sensibility of the artist.

If the drawing of Fagin's head and hand does not seem criminal, however, it does convey a suggestion of caricature. We recall the illustrator's background in the satiric print. But here the education in caricature merely makes possible a simplification that is an intensification. The Fagin of the plate is not a revelation of mania, but a success in dramatic characterization. The plate corresponds to and enriches the novelist's text, without in any way tending to usurp the function of the novelist – but, equally, without being at all inferior to the text. The drawing complements the novel by giving a visible, lasting emphasis to Fagin's end, while the story itself moves forward. The plate is justly admired as a classic illustration to fiction.

APPENDIX III

The Siege of the Tower

'While the siege was thus vigorously carried on, on the north and south, the western side of the fortress was not neglected. Remaining at Cornhill for some hours, Wyat divided his forces into two detachments, and committed one to Captain Bret, whom he directed to proceed to the upper part of Tower Hill, along Lombard-street, Fenchurch-street and Tower-street and to place his men within the churchyard of All-Hallows Barking, and at the rear of the scaffold on Tower Hill; while with the other he himself marched down Gracechurch-street, along Thames-street, taking up a position before the Bulwark Gate.

'As soon as he had reached this point, and arranged his men, he rode off to Bret, and ordered a party, commanded by Captain Cobham, to attack the postern-gate, as before related. Bret was to hold himself in readiness to march down to the Bulwark Gate, or to attack the Leg Mount, a bastion at the north-west angle of the fortress, corresponding (though of somewhat smaller size), with the Brass Mount, as he should receive instructions.

'Having issued these directions, Wyat rode back to his troops — he was now mounted, as were several of his officers, on the steeds captured in the recent skirmish with the Earl of Pembroke — and commanded them to remain perfectly quiet till Admiral Winter's squadron should arrive off the Tower. His injunctions were strictly obeyed, and such perfect silence was observed, that though his men were drawn up within a few yards of the fortress, they were not discovered by the sentinels.

'On the arrival of the squadron, Wyat immediately commenced an attack upon the Bulwark Gate — one of the weakest out-works of the fortress, — and while directing his engines against it, some half-dozen wooden houses adjoining it on the side of the moat, were fired by his men; and the flames quickly extending to the buildings immediately contiguous to the Bulwark Gate, that defence was at once surrendered.

'The first point gained, Wyat despatched a messenger to Bret ordering him to join him instantly; and while a handful of his men, rushing round the semicircular wall, heretofore described as protecting the lesser moat, attacked the embattled gateway fronting the Lions' Tower, with the intention of joining Suffolk's party on the wharf, he directed his main force against the Lion's Gate. This fortification was stoutly defended, and the insurgents were twice repulsed before they could bring their engines to bear against it.

'Bret and his party having arrived, such an irresistible attack was made upon the gate, that in a short time it was carried. With loud shouts, the insurgents drove the royalists before them along the narrow bridge facing the Lions' Tower, and leading to the Middle Tower, putting some to the sword, and throwing others over the walls into the moat.

'The movement was so expeditious, and the rout so unexpected, that the portcullis of the Middle Tower, which was kept up to allow the flying men to pass through it, could not be lowered, and hastily directing those around him to prop it up with a piece of timber, Wyat continued the pursuit to the By-ward Tower.

'Hitherto, complete success had attended his efforts; and if he had passed the fortification he was approaching, in all probability he would have been master of the Tower. Nothing doubting this, he urged his men onwards. On his left rode Bret, and behind them, at a short distance, came Captain Knevet, and two other leaders, likewise on horseback.

'As they arrived within a few paces of the By-ward Tower, three tremendous personages issued from it, and opposed their further progress. They were equipped in corslets of polished steel and morions; and two of them were armed with bucklers and enormous maces, while the third wielded a partizan of equal size. These, it is almost needless to state, were the three giants. The bearer of the partizan was Gog. Behind them came their diminutive attendant, who, it appeared, had been released from his thraldom, particulars of which, and of his adventures subsequent to his meeting with Cicely in the cell beneath the Salt Tower, will be related at a more convenient opportunity.

'Like his gigantic companions, Xit was fully armed, in a steel corslet, cuisses, and gauntlets. His head was sheltered by a helmet, shaded by an immense plume of feathers, which, being considerably too large for him, almost eclipsed his features. He was furthermore provided with a sword almost as long as himself, and a buckler.

'Taking care to keep under the shelter of the giants, Xit strutted about, and brandishing his sword in a valiant manner, shouted, or rather screamed, –

'"Upon them Og! – attack them Gog! – why do you stand still, Magog? Let me pass, and I will show you how you should demean yourselves in the fight!"

'At the sight of the giants, the flying royalists rallied, and a fierce but ineffectual struggle took place. During it, Bret was dismounted and thrown into the moat. Urged by their leader, the insurgents pressed furiously forward. But the giants presented an impassable barrier. Og plied his mace with as much zeal as he did the clubs when he enacted the part of the Tower at Courtenay's masque, and with far more terrible effect. All avoided the sweep of his arm.

'Not content with dealing blows, he dashed among the retreating foe, and hurled some dozen of them into the moat. His prowess excited universal terror and astonishment. Nor was Gog much behind him. Wherever his partizan descended, a foe fell beneath its weight; and as he was incessantly whirling it over his head, and bringing it down, a space was speedily cleared before him.

'Seeing the havoc occasioned by the gigantic brethren, and finding that they completely checked his further advance, Wyat struck spurs into his charger, and dashing upon Magog, tried to hew him down. If the married giant had not caught the blow aimed at him upon his shield, Dame Placida had been made a widow for the second time. Again plunging the spurs rowel-deep into his horse's flanks, Wyat would have ridden over his gigantic antagonist, if the latter, perceiving his intention, had not raised his mace, and with one tremendous blow smashed the skull of the noble animal.

'"Yield you, Sir Thomas Wyat," cried Magog, rushing up to the knight, who was borne to the ground with his slaughtered charger — "you are my prisoner."

'"Back, caitiff!" cried Wyat, disengaging himself and attacking the giant; "I will never yield with life."

'Wyat, however, would have been speedily captured by the giant, if Knevet, seeing his perilous situation, had not pressed forward with several others to his assistance, and rescued him. This accident, however, enabled the retreating party to pass beneath the archway of the By-ward Tower, the portcullis of which was instantly lowered.

'Meanwhile, a body of the insurgents having taken possession of the Middle Tower, had planted themselves at the various loop-holes, and on the roof, and kept up a constant fire on the soldiers stationed on the summit of the By-ward Tower.

'Among those who contrived to distinguish themselves in the action was Xit. Finding his position one of more danger than he had anticipated, he scrambled upon the wall on the right of the By-ward Tower, where, being out of the rush, he could defy at his ease those who were swimming in the moat.

'While he was in this situation, Bret, who, it has been mentioned, was thrown into the moat, swam to the wall, and endeavoured to ascend it. Xit immediately attacked him, and adopting the language of Magog to Wyat, threatened to throw him back again if he did not yield.

'"I do yield", replied Bret.

'"Your name and rank?" demanded the dwarf, in an authoritative tone.

'"Alexander Bret, captain of the London Trained Bands, second in command to Sir Thomas Wyat", replied the other.

'"Here, Magog — Gog — Og — help!" shouted Xit — "I have taken a prisoner. It is Captain Bret, one of the rebel leaders — Help him out of the moat, and let us carry him before the queen! I am certain to be knighted for my valour. Mind, *I* have taken him. He has yielded to me. No one else has had a hand in his capture."'

William Harrison Ainsworth, *The Tower of London* (London, 1840), Book the Second, Chapter XXIX, pp. 316–20.

Notes

The following abbreviations are used in the notes:

Letters – *The Letters of Charles Dickens*, ed. M. House and G. Storey (The Pilgrim Edition, Oxford, i, 1965; ii, 1969).
Nonesuch – *The Letters of Dickens*, ed. W. Dexter (The Nonesuch Dickens, London, 1938).
D — *The Dickensian*.

CHAPTER I

1. Quoted by S. M. Ellis in *William Harrison Ainsworth and his Friends* (London, 1911), i, p. 313.
2. 10 March 1847, *Nonesuch*, ii, pp. 17–18. This letter decisively refutes Kentley Bromhill's claim that 'we do know from the correspondence that is available that [Browne] chose his own subjects in the book for illustration, and that he wrote the captions himself' ('Phiz's Illustrations to *Dombey and Son*', D, XXXVIII, 264 [1942], p. 221).
3. This is not to say that illustrations may not be found in three-volume novels. Mrs Trollope, for instance, experimented with illustrations in the late 1830s, and used the etchings of A. Hervieu in *The Life and Adventures of Jonathan Jefferson Whitlaw* (1836); and such novels as *Michael Armstrong* (1839–40) and *The Widow Married* (1839–40) which were illustrated in their original serial publication, kept their illustrations when reprinted in volume form. But Mrs Trollope ignored illustration completely in her novels after 1845, and the bulk of her output comes after that date; so that the illustrations in her novels are exceptions that prove the rule.
4. Letter to Cadell, 24 March 1831, *The Letters of Sir Walter Scott*, ed. H. J. C. Grierson (London, 1932–7), xi, pp. 493–4.
5. Letter to Mrs Hughes, 9/10 October, 1828, *ibid.*, p. 7.
6. Letter from Cadell to Scott, 28 March 1831, *ibid.*, p. 493n.
7. Agreement of 19 Jan. 1842 for W. H. Maxwell's *Hector O'Halloran*; cf. Agreement with Albert Smith for *Christoper Tadpole*, 10 Aug. 1846: 'it is also mutually agreed . . . that each monthly part shall be so written as to furnish the designer with two effective subjects for pictorial illustration in good and sufficient time to enable him to produce Etchings of the same on steel plates – so that a sufficient number of impressions therefrom can be worked off in time for publication by the 28th day of every month . . .' (The Bentley Papers, in the British Museum, Department of Manuscripts).

8. Letter to Spencer, Dec. 1838, quoted by E. Downey in *Charles Lever His Life in his Letters* (London, 1906), i, p. 107.

9. Letter quoted by R. S. Surtees and E. D. Cuming in *Robert Smith Surtees* (London, 1924), p. 247. Surtees himself felt that the Sponge series, published in Ainsworth's *New Sporting Magazine*, contained 'the substance for a good sporting tale, which Mr Leech's illustrations will, I think, make sell' (*ibid.*, p. 248).

10. *The Quarterly Review*, lix, CXVIII (Oct. 1837), p. 497.

11. *loc. cit.*

12. G. K. Chesterton, *Charles Dickens*, (London, 1906), p. 94; Stephen Marcus, *Dickens: from Pickwick to Dombey* (London, 1965), Chapter I.

13. 'A Piece of China', Jan. 1844, p. 344.

14. *The Finish to Tom and Jerry* (London, 1869 – the earliest edition in the British Museum), p. 82.

15. Thomas Sibson professed astonishment that 'these papers, thus arranged, bursting as they are with incident, and intoxicated as they are with wit, must have come before the public without illustrations for many of their most striking scenes', Preface to *Sibson's Racy Sketches of Expeditions, from the Pickwick Club* (London, 1838).

16. Announcement of *Thirty-Two Illustrations to the Posthumous Papers of the Pickwick Club* by 'Mr Samuel Weller' (Thomas Onwhyn), (London, 1837); quoted by J. Grego in *Pictorial Pickwickiana* (London, 1899). i, p. 372.

17. Preface to First Cheap Edition, 1847.

18. Thackeray recalls the portfolios of caricatures in his review of Leech's *Pictures of Life and Character*, *The Quarterly Review*, xcvi, CXCI (Dec. 1854), especially p. 78.

19. The drunkard in a wheelbarrow is a familiar figure in graphic satire, and is also to be seen in, for instance, 'Gin Lane'.

20. *Glances back through Seventy Years* (London, 1893), i, p. 123.

21. Article I, *Westminster Review*, XXXIV (June 1840), pp. 6–7.

22. The kind of text expected by Dickens's publishers can be seen in 'Alfred Crowquill's' Cockney accompaniment to *Seymour's Sketches* (London, 1838).

23. Letter of 31 May 1834, quoted by Ellis, *op. cit.*, i, p. 267.

24. Letter to Macrone, quoted by Ellis, *ibid.*, i, p. 312.

25. Letter to Seymour, 14 April 1836, *Letters*, i, p. 146.

26. Written on Browne's sketch, *Letters*, i, p. 242.

27. F. G. Kitton, *Dickens and his Illustrators* (London, 1899), p. 71.

28. Letter to Bentley, 14 July 1837, *Letters*, i, p. 283.

29. See, for instance, the review of *Pickwick* in the *Eclectic Review*, April 1837, p. 339; reviewers normally settled for the non-committal term 'periodical' (e.g. *Spectator*, 16 April 1836, p. 373).

30. Agreement of 4 Nov. 1836 (Bentley Papers).

31. Agreement with Henry Cockton for 'The Modern Rake's Progress', 8 Nov. 1839 (Bentley Papers).

32. *ibid.*, item 5.

33. *Novels of the Eighteen Forties* (Oxford, 1954), p. 29.

34. Agreement of 19 Jan. 1842 (Bentley Papers).

35. Letter to Alexander Spencer, 12 Nov. 1838, quoted by Downey, *op. cit.*, i, p. 104.

36. Agreement with W. H. Maxwell, 19 Jan. 1842 (Bentley Papers).

37. Quoted by Surtees and Cuming, *op. cit.*, p. 221.

38. See *Fraser's Magazine*, xviii, CVI (Oct. 1838), pp. 481–8.

39. Letter to Dickens, Feb/March 1841 (Pilgrim Files).

40. See W. Bates, *George Cruikshank* (Birmingham, 1878), pp. 24–5.

41. *Quarterly Review*, lix, CXVIII (Oct. 1837), p. 484.

42. *London and Westminster Review* (July 1837), p. 213.

43. *Monthly Magazine*, New Series, iii, 15 (March 1840), p, 232.

44. 'The shilling number presently had a rival in the shilling magazine, which ran several novels as serials . . . giving better value and soon driving the monthly numbers out of the field.' Q. D. Leavis, *Fiction and the Reading Public* (London, 1932), p. 153.

45. It should be said that most magazines were more expensive than serial parts at this date, but the difference between 1*s*. and, say, 1*s*. 6*d*. (the price of *Ainsworth's Magazine*) could hardly have been the decisive factor. When Ainsworth increased his price to 2*s*. his growing circulation continued to grow (Ellis, *op. cit.*, ii, pp. 15–16).

CHAPTER 2

1. Book iv, lines 631–6.

2. Book iv, lines 71–84.

3. Gillray's respect for Pope is indicated in 'Old Wisdom Blinking at the Stars' (10 March 1782, reproduced by M. D. George in *Hogarth to Cruikshank: Social Change in Graphic Satire* [London, 1967], Fig. 119) where Pope, and Milton behind him, are the two named stars at whom an owlish Johnson is blinking.

4. See R. E. Moore, *Hogarth's Literary Relationships* (London, 1948), p. 22.

5. That the antipathy to Johnson (see Note 3 above) was the result of a strong interest in literature can be seen in the plate 'Apollo and the Muses, inflicting Penance on Dr Pomposo, round Parnassus' (also reproduced by M. D. George, *op. cit.*, Fig. 121), in which Johnson, being scourged by the Muses wears a Dunce's cap bearing the names of the poets he has abused: Milton, Otway, Waller, Gray, Shenstone, and Lyttelton. Johnson's confessional placard tells us where Gillray himself stands: 'For defaming that Genius I could never emulate, by criticism without Judgement. . . .' Criticism *with* Judgement is clearly what the artist offers. Gillray is at pains to be fair, even though he has to use the somewhat clumsy device of two winged books: an open one, on Envy, 'dedicated to Dr. Johnson as an Author', and a closed one on the Milk of Human-kindness 'dedicated to Dr. Johnson as a Man'. Judgement is not a common quality in caricature, but Gillray grew up working for an 18th-century public in which the various standards of Taste and Judgement were presumably represented.

6. *London und Paris* (Weimar, 1806); quoted by Draper Hill in *James Gillray 1756–1815* (London, 1967), p. 11.

7. 'Shakespeare-Sacrificed', 20 June 1789; 'a peep into the Shakespeare-Gallery', 26 April 1791.

8. 'The works of [Rowlandson and Gillray] were so frequently based on Hogarth, that they cannot be imagined without him in so far as raw material is concerned,' F. Antal, *Hogarth, and his place in European Art* (London, 1962), p. 184; Antal discusses in detail the debt of English caricature to Hogarth.

9. The use of Gillray's characteristic manipulations by other artists can be studied conveniently in M. D. George, *op. cit.*, Figs. 164, 174, and 196.

10. See Bates, *op. cit.*, p. 11.

11. e.g. 'John Bull's Progress', 3 June 1793.

12. In addition to his *magna opera* in this form, *The Bottle* and *The Drunkard's Children*, Cruikshank produced, in a lighter vein, *The Bachelor's Own Book or the Progress of Mr. Lambkin (Gent) in the Pursuit of Pleasure and Amusement* (1844), 'The Sailor's Progress' (1819), and 'The Progress of

a Midshipman exemplified in the career of Master Blockhead '(1835). Robert Seymour produced a *Drunkard's Progress* and a *Pugilist's Progress*.

13. See, however, Dickens's discussion of *The Drunkard's Children*, *The Examiner*, 8 July 1848, p. 436.

14. 'Lectures on the Fine Arts. No. 1,' *Blackwood's Edinburgh Magazine*, lxxviii, XIV (July 1823), p. 18.

15. *The Morning Chronicle*, 11 Feb. 1836, third page.

16. F. Wedmore, quoted by W. B. Jerrold, in *The Life of George Cruikshank* (London, 1882), ii, p. 98.

17. *The Quarterly Review*, lxiv, CXXVII (June 1839), p. 102.

18. Letter to M. Feuillet de Couches, 3 Dec. 1847, in Yale University Library.

19. *Anecdotes of William Hogarth, written by himself*, ed. J. B. Nichols (London, 1833), p. 64.

20. Cruikshank wrote 'interesting' on Scollier's letter of 10 Dec. 1847 (George Cruikshank Collection in the University of Virginia Library).

21. Augustus and Henry Mayhew, *The Greatest Plague of Life* (London, 1847), p. 10.

22. *ibid.*, pp. 13–14.

23. Letter of 14 Dec. 1843 (George Cruikshank Collection in the University of Virginia Library).

24. Letter to Macrone, 11 Oct. 1836; *Letters*, i, p. 183n.

25. Letter to Macrone, ?19 Oct. 1836; *Letters*, i. p. 183.

26. Letter to Bentley, ?18 Jan. 1837; *Letters*, i, p. 224.

27. Letter to Cruikshank, ?13 Oct. 1837; *Letters*, i, p. 319.

28. Letter to Cruikshank, ?6 Oct. 1838; *Letters*, i, p. 440.

29. See letter to Cruikshank, 9 Nov. 1838, and Forster's letter to Bentley of previous day, *Letters*, i, pp. 450–1.

30. *The Examiner*, 14 Oct. 1843, p. 645.

31. *The Sunday Times*, 21 Feb. 1836.

32. *The News and Sunday Herald*, 21 Feb. 1836.

33. *The Spectator*, 26 Dec. 1836, p. 1234.

34. *George Cruikshank's Omnibus* (1841–2), *George Cruikshank's Table Book* (1845), *George Cruikshank's Magazine* (1854). *The Comic Almanack*, of which Cruikshank was the principal contributor, had more success, and appeared between 1834 and 1853.

35. *The Times*, 9 April 1872, p. 12.

36. *The Times*, 11 April 1872, p. 12.

37. *The Times*, 13 April 1872, p. 10.

38. Epoch the Third, Chapter VII; *Bentley's Miscellany*, vi (1839), p. 126.

39. Epoch the Third, Chapter VIII; *Bentley's Miscellany*, vi (1839), p. 136.

40. 'A Few Words about George Cruikshank' ('Mr Ainsworth's final explanation, adressed to *B.J.* for publication'), Jerrold, *op. cit.*, i, p. 259.

41. *ibid.*, p. 264.

42. Letter from Ainsworth to Cruikshank, 20 Dec. 1838, quoted by permission of the Widener Collection in the Harvard College Library.

43. He praised especially 'Jonathan Wild discovers Darrell in the loft' ('I have just seen the plates. . . . They are admirable. The loft is one of the most striking scenes even *you* have produced . . .' letter to Cruikshank, 24 Dec. 1838, quoted by permission of the Widener Collection in the Harvard College Library).

44. Of this novel Cruikshank merely said 'No. 3. "Guy Fawkes", suggested by Mr Ainsworth, and illustrated by me, and published in "Bentley's Miscellany".' Here again Cruikshank is modest, for he had decided the precise way in which one of the principal characters dies. He had written to Ainsworth:

'I send you a rough tracing of the only subject which occurs to me out of your account of the attack on "Holbeach." I have supposed Catesby to stagger into the vestibule – and drop dead at the feet of the Virgin (sword broken), – he is followed by Sir John Walsh, (or any body else you like) – *pistol in one hand – fighting* going on in the courtyard. The title might be *The Death of Catesby.*

'If I do not hear from you I shall conclude that I am to go on with it.' (Letter to Ainsworth dated 'Waterloo day – 1841,' in the Collection of the Brown, Picton and Hornby Libraries, Liverpool.)

The title and the text follow Cruikshank's suggestions.

45. Memorandum of Agreement of 19 Nov. 1839 between W. H. Ainsworth, G. Cruikshank, and R. Bentley (Bentley Papers).

46. Ainsworth's biographer, S. M. Ellis, dealt with Cruikshank's claim simply by quoting a letter in which Ainsworth asks Cruikshank to make topographical studies of several parts of the Tower (*op. cit.*, ii, p. 92). But such a request shows no more than that Ainsworth had decided on the settings for the ensuing episodes; it does not disprove Cruikshank's claim that he used to send Ainsworth drawings '*in order that he might write up to them*, and that they should be *accurately described*,' and the evidence of such letters must be weighed against that of the letters concerning the By Ward Tower.

47. Letter (HM 12786) reproduced by permission of The Huntington Library, San Marino, California.

48. Letter (HM 12787) reproduced by permission of The Huntington Library, San Marino, California.

49. Letter to Ainsworth in the Manuscripts Department, Division of Special Collections, Stanford University Libraries, Stanford, California.

50. Book the Second, Chapter XXXIII.

51. Letter quoted by permission of the Widener Collection in Harvard College Library.

52. Book the Second, last chapter.

53. With the following novel, *Old St Paul's*, Ellis allows that 'in the absence of any contradiction from Ainsworth, we may grant that Cruikshank did suggest the idea of a book dealing with the Plague and the Fire. . .' (*op. cit.*, ii, p. 97). The claim for *The Miser's Daughter* he rejects out of hand, as having been conclusively refuted by Ainsworth; but all Ainsworth did in his refutation was to quote his Preface for the cheap edition of 1850. In the Preface, he underlines the moral of the Miser's story, but says nothing about the origin of that part of the novel. He challenges Cruikshank with this Preface in mind: 'If Cruikshank had any claim to the authorship of the tale, why did he not make it then?' ('A Few Words about George Cruikshank', Jerrold, *op. cit.*, i, p. 259). But there was nothing in it that Cruikshank need have objected to. Ainsworth did record there one change of plan in the novel, but since this change concerned an original Jacobite theme which did not involve the theme of avarice, changes here could not confute Cruikshank's claim to have originated the story of the Miser. Assuming that Ainsworth *did* originate the novels in question, he made out a very weak case; but this does not, of course, prove Cruikshank's claims.

54. 'A Few Words about Cruikshank', Jerrold, *op. cit.*, i, p. 264.

55. *loc. cit.*

56. See Appendix II.

CHAPTER 3

1. The affinity with Hogarth has been noted by many critics; see, for instance, George Gissing,

Charles Dickens, A Critical Study (London, 1898), p. 32, and Introduction to *Barnaby Rudge* in the Rochester Edition, p. xix; G. K. Chesterton, *Appreciations and Criticisms of the Works of Charles Dickens* (London, 1911), p. 42; Osbert Sitwell, *Dickens* (London, 1932), p. 36; F. R. Leavis, 'Dombey and Son', *The Sewanee Review*, lxx, I (Jan.–Mar. 1962), c.p. 196.

2. Hogarth's influence on 18th-century fiction and drama is discussed by R. E. Moore, *op. cit.*

3. *Tom Jones*, i, Chapter 11.

4. *Charles Chesterfield* (London, 1841), i, p. 277; cf. 'Paul Pry,' *Oddities of London Life* (London, 1838), ii, p. 4.

5. Letter to Crossley, quoted by Ellis, *op. cit.*, i, p. 328.

6. *ibid.*, i, p. 374.

7. *Bentley's Miscellany*, vi (1839), Epoch the Third, Chapter XVI, p. 448.

8. *Bentley's Miscellany*, v (1839), Epoch the Second, Chapter I, p. 227.

9. Ellis, *op. cit.*, i, p. 381.

10. e.g. G. W. M. Reynolds's *The Drunkard's Progress* (1841); with *Jack Sheppard* had appeared in *Bentley's Miscellany* a novel by Henry Cockton called *Stanley Thorn* which had originally been projected by R. H. Barham under the title 'The Modern Rake's Progress'.

11. cf. George, *op. cit.*, p. 52.

12. [C. White], *The Married Unmarried* (London, 1837), iii, p. 26.

13. 'On the Genius and Character of Hogarth', *The Reflector*, No. 3, (1811), p. 62.

14. '[Hogarth's] merits are indeed so prominent, and have been so often discussed, that it may be thought difficult to point out any new beauties; but, in fact, they contain so much truth of nature, they present the objects to the eye under so many aspects and bearings, admit of so many constructions, and are so pregnant with meaning, that the subject is in a manner inexhaustible.' 'On Hogarth's Marriage a-la-Mode', *The Examiner*, 5 June 1814, p. 366.

15. *The Examiner*, 19 June, 1814, p. 399.

16. As Antal notes (*op. cit.*, pp. 186–7) the view of Lamb and Hazlitt was not necessarily entertained by Royal Academicians; but Walpole, Lamb, and Hazlitt belonged primarily to literature, and their judgement might be expected to dominate literary circles. Lamb's essay was implicitly praised by Dickens when reviewing Cruikshank's *The Drunkard's Children* (*The Examiner*, 8 July 1848, p. 436), and Dickens had in his library the collection of Hazlitt's essays containing the papers on Hogarth. He had a large collection of Hogarths in the hall at Gadshill Place; he also owned the 1726 edition of *Hudibras* with Hogarth's illustrations (see J. H. Stonehouse, ed., *Reprints of the Catalogues of the Libraries of Charles Dickens and W. M. Thackeray* [London, 1935]). It is clear, moreover, that his knowledge of Hogarth was not confined to the plates he possessed, for in his re-review of *The Drunkard's Children* he mentions with evident familiarity 'the detestable advances in the Stages of Cruelty' and the election plates; the influence of the election series is shown in *Pickwick* when Dickens names his election-town 'Eatanswill', emphasizing gluttony in the same way that Hogarth's 'Guzzledown' does.

17. *The Edinburgh Review*, lxviii, CXXXVII (Oct. 1838), p. 77; *The Examiner*, 4 Dec. 1836, p. 776; 3 June 1838, p. 339; 6 Jan. 1839, p. 4; 4 Dec. 1841, p. 773. The *Edinburgh Review* article was by T. H. Lister; another writer for that magazine, Sidney Smith, said in a letter to a friend 'the soul of Hogarth has migrated into the Body of Mr Dickens' (see *Letters*, i, p. 431n).

18. Dickens said in the Preface that he 'had read of thieves by scores' but 'had never met (except in HOGARTH) with the miserable reality'. He presumably had in mind, above all, the 'Night Cellar' in which Thomas Idle is betrayed. Fagin's kitchen is just such a communal den of thieves, 'black with age and dirt', with its fire, deal table, spirit-drinking, and pipe-smoking; it is there that the stolen

goods are brought, counted, and fought over; and there that the Harlots come to visit. There is also a striking similarity between the Artful Dodger and his associates – 'four or five boys . . . smoking long clay pipes and drinking spirits with all the air of middle-aged men' – and the gambling urchins in the foreground of the fourth plate of *The Rake's Progress*. One of them is picking the Rake's pocket, and taking his handkerchief (Fagin's apprentices did a large trade in 'wipes'); one smokes a clay pipe; there is a spirit-glass in the foreground; and 'the air of middle-aged men' is caught with wonderful precision. The group is rendered with amused delight in the precocity of criminal urchins, and it is with just such delight that Dickens renders the Dodger.

19. J. Forster, *The Life of Charles Dickens*, ed. J. W. T. Ley (London, 1928), Book iv, I, p. 291.
20. Quoted by Forster, *ibid.*, Book vi, II, p. 479.
21. Letter to Forster, 25 July 1846; NL, I, p. 771.
22. Chapters XLVI and LVIII.
23. 15 Jan. 1841, and see also letter of 25 Nov. 1840; *Letters*, ii, pp. 154–7, 185–7.
24. Forster, *op. cit.*, Book vi, III, pp. 490–1.
25. *English Graphic Satire* (London, 1874), p. 87.
26. *Dickens: The Dreamer's Stance* (New York, 1965), p. 60.
27. *ibid.*, p. 19.
28. For a fuller analysis of the first plate of *Marriage-à-la-Mode* see W. M. Thackeray, *The English Humourists of the Eighteenth Century* (second edition, revised, London, 1853), p. 223.
29. *The Examiner*, 8 July 1848, p. 436.
30. Chapter XX.
31. Stoehr, *op. cit.*, pp. 16–17; the reference is to H. A. Taine, 'The Novel – Dickens', *History of English Literature*, trans. H. Van Laun (Edinburgh, 1871), ii, p. 344.
32. J. C. Reid, *The Hidden World of Charles Dickens* (Auckland, 1962), pp. 31–2.
33. *Joseph Andrews*, i, Chapter XIII.
34. Moore, *op. cit.*, Chapter IV.
35. G. Santayana, 'Charles Dickens,' *Soliloquies in England and Later Soliloquies* (London, 1922), p. 65.
36. *The Examiner*, 30 Dec. 1848, p. 838.
37. Even in 1850, two years after the Leech review, he acquired the new edition of 600 prints by Gillray which appeared in that year; see Stonehouse, *op. cit.*, p. 50.
38. 'Dickens's Uses of Animism', *Nineteenth Century Fiction*, VII, 4 (March 1953), p. 283.
39. There is also a gigantic animated guillotine, breathing fire, in 'A Radical Reformer', 17 Sept. 1819, to be seen in the British Museum.
40. *The Westminster Review*, XXXIV (June 1840), p. 6.
41. *Nickleby*, Chapter XXXII. In 'Mr. Pickwick and *The Dance of Death*' (*Nineteenth Century Fiction*, XIV, 2 [Sept. 1959], pp. 171–2) Lauriat Lane Jr. suggests that Dickens is here thinking of Holbein. Only the references 'motley dance' and 'stern moral' support this view, and the first is dubious, since although Holbein's series was referred to as 'The *Dance* of Death' few of the figures are actually dancing. Nor are there, in Holbein's series, such 'fantastic groups' as Dickens describes. Holbein merely shows people in various walks of life encountering a skeleton, while Dickens imagines a scene of teeming activity in which not skeletons but animated objects dance. Bruegel's engravings were current in 18th-century England and provided Hogarth with a number of models (see Antal, *op. cit.*, pp. 30, 141, 164–5, 167) and it is to be presumed that some could still be seen in the print-shops of the early nineteenth century.
42. See Lauriat Lane, Jr., 'The Devil in *Oliver Twist*', D, LII, 319 (June 1956), pp. 132–6.

43. *Charles Dickens*, p. 283.

44. Art. III, *The Quarterly Review*, xcvi, CXCI (Dec. 1854), p. 79.

45. See *Letters*, i, p. 9n.

46. 'Man into Beast in Dickensian Caricature', *University of Toronto Quarterly*, XXXI, 3 (April 1962) p. 354.

CHAPTER 4

1. See G. N. Ray, *Thackeray: The Uses of Adversity* (London, 1955), p. 189; see also Thackeray's speech at the Royal Academy Dinner, 1858, which is to be found in L. Melville's *William Makepeace Thackeray* (London, 1910), ii, pp. 115–16.

2. Ray, *op. cit.*, p. 172.

3. 'Thackeray as Draughtsman', *Scribner's Monthly*, XX, 2 (June 1880), p. 258. Sturgis is discussing *The Paris Sketch Book*, and it should be said that his opinion of the *Vanity Fair* illustrations is very much higher.

4. *The Examiner*, 16 Dec. 1854, p. 797.

5. *The Spectator*, 16 Dec. 1854, p. 1330.

6. *The Morning Chronicle*, 28 Dec. 1854, p. 7.

7. 'Thackeray's "Vanity Fair"', *A Review of English Studies*, vi, 1 (Jan. 1965), pp. 19–38.

8. See Stevens, *ibid.*, pp. 35–6.

9. Letter to W. S. Williams, 11 March 1848; *The Brontës, Life and Letters*, ed. Clement Shorter (London, 1908), I, p. 402.

10. Thackeray's intimate knowledge of the works of Hogarth and the caricaturists is apparent in, for instance, his articles on Hogarth (with Smollett and Fielding, in *English Humourists of the Eighteenth Century*), on Cruikshank (*The Westminster Review*, xxxiv, CXVI [June 1840], pp. 1–60), and on Leech (*The Quarterly Review*, xcvi, CXCI [Dec. 1854], pp. 75–86). Gillray was evidently his favourite among the caricaturists, for when, in the essay on Leech, he offers a list of representative caricatures, all those that he remembers in some detail prove, on investigation, to be by Gillray.

'Boney was represented as a fierce dwarf, with goggle eyes, a huge laced hat and tricoloured plume, a crooked sabre, reeking with blood: . . .' (p. 78)

This Boney is frequently to be seen in Gillray's work; there is a particularly clear example of the 'fierce dwarf' in 'Armed-Heroes' (18 May 1803). When Thackeray recalls how 'good old George, King of Brobdingnag, laughed at Gulliver-Boney, sailing about in his tank to make sport for their Majesties' (p. 79), he had in mind the second of two Gillray plates on this theme, 'The King of Brobdingnag and Gulliver' (10 Feb. 1804). He continues:

'. . . we remember in those old portfolios, pictures representing Boney and his family in rags, gnawing raw bones in a Corsican hut; Boney murdering the sick at Jaffa; Boney with a hookah and a large turban, having adopted the Turkish religion, &c.' (p. 79)

Presumably the recollection here is of 'Democracy; – or – a Sketch of the Life of Buonaparte' (12 May 1800), a plate in the comic-strip (and Hogarthian Progress) manner, showing various scenes from Boney's life. In his next sentence Thackeray explicitly calls the sequence 'the Gilray [sic] chronicle', although it had not been announced as this at the start, and the prints he goes on to mention are all by Gillray.

Although these identifications have been offered confidently, there are discrepancies. In the

Brobdingnag plate everyone is laughing at Boney *except* the king, and although the plate showing Boney's life can be identified as Gillray's by the first picture ('Boney and his family in rags, gnawing raw bones in a Corsican hut'), and by the 'hookah' and the 'large turban', Boney is not here shown 'murdering the sick at Jaffa'.

There are, moreover, similar discrepancies in the plates explicitly stated to be by Gillray. Thackeray describes Fox and his supporters 'scaling heaven, from which the angelic Pitt hurled them down' (p. 79), and there is only one Gillray that could have suggested this: 'Confederated Coalitions; or The Giants storming Heaven . . .' (1 May 1804). But as the title suggests, Pitt is here one of the storming Giants, and not one of the defending angels. Gillray's Fox is described as having 'hairy cloven feet, and a tail and horns', and although Fox may be seen elsewhere in his demoniacal aspect – as in 'The Table's Turn'd' (4 March 1797, Fig. 57) – in 'Confederated Coalition' itself he has hirsute legs, but is without the other accoutrements. These discrepancies need not be seriously disturbing; they simply suggest that Thackeray was describing the prints from memory and not merely looking them up, and thus, being minor details, they give confirming evidence of the strong impression the prints had originally made.

11. *The Oxford and Cambridge Magazine, Jan.* 1856, p. 61.
12. Stevens, *op. cit.,* (see Note 7), pp. 30–2.
13. The genesis of *Vanity Fair* is discussed by Ray, *op. cit.,* pp. 384–5.
14. M. H. Spielmann, *The History of Punch* (London, 1895), p. 253.
15. *Punch,* iii (July–Dec. 1842), p. 73.
16. The marks for blocks in the *Vanity Fair* manuscript are discussed by Joan Stevens in 'Thackeray's "Vanity Fair"'; the manuscript of *Pendennis* in the Widener Collection is similarly marked, with small squares inserted at the point where the wood-engravings must go, and sometimes also the word 'block'. The manuscript of *The Newcomes* is at Charterhouse.
17. 'The Best of Richard Doyle', *The Art Journal,* 1902, p. 251.
18. 'Hogarth, Smollett, and Fielding.'
19. *The Oxford and Cambridge Magazine,* Jan. 1856, p. 56.
20. *The Examiner,* 1 Sept. 1855, p. 548.
21. *The Times,* 23 Nov. 1853, p. 9.
22. 'Hogarth, Smollett, and Fielding.'
23. *The Miser's Daughter,* i, Book I, Chapter XII.
24. The manuscript of *The Virginians* is in the Pierpont Morgan Library, New York.
25. *Thackeray and the Form of Fiction* (Princeton, 1964), p. v.
26. The capitals contain, for instance, most of that 'set of recurring symbols' which, as Geoffrey Tillotson felt, 'dominated' the novels: the Mermaid (*Pendennis,* i, Chapter XIX; ii, Chapter XVI; *The Newcomes,* ii, Chapter XII), the Turkish Marriage Market (*The Newcomes,* ii, Chapter V), the theatre (*Pendennis,* i, Chapters IV, XII, XIV; ii, Chapters XII, XXVII), *Othello* (*Pendennis,* i, Chapter XXV), classical poetry and history (*Pendennis,* i, Chapter XXX; *The Virginians,* ii, Chapters XIV, XV, XXVII, XXXVI) and the Good Samaritan. Animal fables appeared each month on the cover of *The Newcomes,* and textural use of *The Rape of the Lock* is supplemented with many cuts showing a charming and elegant pair of 18th-century lovers. (See Geoffrey Tillotson, *Thackeray the Novelist* [London, 1954], p. 37.)
27. The capitals assist also in that habitual use of 'parodic modes' analysed by Mr Loofbourow in *Thackeray and the Form of Fiction* (*passim*), although their function is more than parodic. In Mr Loofbourow's category of 'chivalric romance' the knight-in-armour subjects and the associated knight-and-dragon subjects (*Vanity Fair,* i, Chapter XXIV; *Pendennis,* i, Chapters XXIX and

XXX; *The Newcomes*, i, Chapter XXXVII; ii, Chapters XVIII, XX, XXXI; *The Virginians*, i, Chapter XIII) vary delicately in their application, and the figure of the knight may be introduced simply to ensure that the reader gives a fair recognition to a real nobility in the hero's actions (as in *The Virginians*, i, Chapter XIII).

28. The capitals are frequently used serially with lighter subjects; cf. *Pendennis*, ii, Chapters XXIX and XXX, where the two stages of Major Pendennis's encounter with Morgan are reflected in two cuts, one of a highwayman lying in wait, the other of the highwayman prostrate beneath his armed victim.

CHAPTER 5

1. *The Listener*, 22 July 1965, p. 131.
2. The passage comes from *Narrative Pictures* (London, 1937), pp. 21–2; for expressions of the dominant attitude to 'Phiz' in *The Dickensian* see W. A. Fraser, 'Hablôt K. Browne', ii, 7 (July 1906), pp. 176–83, and J. N. B. Millican, '"Phiz" without sparkle', xii, 276 (Sept. 1945), pp. 193–6.
3. Browne's first illustrations for *Pickwick* came in the third number, replacing the plates by Buss which were quickly cancelled; the plates by Browne were 'The Fat Boy Awake on This Occasion Only' and 'Mr Wardle and his Friends Under the Influence of "the Salmon".'
4. The fullest account of the duplicate plates is given in Professor Johannsen's book *Phiz: Illustrations from the Novels of Charles Dickens* (Chicago, 1956), but, being primarily concerned to distinguish between the plates from a collector's point of view, he notes differences in, for instance, the number of buttons a man has, while ignoring large changes of style.
5. *Critical Studies of the Works of Charles Dickens* (New York, 1924), p. 58.
6. 'The old woman with her wrinkled face close to the bars of the stove, puffing at the dull embers which had not yet caught the wood – Squeers stooping down to the candle, which brought out the full ugliness of his face, as the light of the fire did that of his companion – both intently engaged, and wearing faces of exultation which contrasted strongly with the anxious looks of those behind . . . – this, with large bare room, damp walls, and flickering doubtful light, combined to form a scene which the most careless and indifferent spectator – could any have been present – could scarcely have failed to derive some interest from, and would not readily have forgotten.' (Chapter LVII)
7. Letter of 13 Jan. 1840; *Letters*, ii, p. 8. This decision must have been influenced partly by the change from monthly to weekly publication, for a wood-engraving can be produced at shorter notice than an etching, and unless the etching itself were huge, it would look absurd on a page as large as those in the *Clock*, while it would have been virtually impossible to print plate and text on one sheet (since the text requires surface printing and the etching intaglio).
8. See letters to George Cattemole of 21 and 22 Dec. 1840, 6 and 19 Aug. 1841; to Samuel Williams of 31 March 1840 (*Letters*, ii).
9. '"Woodcuts dropped into the Text": The Illustrations in *The Old Curiosity Shop* and *Barnaby Rudge*', *Studies in Bibliography*, xx (1967), pp. 113–34.
10. 'I intend asking Maclise to join me likewise', letter of 13 Jan. 1840; *Letters*, ii, p. 8.
11. Note of 6 Nov. 1840; *Letters*, ii, pp. 145–6.
12. Later note of ?6 Nov. 1840; *Letters*, ii, p. 146. A further request in this note, disappointed in the final cut, illustrates Dickens's desire for pictorial detail of an allegorical kind: 'Will you put on some shelf or nook, an old broken hour glass?'

13. *Clock*, ii, p. 103.
14. The quotations are from the opening pages of *Clock* (pp. 3 and 1).
15. Letter to Forster, ?10 Jan. 1840; *Letters*, ii, p. 4.
16. Quotations from *Clock*, i, pp. 4 and 54.
17. Letter to Forster, 2 June, 1845; *Nonesuch*, p. 680.
18. Letter of 13 Jan. 1840; *Letters*. ii, p. 8.
19. Illustrations in *Clock*, i, pp. 13, 17 and 36; see letter to Cattermole, 9 March 1840; *Letters*, ii, pp. 41–2.
20. Illustration in *Clock*, i, p. 37.
21. Letter of ?7 August 1840; *Letters*, ii, p. 110.
22. Letter to Cattermole of 30 Jan. 1841; *Letters*, ii p. 199.
23. Letter to Cattermole of ?22 Dec. 1840; *Letters*, ii, p. 171.
24. *Household Words*, i (15 June 1850), p. 265.
25. Letter of 14 Jan. 1842; *Letters*, ii, pp. 183–4.
26. *The Examiner*, 4 Dec. 1841, p. 772; the attribution of this review to Forster is my own, but the text tallies so closely with that in the *Life* that the attribution seems certain.
27. 7 Nov. 1840, p. 887.
28. Forster's line of thought is similar to Hood's, and in reprinting his review in the *Life* Forster added a passage that shows a clear debt to Hood: 'Nor could the genius of Hogarth himself have given it higher expression than in the scenes by the cottage door, the furnace fire, and the burial place in the old church, over whose tombs and gravestones hang the puppets of Mr. Punch's show while the exhibitiors are mending and repairing them.' Hood had written: 'As a companion picture, we would select the Mending of the Puppets in the Churchyard, with the mocking figure of Punch perched on a grave-stone – a touch quite Hogarthian in its satirical significance.'
29. See *Letters*, ii, p. 220. The insertion runs from 'I sat down in my easy-chair . . .' to '. . . . resolved to go to bed, and court forgetfulness'. The first book-edition was printed from stereotype plates of the serial version, and since the page on which this passage comes had originally some material referring to Master Humphrey that needed to be removed from the bound novel, an addition of some kind was necessary; but this consideration should not detract from the significance of the passage actually inserted by Dickens.
30. Letter of 31 March 1840; *Letters*, ii, p. 49.
31. Letter of 6 Aug. 1841; *Letters*, ii, p. 352.
32. Letter to Cattermole, 14 Jan. 1841; *Letters*, ii, p. 183.
33. Gissing, *op. cit.*, p. 109.
34. 'I am warming up very much about *Barnaby*. Oh! If I only had him, from this time to the end, in monthly numbers.' Letter to Forster, 5 August 1841, *Letters*, ii, p. 351.

CHAPTER 6
1. xxxii (1839), p. 304.
2. 'Dickens and Daumier', *Studies in the Comic* (California, 1941), pp. 273–98.
3. Marcus, *op. cit.*, p. 216.
4. Review of *The Drunkard's Children*, *The Examiner*, 8 July 1848, p. 436.
5. Letter to Browne, 7 Feb. 1843; *Nonesuch*, i, p. 506–7.
6. Letters to Forster (18 July 1846; *Nonesuch*, i, p. 768) and to Browne (10 March 1847; *Nonesuch*, ii, p. 17).

7. Letters to Forster (Nov. 1846; *Nonesuch*, i, p. 809), to Browne (15 March 1847; *Nonesuch*, ii, p. 19), and to Forster (21 Dec. 1847; *Nonesuch*, ii, p. 63).

8. This point is not sufficiently allowed for by Kitton, who in *Dickens and his Illustrators* devoted several pages to listing the small inconsistencies between text and picture (see pages 76–7, 81, 87–8, 91, 103–4).

9. I am grateful to Mrs Leavis for this point.

10. 29 Oct. 1846; *Nonesuch*, i, p. 806.

11. Quoted by Kitton in note to Plate XXXII, *op. cit.*, facing p. 76.

12. This practice is also to be found in Charles Lever's *The Knight of Gwynne*, in the plate 'Paul discovers a "pose plastique"' and in the accompanying textual description of the 'pose' (Chapter LVI, p. 466).

13. This assumes that the woman who bathes Christ's feet was the Magdalen, an identification belonging to popular tradition rather than to the Bible.

14. Letter to W. F. De Cerjat, 29 Dec. 1849; *Nonesuch*, ii, p. 194.

15. Forster, *op. cit.*, Book vi, VII p. 548.

16. J. Butt and K. Tillotson, *Dickens at Work* (London, 1957), p. 141.

17. The picture has been variously identified, Kentley Bromhill calling it 'a scene from Shakespeare in the elegant Italian fashion' ('Phiz's Illustrations to *David Copperfield*', D, XL, 269 [Dec. 1943] p. 50), and Professor Johannsen, a scene from *Faust* (*op. cit.*, pp. 336–7); the identification as a scene from *Faust* may be confirmed by an inspection of the illustration 'The Picture Gallery – Sir Andrew puzzled' for Charles Lever's *Roland Cashel*. The text says of the right-hand painting in the illustration that 'the subject was a scene from Faust' (Chapter XXII). The *Cashel* plate appeared in November 1848, that for *Copperfield* in December 1849.

18. Browne's sketch for this plate is in the Free Library of Philadelphia. It is clear from Dickens's reference to Gounod's *Faust* in 1863 – 'a very sad and noble rendering of that sad and noble story' (letter to Macready, 19 Feb. 1863; *Nonesuch*, iii, p. 342) – that he himself had long found the original moving.

It might, however, be asked whether Dickens could count on his public recognizing the scene from *Faust*: was the German tragedy sufficiently well-known? *Faust* (Part I) began to be known in the 1820s, but there were few full translations then; in the 1830s, however, no less than nine book-length translations appeared, and in the 1840s five more came out, not counting the many translated extracts (see Bayard Quincy Morgan's *Critical Bibliography of German Literature in English Translation* 1481–1927 [London, 1938]). Moreover, the readers of the time had a clear picture of the principal characters, for the outline engravings of Retsch, which were used in a number of early editions and remained in use till the 1890s, had in fact introduced *Faust* to England (see Jean-Marie Carré, *Goethe en Angleterre* [Paris, 1920], p. 82). These engravings served as the model for George Soane's adaptation at Drury Lane in 1825: *The Examiner* noted that Mephistopheles appeared 'in a costume admirably modelled from the outlines of RETSH [sic]' (22 May 1825, p. 321). Browne does not clothe his Faust exactly in the manner of Retsch, but the similarity is close enough to leave little doubt that a public so familiar with *Faust* and Retsch would recognize the picture above Miss Mowcher, and take its point.

The picture further serves, of course, to make clear Steerforth's connection with the Romantic conception of a tragic hero with demonic associations that had prevailed in the earlier years of the century.

19. Ideas gained from Dickens's works revolved in Browne's mind and worked their effects gradually. One of his sketch-books in the Victoria and Albert Museum shows him experimenting with various

motifs from *Dombey*. Although the sketch-book is dated 1853 the studies 'Draw the curtain!' and 'The Shadow on the Wall' recall the death of Mrs Skewton and 'The Shadow in the little Parlor'.

20. *Nonesuch*, ii, p. 471.
21. *Life and Labours of Hablôt Knight Browne* (London, 1884), p. 135.
22. The quotations come respectively from Chapters II, XLVIII, XII, and XVI; the portraits frown in Chapter XXIX.
23. The engraving of this painting is in reverse, so that there the Earl holds his left hand to his chest.
24. George Gissing, *Charles Dickens: A Critical Study* (London, 1898), p. 100.

CHAPTER 7

1. *Illustrators of the Sixties* (London, 1928), p. 6.
2. *Modern Illustration* (London, 1895), p. 83.
3. *English Illustration 'The Sixties'*: 1855–70 (London, 1897), p. 139.
4. W. Minto, ed., *Autobiographical Notes of the Life of William Bell Scott* (London, 1892), I, p. 206.
5. Letter to Professor Bates, 30 April 1873, quoted by W. Bates, *op. cit.*, p. 6n.
6. White, *op. cit.*, p. 22.
7. *ibid.*, p. 18.
8. *ibid.*, p. 138.
9. Quoted by Kitton, *op. cit.*, pp. 112–13.
10. The letter to Carpenter is in the files of the Pilgrim Edition of Dickens's Letters, and I am grateful to the Editors for permission to publish part of a letter previously unpublished. Since the letters have not as yet had their dates assigned to them authoritatively, I offer my own provisional dating, taking first the letter to Robert Young.

In an unpublished letter to Stone of 14 February 1864 (also in the Pilgrim Files) Dickens says he has given directions for Stone's name to be inserted in future advertisements for *Our Mutual Friend*. This would suggest that Stone was engaged after the advertisements for the novel had begun to appear. *Our Mutual Friend* was first advertised in *All the Year Round* on 23 January, and the advertisement was reprinted each week until 5 March, when Stone's name was added. The letter just cited also makes it clear that, at the time of writing, Dickens had not yet had his first consultation with Stone about the illustrations. Stone had evidently been engaged very recently.

Browne could hardly have been so sure that Stone was to have the commission before the decision was taken; equally, he would not have said 'no doubt' after Stone's name had been definitely mentioned in the advertisements. These considerations would place Browne's letter in February or early March, 1864. The reference to Trollope would suggest a late date in this period, for *Can You Forgive Her?* (the only work of Trollope's that Browne illustrated) commenced issue in monthly parts in January, 1864, and Browne speaks as though the venture were well under way. His relations with Trollope seem already well started on that deterioration which ended in Browne's expulsion from the novel in October 1864.

On the other hand, the letter to Carpenter must almost certainly come before 1864. Browne's address provides a clue; it is given in the letter as '1 Horbury Crescent, Notting Hill'. In the *Post Office London Directory* for 1864, Horbury Crescent is renumbered, and Browne is given Number 2: the Directory is dated from the December of the previous year, and the Crescent would need to have been renumbered by then. The correspondent is presumably the Alfred Carpenter who was on the General Committee of the Croydon Literary and Scientific Institution from 1859 to 1862; he held no office in 1863, although he reappears in April 1864 as a Director (records in Central Library, Croydon Town Hall). One would assume that Carpenter's application to Browne belongs to his Committee days, since Browne did not move to Horbury Crescent until Christmas 1859 (Thomson, *op. cit.*, p. 27), and this would indicate that Browne's (belated) reply was written between the beginning of 1860 and the early part of 1863. It is likely that Browne did not need to reside in Croydon very long before such an application was made to him.

11. Dickens did, for instance, have difficulty in locating Browne at the start of the serial. He wrote to Wills:

> 'Will you give my address to B. and E. without loss of time, and tell them that although I have communicated at full explanatory length with Browne, I have heard *nothing of or from him*. Will you add that I am uneasy and wish they would communicate with Mr Young, his partner, at once. Also that I beg them to be so good as to send Browne my present address.' (19 Oct. 1855; *Nonesuch*, ii, p. 698)

12. 'How Edwin Drood was illustrated', *Century Magazine*, XXVII, 4 (Feb. 1884), p. 523.

13. 'Mr Marcus Stone affirms that he was much hampered by Dickens with respect to these designs, for the novelist, hitherto accustomed to the diminutive scale of the figures in Hablôt Browne's etchings, was somewhat imperative in his demand for a similar treatment of the illustrations for "Our Mutual Friend".' Kitton, *op. cit.*, p. 197.

14. I am drawing, in this paragraph, on a series of unpublished letters to Stone, which will appear in the relevant volume of the Pilgrim Letters.

15. 'Book Illustrations', *All the Year Round*, 10 Aug. 1867, pp. 151–5.

16. See for instance Dickens's 'Old Lamps for New Ones', *Household Words*, 15 June 1850, pp. 265–7; Harriet Martineau's 'Tubal Cain', *Household Words*, 15 May 1852, pp. 192–7; 'Holding up the Cracked Mirror', *All the Year Round*, 19 May 1866, pp. 445–8; 'A Florentine Procession', *All the Year Round*, 14 Dec. 1867, pp. 5–6.

17. Letter of Oct. 1855; *Nonesuch*, ii, p. 700.

18. Part ii, Chapter XXII (Constance Garnett's translation).

19. E. J. Simmons, *Leo Tolstoy* (London, 1949), p. 110.

20. *Tolstoy's 'War and Peace': A Study* (Oxford, 1962), p. 148.

21. I have tried to suggest elsewhere, however, that where draughtsmanly standards were less exacting, in the *Punch* cartoons, Du Maurier could be more poetic ('The Novel and the Cartoon', *The Cambridge Quarterly*, Autumn/Winter 1969–70, pp. 419–29).

Appendix I

1. W. Hamilton, *A Memoir of George Cruikshank* (Second Edition, London, 1878), p. 22.

2. *ibid.*, pp. 15–16.

3. See Thomas Hatton in *Retrospectus and Prospectus: the Nonesuch Dickens* (London, 1937), p. 55.

4. Memorandum of Agreement between T. C. Wilson and R. Bentley, 26 Feb. 1838 (Bentley Papers).

5. A. Johannsen, *Phiz* (Chicago, 1956), p. v.

6. The two steels for a number of *Dombey* cost £1.8s. od., 'Accounts of Sales of the Works of Charles Dickens, Bradbury and Evans, 1845–1861', Forster Collection, Victoria and Albert Museum.

7. Blanchard Jerrold, *The Life of George Cruikshank* (London, 1882), ii, p. 37; see D. C. Thomson, *The Life and Labours of H. K. Browne* (London, 1884), p. 84.

8. Memorandum cited in Note 4.

9. Agreement of 25 Aug. 1841 (Bentley Papers).

10. Agreement of 7 Nov. 1842 (Bentley Papers).

11. R. S. Surtees and E. D. Cuming, *Robert Smith Surtees* (London, 1924), p. 217.

12. F. G. Kitton, *Dickens and his Illustrators* (London, 1899), p. 40.

13. *loc. cit.*

14. Bohn's 'Biographical Notice' in *Seymour's Humorous Sketches* (London, 1872), p. vi.

15. Thomson, *op. cit.*, p. 29. He also gives the details of the Smedley plates (which, to my mind, simply show the usual sum Browne would expect to receive) on page 183; 'For each etching [for *Lewis Arundel*] "Phiz" received £8.18s.6d., and the same price was maintained for the "Harry Coverdale" plates. . . .'

16. Agreements of 26 December 1835; 6 May, 23 May, 20 July, 1837 (Bentley Papers).

17. Agreement of 9 Nov. 1836 (Bentley Papers).

18. *Letters*, i, p. 230.

19. Letter of 1 June 1841, in the Baker Memorial Library, Dartmouth College, Hanover, New Hampshire.

20. Memorandum of an Agreement between W. H. Ainsworth, G. Cruikshank and R. Bentley, 19 Nov. 1839 (Bentley Papers).

21. Thomson, *op. cit.*, p. 234.

22. Jerrold, *op. cit.*, i, pp. 33–4.

23. Thomson, *op. cit.*, p. 35.

24. See Surtees and Cuming, *op. cit.*, especially pp. 313–20.

25. *The London and Westminster Review*, 1838, p. 266.

26. Hamilton, *op. cit.*, p. 16.

27. p. 268.

28. Hamilton, *op. cit.*, p. 16.

29. Johannsen, *op. cit.*, p. 1.

30. There is the case of *Nickleby* plate 4, supposed by Thomson and by Hatton and Cleaver to have been etched in triplicate (T. H. Hatton and A. H. Cleaver, *A Bibliography of the Periodical Works of Charles Dickens* [London, 1933], p. 134). Professor Johannsen maintains that only two steels were etched, and that the differences between them were due to retouching. I can only offer my opinion that the differences, though minute, involve more than retouching, and that a further inspection of the plates would show that it is not true to say that 'the third plate . . . meticulously follows the lines of the second, even to the lines of the shading . . .' (*op. cit.*, p. 83). The lines of the shading are different, while the close similarity of the plates is not surprising when one considers the same tracing would have been impressed on the etching ground of each.

31. Thomson, *op. cit.*, p. 235n.

32. July 1823, p. 385.

33. March 1824, p. 137.

34. Bohn, *op. cit.*, p. vi.

35. *The London and Westminster Review*, XXXII (1839), p. 283.

36. Letter to Edward Chapman, 11 May 1850; *Nonesuch*, ii, p. 215.

37. Letter to Chapman, 22 July 1850; *Nonesuch*, ii, p. 223.

38. Article cited in Note 25, p. 277.

39. p. 278.

40. Hatton and Cleaver, *op. cit.*, p. 165.

41. *The Brothers Dalziel* (London, 1901), pp. 6–8.

42. Letter to Chapman, 14 March 1870; *Nonesuch*, iii, p. 766.

43. Letter from Dickens to F. M. Evans, 24 Feb. 1846; *Nonesuch*, i, p. 737.

44. Letter from Dickens to Leech, 19 Nov. 1845; *Nonesuch*, i, p. 722.

45. p. 275.

Appendix II

1. *Oliver Twist* (The Clarendon Dickens; Oxford, 1966), pp. 394–5; a further private statement of the claim may be seen in a letter from Cruikshank to W. J. McClellan, dated 12 Nov. 1870, quoted by W. G. Wilkins, 'Cruikshank versus Dickens', D, XVI, 2 (April, 1920), pp. 80–1.

2. F. G Stevens, *A Memoir of George Cruikshank* (London, 1891), p. 14.

3. *Oliver Twist* (The Clarendon Dickens), p. 395.

4. Quoted by permission of the Widener Collection in the Harvard College Library.

5. Jan. 1866, p. 138.

6. *Memoir of Thomas Joseph Pettigrew* (New York; extracted from *Medical Life*, Jan. and Feb. 1931), p. 79.

7. Dawson, *op. cit.*, pp. 80–1.

8. Chapter II; *Bentley's Miscellany*, i (1837), p. 108.

9. Chapter II; *Bentley's Miscellany*, i (1837), p. 114.

10. *ibid.*, p. 115.

11. *ibid.*, p. 109.

12. Ch. V; *Bentley's Miscellany*, i (1837), p. 329.

13. Marcus Stone, R.A., 'Some Recollections of Dickens', D, vi, 3 (March, 1910), pp. 62–3.

14. Cruikshank, *The Artist and the Author. A Statement of Facts* (London, 1872), p. 5.

15. George Hodder, *Memories of my Time* (London, 1870), p. 108; when questioned on this point by Austin Dobson, however, Cruikshank insisted that 'he had never been perplexed in the matter, or had any doubts as to his design', Jerrold, *op. cit.*, i, p. 229.

16. Kitton, *op. cit.*, p. 15.

17. *Oliver Twist* (The Clarendon Dickens), p. xxii.

18. Kitton, *op. cit.*, pp. 14–15.

19. This must apply to a drawing in the Widener Collection, entitled (in Cruikshank's hand) 'Sketches for "Oliver Twist" – Suggestions to Mr. C. Dickens – the *writer*': the sketches there are clearly Cruikshank's working drawings for Ch. XVIII (*Bentley's Miscellany*, ii (1837), pp. 534–40) with, first, several studies of a miserable Oliver huddled in what is, presumably, the back-garret (p. 535), then several studies for 'Master Bates explaining a professional technicality', the plate illustrating Ch. XVIII.

20. This assumes that the sketch in question was made before the etching, but it could belong to a later date, and be a sketch for the cover; the scale and the general similarity to the Sikes sketch do, however, suggest that it belongs most probably to the earlier phase.

21. Chapter L, originally Book the Third, Chapter the Twelfth; *Bentley's Miscellany*, v (1839), p. 158.

22. 'Charles Dickens and his Works', *Fraser's Magazine*, xxi, CXXIV (April 1840), pp. 397–400.

23. Chapter XLVII, originally Book the Third, Chapter the Ninth; *Bentley's Miscellany*, v (1839), p. 70.

24. Philip Collins, *Dickens and Crime* (London, 1962), p. 175.

25. *Oliver Twist* (The Clarendon Dickens), p. xxii.

26. See *Letters*, i, p. 277n.

27. Chesterton, *Charles Dickens*, p. 111.

Select Bibliography

1. UNPUBLISHED MATERIAL

The original drawings, letters, and literary manuscripts of the artists and authors mentioned in this study are widely scattered. I have been especially grateful for the opportunity to consult unpublished material in the following collections:

The Arents Collection, New York Public Library; the Baker Memorial Library, Dartmouth College; the City of Bath Municipal Libraries and Victoria Art Gallery; Boston Public Library; the British Museum; the London Borough of Camden, Libraries and Arts Department; Charterhouse Library; Cornel University Library; Croydon Central Library; the Dexter Collection, in the possession of Mr Alan Stern; Haverford College Library; the Houghton Library, Harvard; the Henry E. Huntington Library and Art Gallery; Indiana University Libraries; University of Iowa Libraries (letter from Ainsworth to 'George' – Cruikshank, by my identification, since the letter concerns illustration); Liverpool Public Library; the National Library of Scotland; University of North Carolina Library; the Free Library of Philadelphia; the Pierpont Morgan Library, New York; the files of the Pilgrim Edition of Dickens's Letters; Stanford University Library; the Miriam Lutcher Stark Library, University of Texas; the Victoria and Albert Museum; University of Virginia Library; the Widener Collection, Harvard; Yale University Library.

2. ILLUSTRATED NOVELS

The name of the illustrator follows the date of a given edition.

Ainsworth, W. H. *Rookwood*. 1834 (without illustrations). 1836, G. Cruikshank.
———— *Crichton*. 1837. *Ainsworth's Magazine*, 1848, H. K. Browne.
———— *Jack Sheppard. Bentley's Miscellany*, 1839–40, G. Cruikshank.
———— *The Tower of London*. Monthly parts, 1840, G. Cruikshank.
———— *Guy Fawkes. Bentley's Miscellany*, 1840–1, G. Cruikshank.
———— *Old Saint Paul's*. Monthly parts, 1841, John Franklin.
———— *The Miser's Daughter. Ainsworth's Magazine*, 1842, G. Cruikshank.
———— *Windsor Castle. Ainsworth's Magazine*, 1842–3, G. Cruikshank, Tony Johannot, W. A. Delamotte.

Ainsworth, W. H. *Saint James's. Ainsworth's Magazine*, 1844, G. Cruikshank.

——— *The Revelations of London. Ainsworth's Magazine*, 1844, H. K. Browne; as *Auriol, The New Monthly Magazine*, 1845–6. H. K. Browne.

——— *James the Second. Ainsworth's Magazine*, 1847, R. W. Buss.

——— *Mervyn Clitheroe*. Monthly parts, Dec. 1851 – March 1852 (Parts 1–4) and Dec. 1857–June 1858 (Parts 5–11/12), H. K. Browne. *Mervyn Clitheroe* was the last of Ainsworth's novels to be published in monthly parts; bibliographical information on the occasional use of illustration in Ainsworth's later fictions may be found in Harold Locke's *A Bibliographical Catalogue of the Published Novels and Ballads of W. H. Ainsworth* (London, 1925).

Cockton, Henry. *The Life and Adventures of Valentine Vox, the Ventriloquist*. Monthly parts, 1839–40, T. Onwhyn.

——— *Stanley Thorn. Bentley's Miscellany*, 1840–2, G. Cruikshank.

——— *George St. George Julian, the Prince*. Monthly parts, 1841, T. Onwhyn.

——— *The Sisters; or, the Fatal marriages*. ?Monthly parts, 1843–4, T. Onwhyn. *Illustrated London News*, 1843, Kenny Meadows and 'Alfred Crowquill'.

——— *Sylvester Sound, the Somnambulist. Monthly parts*, 1843–4, T. Onwhyn.

——— *The Love Match*. ?Monthly parts, 1844–5, T. Onwhyn.

——— *The Steward: a Romance of Real Life*. Monthly parts, 1850, T. Onwhyn.

Dickens, Charles. *The Posthumous Papers of the Pickwick Club*. Monthly parts, 1836–7, R. Seymour, R. W. Buss, H. K. Browne.

——— *Oliver Twist. Bentley's Miscellany*, 1837–9, G. Cruikshank.

——— *The Life and Adventures of Nicholas Nickleby*. Monthly parts, 1838–9, H. K. Browne.

——— *The Old Curiosity Shop. Master Humphrey's Clock*, weekly and monthly parts, 1840–1, G. Cattermole, H. K. Browne, S. Williams, D. Maclise.

——— *Barnaby Rudge. Master Humphrey's Clock*, weekly and monthly parts, 1841, G. Cattermole and H. K. Browne.

——— *The Life and Adventures of Martin Chuzzlewit*. Monthly parts, 1843–4, H. K. Browne.

——— *Dealings with the firm of Dombey and Son*. Monthly parts, 1846–8, H. K. Browne.

——— *The personal History, Adventures, Experiences, and Observations of David Copperfield the Younger*. Monthly parts, 1849–50, H. K. Browne.

——— *Bleak House*. Monthly parts, 1852–3, H. K. Browne.

——— *Little Dorrit*. Monthly parts, 1855–7, H. K. Browne.

——— *A Tale of Two Cities. All the Year Round*, 1859. Monthly parts, 1859, H. K. Browne.

——— *Great Expectations. All the Year Round*, 1860–1. Published in volume form without illustrations, 1861; with illustrations by Marcus Stone, 1862.

——— *Our Mutual Friend*. Monthly parts, 1864–5, M. Stone.

——— *The Mystery of Edwin Drood*. Monthly parts, 1870, L. Fildes (cover from design by C. Collins).

Egan, Pierce, the elder. *Life in London*. Monthly parts, 1820–1, R. and G. Cruikshank.

——— *The Pilgrims of the Thames*. Monthly parts, 1836–7, Pierce Egan the younger.

——— *The Finish to the Adventures of Tom, Jerry and Logic*. ?Monthly parts, ?early 1830s, R. Cruikshank (the earliest edition in the British Museum is a reprint of 1869).

James, G. P. R. *The Commissioner: or, De Lunatico Inquirendo*. Monthly parts, 1841–3, H. K. Browne.

Lever, Charles. *The Confessions of Harry Lorrequer. Dublin University Magazine*, 1837–40. Monthly parts, 1839–40, H. K. Browne.

——— *Charles O'Malley*. Monthly parts, 1840–1, H. K. Browne.

Lever, Charles. *Jack Hinton, the Guardsman* (part of *Our Mess*). Monthly parts, 1842, H. K. Browne.

———— *Tom Burke of 'Ours'* (part of *Our Mess*). Monthly parts, 1843–4, H. K. Browne.

———— *Arthur O'Leary. Dublin University Magazine*, 1843. 1844, G. Cruikshank.

———— *Tales of the Trains. Dublin University Magazine*, 1845. Monthly parts, 1845, H. K. Browne.

———— *The O'Donogue: A Tale of Ireland Fifty Years Ago*. Monthly parts, 1845, H. K. Browne.

———— *The Knight of Gwynne. Monthly parts*, 1846–7, H. K. Browne.

———— *Roland Cashel*. Monthly parts, 1848–9, H. K. Browne.

———— *Confessions of Con Cregan: the Irish Gil Blas*. Monthly parts, 1849–50, H. K. Browne.

———— *The Daltons, or Three Roads in Life*. Monthly parts, 1851–2, H. K. Browne.

———— *The Dodd Family Abroad*. Monthly parts, 1852–4, H. K. Browne.

———— *The Martins of Cro' Martin*. Monthly parts, 1854–6, H. K. Browne.

———— *Davenport Dunn: A Man of Our Day*. Monthly parts, 1857–9, H. K. Browne.

———— *One of Them*. Monthly parts, 1859–61, H. K. Browne.

———— *Barrington*. Monthly parts, 1862–3, H. K. Browne.

———— *Luttrell of Arran*. Monthly parts, 1863–5, H. K. Browne. The last of Lever's novels to appear in monthly parts, although all his subsequent novels (except for *A Rent in a Cloud*, 1865) were serialized in various magazines.

Maxwell, W. H. *The Fortunes of Hector O'Halloran and His Man Mark Anthony O'Toole*. Monthly parts, 1842–3, 'Dick Kitcat' (R. Doyle), J. Leech.

Mayhew, Augustus. *Paved with Gold or the Romance and Reality of the London Streets*. Monthly parts, 1857–8, H. K. Browne.

Mayhew, Augustus and Henry. *The Greatest Plague of Life*. Monthly parts, 1847, G. Cruikshank.

———— *Whom to Marry and How to Get Married!* Monthly parts, 1847–8, G. Cruikshank.

———— *The Image of His Father*. Monthly parts, 1848, H. K. Browne.

Miller, Thomas. *Godfrey Malvern; or, the Life of an Author*. Monthly parts, 1842–3, H. K. Browne.

Neale, W. Johnson. *Paul Periwinkle*. Monthly parts, 1839–41, H. K. Browne.

Reynolds, G. W. M. *Pickwick Abroad. The Monthly Magazine*, 1837–8, 'A. Crowquill', J. Phillips, Bonner. Monthly parts, 1838–9, 'A. Crowquill', J. Phillips, Bonner.

———— *Robert Macaire in England*. 1840, H. K. Browne.

———— *The Days of Hogarth*. Undated, W. G. Standfast.

Rowcroft, Charles. *Fanny, the little Milliner*. 1846, H. K. Browne, T. Onwhyn.

Smedley, F. E. *Frank Fairlegh. Sharpe's London Magazine*, 1846–8. Monthly parts, 1849–50, G. Cruikshank.

———— *Lewis Arundel. Sharpe's London Magazine*, 1848–51. Monthly parts, 1851–2, H. K. Browne.

Smith, Albert Richard. *The Struggles and Adventures of Christopher Tadpole at Home or Abroad*. Monthly parts, 1846–7, J. Leech.

———— *The Pottleton Legacy*. Monthly parts, 1848–9. H. K. Browne.

Surtees, R. S. *Jorrocks's Jaunts and Jollities. The New Sporting Magazine*, 1831–4, 1838, H. K. Browne.

———— *Handley Cross. The New Sporting Magazine* (as 'The Gin-and-Water Hunt' and 'The Handley Cross Hounds'), 1838–9. Monthly parts, 1853–4, J. Leech.

———— *Mr Sponge's Sporting Tour. The New Monthly*, 1849–51. Monthly parts, 1852–3, J. Leech.

———— *'Ask Mamma'*. Monthly parts, 1857–8, J. Leech.

———— *'Plain or Ringlets '* Monthly parts, 1859–60, J. Leech.

Surtees, R. S. *Mr Facey Romford's Hounds*. Monthly parts, 1864–5, J. Leech, H. K. Browne.

Thackeray, W. M. *Catherine*. Fraser's Magazine, 1839–40, W. M. Thackeray.

—————— *The History of Samuel Titmarsh and the Great Hoggarty Diamond*. Fraser's Magazine, 1841. 1849, W. M. Thackeray.

——————*Vanity Fair: Pen and Pencil Sketches of English Society*. Monthly parts, 1847–8, W. M. Thackeray.

—————— *The History of Pendennis*. Monthly parts, 1848–50, W. M. Thackeray.

—————— *The Newcomes*. Monthly parts, 1853–5, R. Doyle.

—————— *The Virginians*. Monthly parts, 1857–9, W. M. Thackeray.

—————— *Lovel the Widower*. Cornhill, 1860, W. M. Thackeray.

—————— *The Adventures of Philip on his Way Through the World*. Cornhill, 1861–2, F. Walker and W. M. Thackeray.

—————— *Denis Duval*. Cornhill, 1864, F. Walker and W. M. Thackeray.

Trollope, Frances, *The Life and Adventures of Jonathan Jefferson Whitlaw*. 1836, A. Hervieu.

—————— *The Vicar of Wrexhill*. 1837, A. Hervieu.

—————— *The Life and Adventures of Michael Armstrong*. Monthly parts, 1839–40, A. Hervieu, T. Onwhyn, R. W. Buss.

—————— *The Widow Married*. The New Monthly Magazine, 1839–40, R. W. Buss.

—————— *Charles Chesterfield*. The New Monthly Magazine, 1840–41, H. K. Browne.

—————— *The Barnabys in America*. The New Monthly Magazine, 1842–3, J. Leech.

References to other relevant publications of the authors and artists discussed will be found in the notes to the text. The illustrated serials of Anthony Trollope are not listed since, coming in the sixties and seventies, they belong to a later phase than that discussed here.

3. CRITICISM

Antal, F. *Hogarth, and his place in European Art*. London, 1962.

Bates, W. *George Cruikshank: The Artist, the Humourist, and the Man*. Birmingham, 1878.

Browne, E. *Phiz and Dickens*. London, 1913.

Bursill, J. F. *George Cruikshank, Artist – Humourist – Moralist*. London, 1878.

Buss, R. W. *English Graphic Satire*. London, 1874.

Butt, J., and K. Tillotson. *Dickens at Work*. London, 1957.

Chesson, W. H. *George Cruikshank*. London, 1908.

Cohen, Jane R. '"All-of-a-Twist" – The Relationship of George Cruikshank and Charles Dickens', *Harvard Library Bulletin*, XVII (1969), 2 (pp. 169–94), 3 (pp. 320–42).

Dalziel, G. and E. *The Brothers Dalziel*. London, 1901

Davis, E. R. 'Dickens and the Evolution of Caricature', *PMLA*, LV, 1 (March 1940), pp. 231–40.

Douglas, R. J. H. *The Works of George Cruikshank*. London, 1903.

Everitt, G. *English Caricaturists and Graphic Humourists of the Nineteenth Century*. London, 1886.

Fielding, K. J. 'Charles Dickens and the Department of Practical Art', *The Modern Language Review*, XLVIII, 3 (July 1953), pp. 270–7.

Fildes, L. V. *Luke Fildes, R.A.* London, 1968.

George, M. D. *Hogarth to Cruikshank: Social Change in Graphic Satire*. London, 1967.

Gettman, R. A. *A Victorian Publisher: a study of the Bentley Papers*. Cambridge, 1960.

Gibson, P. 'Dickens's Uses of Animism', *Nineteenth Century Fiction*, VII, 4 (March 1953), pp. 283–91.

Grego, J. *Pictorial Pickwickiana*. London, 1899.

Hambourg, D. *Richard Doyle. His Life and Work*. London, 1948.

Hamilton, W. *A Memoir of G. Cruikshank*. London, 1878.

Hill, D. *Mr Gillray the Caricaturist*. London, 1965.

Jackson, M. *The Pictorial Press*. London, 1885.

James, P. *English Book Illustration* 1800–1900. London, 1947.

Jerrold, W. B. *The Life of George Cruikshank*. London, 1882.

Johannsen, A. *Phiz: Illustrations from the Novels of Charles Dickens*. Chicago, 1956.

Kitton, F. G. *Charles Dickens by Pen and Pencil*. London, 1890.

———— *Dickens and his Illustrators*. London, 1899.

———— *Dickens and his Illustrators* ('A Paper read at the Inaugural Meeting of the Dickens Fellowship, held in London, November 5th, 1902). London, undated.

———— *John Leech, Artist and Humourist*. London, 1883.

———— '*Phiz*' (*H. K. Browne*), *A Memoir*. London, 1882.

Klingender, F. D. *Hogarth and English Caricature*. London, 1944.

Layard, G. S. *George Cruikshank's Portraits of Himself*. London, 1897.

———— *Suppressed Plates*. London, 1907.

Leavis, F. R. 'Dombey and Son,' *The Sewanee Review*, LXX, i (Jan.–Mar. 1962), pp. 177–201.

Lusk, L. 'The Best of Richard Doyle', *The Art Journal*, 1902, pp. 248–52.

McKenzie, G. 'Dickens and Daumier', *Studies in the Comic* (*University of California Publications in English*, VIII, California, 1941), pp. 273–98.

Maclean, R. *George Cruikshank*. London, 1948.

McMaster, R. D. 'Man into Beast in Dickensian Caricature', *University of Toronto Quarterly*, XXXI, 3 (April 1962), pp. 354–61.

Marchmont, F. *The Three Cruikshanks*. London, 1897.

Matz, B. W. ' "Phiz." The Centenary of Hablôt Knight Browne', *The Bookman*, XLVIII, 285 (June 1915), pp. 69–74.

Melville, L. 'Thackeray as Artist', *The Connoisseur*, VIII, 29 (Jan. 1904), pp. 29–31; 31 (March 1904), pp. 152–5.

Meynell, A. 'How Edwin Drood was illustrated', *Century Magazine*, XXVII, 4 (Feb. 1884), pp. 522–8.

Moore, R. E. *Hogarth's Literary Relations*. London, 1948.

Pennell, J. *Modern Illustration*. London, 1895.

Price, R. G. G. *A History of 'Punch'*. London, 1957.

Reid, F. *Illustrators of the Sixties*. London, 1928.

Reid, J. C. *The Hidden World of Charles Dickens* (*University of Auckland Bulletin* No. 61, English Series No. 10). Auckland, 1962.

Retrospectus and Prospectus, the Nonesuch Dickens. London, 1937.

Robb, B. 'George Cruikshank's etchings for "Oliver Twist",' *The Listener*, 22 July 1965, pp. 130–1.

Roe, F. G. 'Seymour, the "Inventor" of "Pickwick",' *The Connoisseur*, LXXVII, 306 (Feb. 1927), pp. 67–71.

———— 'Portrait Painter to "Pickwick;" or, Robert Seymour's Career,' *The Connoisseur*, LXXVII, 307 (March 1927), pp. 152–7.

Sarzano, F. *Sir John Tenniel*. London, 1948.

Spielman, M. H. *The History of Punch*. London, 1895.

Steig, M. 'Phiz's Marchioness', *Dickens Studies*, II, 3 (Sept. 1966), pp. 141–6.

———— 'The Iconography of the Hidden Face in *Bleak House*', *Dickens Studies*, IV, 1 (March 1968), pp. 19–22.

Stevens, F. G. *A Memoir of George Cruikshank*. London, 1891.

Stevens, J. 'Thackeray's "Vanity Fair",' *A Review of English Studies*, VI, 1 (Jan. 1965), pp. 19–38.

————— '"Woodcuts dropped into the Text": The Illustrations in *The Old Curiosity Shop And Barnaby Rudge*', *Studies in Bibliography*, XX (1967), pp. 113–34.

Sturgis, R. 'Thackeray as a Draughtsman', *Scribner's Monthly*, XX, 2 (June 1880), pp. 256–74.

Thomson, D. C. *Life and Labours of H. K. Browne*. London, 1884.

White, G. *English Illustration 'The Sixties': 1855–70*. London, 1897.

Wright, T. *A History of Caricature and Grotesque in Literature and Art*. London, 1865.

References to other articles, relevant correspondence in periodicals, and other books touching on the subjects discussed, will be found in the notes to the text. Many items relating to the illustration of Dickens's work may be found in the files of the *Dickensian*; they are too numerous to list here but may easily be traced through the magazine's index.

Index